DISCARD

Prince George Public Library
887 Dominion Street
Prince George BC V2L 5L1
(250) 563-9251

HEIRS OF ACHILLES

HEIRS OF ACHILLES

Alan E. Samuel

Edgar Kent
TORONTO
2008

Published by Edgar Kent, Inc., Publishers
13412 Guelph Line, Campbellville, Ontario L0P 1B0 Canada
University of Toronto Press, 2250 Military Rd. Tonawanda, N.Y. 14150 U.S.A.
5201 Dufferin Street, Toronto, Ontario M5H 5T6 Canada
www.edgarkent.ca service@edgarkent.ca

Copyright © 2008 by Alan E. Samuel
All rights reserved. No part of this publication may be reproduced by any means, electronic, mechanical, photocopying, recording or in any other way, or stored in, included in a retrieval system, or transmitted in any form or by any means, without the written permission of both the author and the above publisher of this book.

Printed in The United States of America

Jacket design, Peter Maher
Monoprint "The Mask of Achilles " by Peter Maher

Library and Archives Canada Cataloguing in Publication

Samuel, Alan Edouard   Heirs of Achilles / Alan E. Samuel.

Includes bibliographical references and index. ISBN 978-0-88866-658-1

1. Civilization, Western--History. 2. Civilization, Western-- Philosophy. 3. Civilization, Western--Psychological aspects. I. Title.

CB151.S35 2008   909'.09821   C2008-900414-0

To Sandra

Take my hand
and dive with me
below the rolling surface of the sea
down past the last bright sparkles of the light.
Swim with me
and hidden fish
through the purple tunnels of the deep
and find the sunken castles I once knew.
Rise with me,
the sapphire waves
throw silver sprinkles to the azure sky
and we can swim until we reach the sun.

Contents

Introduction

1. Preliminary Observations 3
2. Plans and Disagreements 7

Part One: The Individual and the Self

3. The Pursuit of Self–Knowledge 25
4. The Knowing Self 48

Part Two: The Self in Community

5. The Psychology of the Self 62
6. The Harmonious Family 74
7. The Knowledge of Good and Evil 86

Part Three: State and Society

8. The Possibility of Justice 106
9. Autocracy 125
10. Democracy 146
11. Equality 168

Part Four: "You Are Not Alone"

12. The Human Condition and Cosmic Justice ... 186
13. God's Holy Truth 202
14. To Live in Christian Times 230
15. Saving Humanity 242
16. The Great Chain of Being 259

Part Five: The Individual and the Cosmos

17. Epic Times 271
18. The Optimism of Pessimism 289

Criticizing the Tradition 312

Appendix: Mentality 320

Bibliography 324

Index 337

Preface and Acknowledgements

I think it was the late 1970s that John Naylor, then of Methuen, suggested I write about antiquity as I saw it. I was just to write what I knew and believed, a narrative reflecting a near-lifetime of teaching, research and just thinking about the ancient world and its texts. The result of that conversation was *The Promise of the West*, and I have always been grateful to John for encouraging me to step out of my accustomed tracks and try something new. Naylor not only started me on that book and brought it through the difficulties of publication, he caused me to reexamine my ideas and my knowledge – and to read, read again the literature of the world I had been studying so long. And of course, as I moved ahead in the formulation of the book, I read in a new way. For example, I read the entire Bible as a single book, both Old and New Testaments, and I still remember the impact that had on me.

I learned a lot over the years I was working on that book, and I owe many debts to those who helped make it possible. My children put up with my preoccupation, and my friends listened to my orations as I tried to present verbally what I was learning. The Canada Council and the Guggenheim Foundation gave me the time to do all that reading and thinking. Colleagues Leonard Woodbury, Naphtali Lewis and John Rist were wonderfully generous in reading drafts and warning me of mistakes I was ready to put into print. The editors of Routledge helped bring the writing out as a book in a more elegant format than I had expected.

I had the notion, after some years, of putting together a second edition, but as I worked on that, I realized that some of my ideas had changed, and that I had a different focus for my historical writing. Still, some of the comments, some of the information in *The Promise of the West* still had validity for me, and I have felt free to plagiarize my own work to produce some of the pages for this book. I tried not to simply transfer text, but I was not always patient enough to rewrite completely to say the same thing. And I owe the same thanks for this as I offered for my previous work, however different my approach and intent are in producing this new book. In fact, I owe thanks to a lifetime of friends, colleagues, political associates and family with whom I have probed again and again the issues I examine here.

This is a different book, however, and I am much clearer in my own mind about its purpose. As a new project, the writing produced a whole new set of obligations, and I am very grateful to those who devoted time and attention to what I was doing: Robert Morell, for reponding to requests for advice; Lee Haviland and Peter Maher, for reading and commenting on several drafts; Bernard Chamberlain for his advice. Most of all, I thank my wife Sandra for encouraging me to step out of my customary disguise of objective historian and write from a more personal point of view.

Introduction

–1–
Preliminary Observations

A friend with whom I play euchre always refers to himself and his partner as "the good guys," and the opponents as "the bad guys." When he wins a hand, it's "one for the good guys," and if he loses, its "one for the bad guys." If I play as his partner, I become one of the good guys. If I am his opponent, I'm a "bad guy." I don't find this shifting moral position hard to live with as I sit playing cards by the side of a lake in Northern Ontario, but in the game of life, the game I play most of the time, and for real, I want to be sure I am one of the good guys. More than that, I am repeatedly tempted to enlist myself in the fight against the bad guys, especially since I am pretty sure I know who the bad guys are. But then I think to myself, the author of *Mein Kampf* also thought he was one of the good guys, and certainly was sure who the bad guys were. In fact, I would have been one of them. So my moral certainty blurs a little bit, and I start repeating to myself questions I asked myself as an undergraduate, more years ago than I like to remember. "Good grief," I think to myself, "have I got no further with this after all these years?"

Not much. I admit that. But I have read a great deal, and despite my tendency to forget the details of most of what I read, the words of philosophers, poets, historians, novelists, and so on have had some effect on my brain processes. At least I think they have had an effect, one that shakes the certainty I had at the age of thirty. They also lead me to some conclusions for which I could claim the character of insight. That is quite an assertion, or at least so it seems to me, until I produce a disclaimer: Any insights I have, I tell you as you start this book, are not into the nature of the cosmos, or reality, but into my own thoughts, my own understandings, the lessons I personally draw from the books I have read and conversations I have had, and from the stories that I think had influence on me.

I am writing this without knowing who you are. I suspect that if you are male like me, what I have to say will make a certain amount of sense, and may achieve in part what I claim this reading and thinking has had on me: some perception of the influences that not only have made you and me what we are, but even more important, make it so difficult – and dangerous – for us to change. If you are female, on the other hand, what I write may not have that effect, but may help you peer around the edge of the coin to see what is on the reverse side.

I started all this years ago, with that confidence in a theory that is very characteristic of the human makeup I am writing about here. I had been worried about good and evil, right and wrong, and how to find some secure principle on which to base discrimination between the two. I had been engaged in a discussion – argument, really – with a friend, on the subject of female genital mutilation, a subject then of much controversy in Toronto. I said it was wrong, and my friend argued that I made this judgment only according to the lights of my culture: in the culture in which the practice lived, it was right, and there was no absolute that could be imposed here. In my subsequent search for a means of defending my view, I was looking, I suppose, for what contemporaries call a "grand narrative."

For most of my life I have been content to live without absolutes. I could live my life without the ten commandments, and if I did things that in retrospect I considered wrong – well, it was not a violation of an absolute I had been guilty of, but the breaking of a rule of life I ordinarily lived by. But female genital mutilation? My feelings – and here I choose my word carefully – insisted that the practice was wrong, not only in Toronto, but everywhere. This was an absolute, and for a person who did not believe in absolutes, insisting on one created a difficult intellectual position. Yet there I was, doing that, and I worried the issue thereafter, repeating the question: how could I insist upon some rule, some moral stance, some judgment, in a world in which morality was subject to human opinion, and was therefore transitory and relative?

That question was the first step on a journey. For a long time, I rested at a way-station that served as an answer: History, the experience of my civilization, so fashioned me and those who shared my tradition, that without the fundamental attitudes generated by that history, we could not exist as we are. Thus we exercise some absolutes by necessity, and we could not exist or maintain the civilization we have without the attitudes that grow out of our past. This is a sort of intellectual fun, and it was even more satisfying for the fact that I could find all sorts of attitudes I liked, and social and philosophical virtues in which I believed, justified by the historical and literary tradition in which I placed myself. I think I still believe in the respite offered by this way-station, that I act according to the attitudes established by the stories fundamental to my culture. But I had to leave this comfortable way-station as I perceived the fuzziness of the term "my culture," the assembly of ideas and events an academic classicist is inclined to name as "western civilization." Western civilization? "My culture?" Who is "me?" Who is "us," "we," "our culture," to whom I referred in earlier versions of this book? If I were to adhere to the principles I had followed in earlier drafts, tracing the impact of attitudes on the people who framed their lives according to the attitudes underlying fundamental texts, "we," and "our tradition" could apply only to those who were familiar with those texts. What I found fundamental in the *Iliad*, the *Oresteia* trilogy of Aeschylus, Plato, the Bible, and so on could only apply with confidence to those who could and did read them. Who would they be? Until the last two centuries, for the most part they would only be men, and only a few, "educated," men of the class prosperous enough to send its boys through school.

Aha! you say. This is going to be an attack on patriarchy, hierarchy, domination, and all the bad things. He's going to show how to put aside all these stories that have had such a bad influence, stories that, as Thomas Berry has said, must be removed for at least two centuries to allow new growth. Sorry. I am not going to do that. I could aim at that result, and it might even be fairly easy to do so. But that, no more than my first way-station, is not the place I have stopped. Instead, I am just going to tell you what the stories mean to me, and to make that clear, I am going to tell you some other narratives I have encountered during my journey. I hope I can show you how these stories make me, and you too to some extent, what we are. I hope I can also show that a better idea of what we are is needed if we want to change without losing all the good the stories have created.

–2–
Plans and Disagreements

We live in an anti-historical age. Dramatic portrayals of contemporary events fill our television screens 24 hours a day – "real-time" pictures of explosions, rolling tanks, forest fires, disastrous hurricanes, crowded hospital corridors, hijacked aircraft. The kaleidoscope of current life whirls in front of us, illustrated by 3-D maps, film clips of events of the recent past, portraits of noted personalities, talking heads analyzing events as they occur. But there is no background, no explanations drawn from looking back over the road we have traveled to reach the point at which we stand, bewildered by the thrust of events and doubtful of the course to be taken to move ahead with our lives or plan the world's future. Of the hundreds of channels on the TV, only one calls itself "History," and that is mostly filled with recent movies, often fiction, portraying the high dramas of the past century.

Some of us deplore this situation; naturally I, having made my living from history, would like to think there is a loss incurred in the absence of any depth to our knowledge of our past. This is not a matter of avoiding repetitions of mistakes by learning from the past; it is a question of understanding ourselves and our society in the way that we comprehend and make decisions for ourselves and our children – taking account of what we are and making our judgments according to that understanding. It is a matter of thought, a question of words, not pictures, understanding what is important and what is not. History can be a form of philosophy, expressing by its rendition of our past a judgment about what we have been, and therefore, what we are. It is a part of our journey through life, extended from our own short lives to connect with the lives of those ancestors who have formed us, just as our parents formed us for our current existence.

The major goal I have set myself in writing this book is to trace characteristics of Hellenic civilization – and also, because they too are so influential, characteristic Jewish and Christian ideas. These influences from the past have become so basic to my thought and attitudes that they have massively influenced my development, and probably the development of many others as well. In my view, there are attitudes and assumptions about the nature of human beings and the world in which we live that emerged during the some thousand years in which Greek civilization was vital and creative. Many of these assumptions and attitudes survived two millennia to become part of the basis of the way many people think today about themselves, their institutions, their standards of good and bad and the proper way to reason and evaluate experience.

I must initially acknowledge the objection that I, like so many other historians, use the broad term "western" in connection with culture or history when the culture I describe might be, at the very widest, the culture of Europe and the regions to which it penetrated. It is also true that the limited group of European nations and their offspring cannot conveniently be tied up in a bag labeled "western" and treated as a unity. Nevertheless, the issues I intend to treat are so basic to modes of thought that they transcend the diversities in the groups they affect. By "western" then, I mean the cultures and traditions influenced by the texts and ideas I treat in the following pages. This may be a circular definition, but it does circumscribe the topic.

The definition also allows a comparison with Chinese civilization, because that tradition can be safely excluded from any possibility of description as "western" and distinguishes the realms to which my comments apply. I should also here repeat my earlier observation, that most of what I write reflects not only the views of a male, but belongs in the whole tradition of male ideas that have formed the central influences of the societies that can be called "western." Each reader will have to decide for himself or herself whether the ideas and texts I assert as influential on "us" do indeed dominate in forming his or her attitudes. But I remind my reader again that the word "we" that appears so often in what follows should probably be read almost always as "we men," and perhaps only as "I."

Not everything characteristic of the West owes its genesis to Greek civilization. In my first attempt to explore this approach to history, I included Hebrew and Christian texts in my purview, and when I returned to the work, I planned at first to limit myself to Greek texts. But I saw how lazy this decision was as I read James Hillman's diatribe against monotheistic Christianity, almost at the end of his book exploring the grip war holds on us.[1] I had already written most of the book that still lies ahead of you, but I decided I had missed a big piece of the story. Much as I wanted to evade the difficulty of including the texts of the biblical religions in examining the origins of many of the attitudes of my culture, I saw that I could not neglect them. So this book became longer to write and to read.

Later periods, however, I will not treat in this book. There was a great upheaval in human notions during the mediaeval period, an upheaval that began, I believe, with such writers as Philo of Alexandria and the Christian fathers who followed him closely in time, and lasted several hundred years beyond the fall of Rome and the death of St. Augustine, and reaching down into the century of Luther, Gutenberg, the evacuation of Spain by the Moors, and the discovery of America. Despite the importance of the experience of those centuries and the impact of Christianity and the mediaeval way of thinking, the influence of Hellenism persisted, and it is this influence that I intend to trace in this book. But the influence I aim to discuss is an influence at the most basic level, and I will not be following literary influences, the impact of the classical on art and sculpture, or even, aside from noting briefly where it seems appropriate, the survival or impact of specific philosophical ideas.

I acknowledge that this book does not conform to the current state of historical writing, at least as I see it. Perhaps the most notable change in historical writing during my lifetime in the academic trough has been the demotion of political history. The parade of wars, kings, dates and discoveries that was "History" to students of earlier generations (and still may be so to some in high school) has marched past. Nowadays scholars spend a great deal of time examining society and the economy, classes, groups, families and the like, or patterns of trade, price cycles, means of production and exchange, to find explanations for events in the past, assembling data in quantities that can be evaluated and used to demonstrate changes and shifts. This is most noticeable, of course, in work on modern (i.e., post fifteenth-century) history, for which enough data usually exist to provide analysis, if not consensus on the results of study. As we move further back in time, through medieval history, this approach is less and less satisfactory, although for the story of Egypt in the Greek, Roman and Byzantine periods there may be more evidence than for any other pre-modern society. Still, the shortage of good evidence also affects the conclusions of other lines of approach to the past, the application of results and parallels from anthropology, psychology and sociology, to name a few disciplines through which modern people attempt to understand themselves and their world. Since, in fact, we have such little information about the past, whether quantifiable or allegorizable, our historical analysis, certainly for antiquity if not for later periods, can yield a result which as Chester Starr has written, "may be intellectually magnificent, but it remains a gossamer."[2]

Recent trends in attempting to understand the ancient world scrutinize individual and group power relations, the significance of imbalances among gender groups and among various ethnic, religious and racial groups. Some writers reject the notion of truth in history and deny the value of attempting to provide any coherent account to relate meaning between past and present. All these doubts increased my hesitation to use straight "History" as the basis for my delineation of the influence of the past. I was not very satisfied with the results of social or economic analysis, nor utility of parallels from other disciplines, nor even the more recent questioning of the validity of the concept "History" at all. For a start, they responded very badly to the question: "What do we really know?" Once I had asked that question and demanded a reliable answer, I found myself relying more and more on texts – texts, in fact, primarily as a form of realia. As realia, they are conclusive evidence of what can be found in manuscripts of what a writer, known or unknown, actually wrote. Not what was thought, believed, or meant, but written. While there must always be some doubt about some details of the physical text, and there are a few cruces in which manuscript uncertainty affects meaning significantly, the texts are, for the most part, independent expressions of ideas which were transmitted, not only ultimately to our society, but were available also to many generations before us.

Of course, the texts must be read or known, a process that inevitably generates as many understandings of the written signs as there are readers. The texts themselves affect different people in different ways. As Karen Armstrong points out, "our inner world is created by fragments of many different texts, which live together in our minds, one qualifying another.... We rarely absorb texts whole: isolated images, phrases and gobbets live in our minds in myriad, fluid groupings, acting and reacting on one another."[3] I agree that everything I say in what follows depends on my particular understanding of each text I discuss. Insofar as my understanding of a specific text has features in common with the interpretations of readers over the centuries as well as of my contemporaries, my comments will have significance for the attitudes of others. But even there, my understandings of the attitudes and assumptions of others, past and present, are acts by which I assert statements that are themselves interpretive. I am going to try to write this history, then, with an awareness of the individuality of my comments, and will from time to time repeat the point that a statement is only my understanding of a text. I hope the reader will take my occasional reminders of this as a suggestion to carry the awareness throughout the reading. But I always will maintain an approach to this project that proposes a connection between the impact of this material on me personally, only suggesting the possibility of its effect on others as well.

My examination of antiquity focuses on texts in a search for the roots of attitudes, and that pursuit will give an incomplete picture of the ancient world at best. However, my interest is not in the ancient world *per se* but in those aspects of it which I believe have had a strong impact on me. Still, there are some events and legacies from antiquity more readily recognized as "History" that have had a great impact on me and, as they have been generally understood, they have become text in themselves. In other cases, events have so molded the texts that the texts make no sense without their context. As a result, in the pages that follow, I tell some narrative history as well as peruse the contents of texts.

The idea of approaching these issues is by no means original with me. I think immediately of three recent writers who approach the study of history with precisely the same interest in the impact of attitudes as impel me to write this book. J. Peter Euben put the issue well in his discussion of texts: "If we are to understand ourselves as interpretive beings, we must recognize the traditions that have made us what we are, the stories in which we play a part, and the prejudgments, interests, and reasons that initially draw us to a text or text analogue."[4] Stressing the lineage of thought, Christian Meier asks questions about the reason fifth century Athenian texts – and art – are so open to our understanding, "why these works retain their appeal for us, whether they are really so essentially accessible in themselves or whether our European culture has taken up too much from the culture of the Greeks for it to strike us as strange."[5] The thrust of my discussion is not to ask such a question, or to concern myself with whether we have taken up "too much" of Greek culture. We are what we are, and we have done what we have done. It is what we will do that is at issue, and I take it as my project to show us more of what we are so that knowing ourselves, we will act and live in the future in ways that can accommodate the past.

Finally, because so much of recent writing about the impact of Greek thought and institutions has treated the question of Greek responsibility for what modern political thinkers call liberalism, it is worth noting what a student of ancient Athenian politics writes about the matter. Josiah Obers, whose work has contributed so much to our understanding of Athenian democracy, in his even-handed phrase describing Athens as "a society that developed norms strikingly similar to those of modern liberalism, but predicated those familiar norms on radically unfamiliar grounds,"[6] is looking at the issue to understand Athens, rather than to deal with the essential dictation of the ancient Athenian experience to the modern. Even so, his citation of the resemblances between ancient and modern norms is a support for the importance of understanding that ancient set of ideas, despite the fact that Athenian liberalism comes out of ancient practice while modern liberalism emerges out of the Athenian as mediated by 2000 years of experience, for the most part interrupted by rejection of that Athenian past.

An idealization of Athens, or even of Classical Greece, sees the fifth century as the culmination of a history that made it possible for all sorts of questions about the world and the human condition to be given in a new form:

> The answers were formed by the spirit of reason which suffused the citizenries, which, notwithstanding the superiority of many individuals, was common property, and which set its sights on permeating the world at large.... The fact that the spirit of reason was so general and so successful, so concrete for the majority and so abstract for a minority, operating in new fields such as the recording of

history, Sophistic theorizing, philosophy and various sciences, set the whole tone of life in Athens and contributed at the same time to the openness and accessibility of its culture.[7]

It will be clear from what follows that I do not see the fifth century as so individual a time; much of what makes Hellenism meaningful to us, and a motive force in the framing of our ideas, developed long before the fifth century. Some aspects, though formed in good measure by early Hellenism, came after the fifth century, and continued through the ages to contribute to the complex of assumptions and attitudes that make our culture what it is. The strength of the attitudes that form us is revealed by the impact the ideas had on the Greeks themselves; what Homer's audience might absorb from the story of Achilles remained fundamental to Greek attitudes for a thousand years, an inherent aspect of Hellenism that survived additions, and even contradictions, as history moved through successive centuries and new notions enlarged the scope of what was possible for a Greek to think. I see my project as calling for the tracing of that development as part of the demonstration of the manner in which ideas and attitudes erupted over the centuries and became part of my intellectual and moral inheritance.

Some might use the word "mentality" to describe the impact of Hellenism on western civilization, but that concept has recently come under attack from Geoffrey Lloyd.[8] My own treatment of the Hellenic impact on my "mentality" accepts the existence of attitudes and assumptions that continued from ancient times into modern, and I think the attack on the term unwarranted.[9] This is almost the same concept, perhaps in fact the same, as the term "tradition" which Karl Popper uses: "…we speak of traditions mainly when we wish to describe a uniformity of people's attitudes, or ways of behaviour, or aims or values, or tastes."[10]

Another way that frames the way people see the world is language. Lloyd also introduced this consideration at the end of his discussion of mentality. In an attempt to test his hypothesis by comparing Greek ideas with Chinese, he sought to find explanations for the differences between the two cultures that can be explained apart from mentality. In comparing Greek texts to Chinese, he argues:

> Yet clearly insofar as the ideas a philosopher produced were directed at a ruler whom he was hoping to influence, and insofar as the ruler himself was the final arbiter of the value of those ideas, those factors may well have imposed certain constraints on the ideas considered worth putting forward, constraints that may be thought to have inhibited, if not excluded, the development both of radical solutions to problems and of theoretical, abstract, impractical ones. Conversely, there are no analogues, in China, for the highly open-ended situation that, in the classical period at least, many Greek individuals faced, where their goal, when not to reach the abstract truth itself, was to persuade an undifferentiated general audience, even if one imagined to be no tyros in the evaluation of evidence and arguments.[11]

Lloyd is here reacting to the enormous gap between the Greek and Chinese ideas and their modes of expression. I will be discussing some of the differences between Greek ideas and Chinese as an aid to clarifying the significance of some of the attitudes that can be determined as Hellenic; for the moment, it is enough to point to the fundamental difference between the Greek separation of the universe from the individual observer who seeks to distinguish and comprehend what lies outside the viewer, and the concern of the Chinese thinker, who stresses the connections and unity between the human person, other humans, and the rest of creation. This fundamental difference in the way of seeing the world has led some to argue that language actually plays a large part in determine how people think and even what they think. A first reaction to the Chinese language commonly produces the conclusion that in Chinese, a language of expressing human ideas and thoughts extraordinarily different from Indo-European languages, the language itself molds what can be thought and said. This view has been expressed repeatedly from the sixteenth century.[12] In modern times it has taken one form or another of the hypothesis that the language of thinking provides "guidance and constraint" for the formulation of thought, a view of language and thinking argued by Benjamin Whorf.[13]

These linguistic issues and the dispute over incommensurability of language or the possible translatability – or non-translatability – from one language to the next have been mooted recently by Wardy's [14] exposition of the Chinese translation of Aristotle's *Categories*. Wardy argues that even some of the most specific Greek terminology can be rendered into Chinese, even if the translation would not be understandable in all cases to those not initiated into the concepts, a claim disputed in reviews of the book.[15] Chinese is very different from Greek or any other Indo-European language.[16] and the construing of classical Chinese is a particularly difficult matter, not only because of the structure of the language itself but the shifting understanding of the origin, antiquity and composition of the texts themselves.[17] In some cases, meanings are impossible to determine with complete confidence. There are many instances in which the ancient or modern Chinese commentators on a passage of Confucius, Mencius or Lao-Tzu differ strikingly in their interpretations of a text, and there are even cases in which one commentator takes a text as a positive statement, while another understands it as a negative. Not a few students of the language claim that there is a certain incommensurability between Chinese and Indo-European languages that make it impossible to translate certain ideas.

It is probably the case that there is some truth to the notion that for Chinese, as for the speakers of any language, "guidance and constraint" applies to conceptualization in some measure. It may not be that some ideas are impossible of expression or conceptualization by speakers of certain language, but it is entirely reasonable to suppose that for the Chinese, some Greek ideas would be difficult to comprehend, just as Greeks would find some Chinese concepts very hard to apply their reason to. At the very least, it must be true that some ideas are easier to express in some languages than others. A. C. Graham makes this point rather cleverly, pointing out that a perfect speaker of French "can no more translate it perfectly into English than his scientific into liturgical language or his poetry into officialese,"[18] an observation that extends to understanding that any shift in a medium of communication imposes some limits on what can be said or communicated, and in original composition, what can be thought as well. Culture, political arrangements and experience interact with language and mentality to share in the very complex matter of molding human ideas and experience, so we must leave room in our understanding of Greek or Chinese culture for the effects of culture, language, mentality and experience. All these aspects of life interact.

These are the premises of the manner in which I have written this book. I hope that my introduction of the Chinese ideas creates a contrast to Hellenism sufficient to emphasize the individuality of cultures. I wish to stress, however, that the introduction of the Chinese ideas as comparative makes no claim that the assumptions and attitudes of the West are in any way superior to those of the Chinese. It is merely an attempt to limn the Hellenic characteristics more clearly by setting them against alternative views, perhaps, indeed, suggesting that one set of attitudes cannot really be interpreted without reference to radically different views. This is intended to be an explication of differences without asserting values – except that in the long run, values emerge from being true to one's self and history, "sincerity," perhaps, as the Confucian might say.

This is not pure relativism, because the argument involves the possibility of insisting on adherence to an idea or a form of behavior in the given society even while allowing that the norm might not be valid for another. An understanding of a society's past can reveal the impact of borrowings, at least of important concepts or patterns, from one society by another. It may not be so easy for Singapore, by example, to import democratic institutions without abandoning some control over personal life to maintain standards of appropriate behavior; the government of China itself seems to have no intention of exposing the traditional stability of Chinese society to the turbulence of democratic institutions. The modern Confucian sage (and erstwhile Guomindang official) Chen Li-fu, while claiming that "Communism will not be tolerated in China,"[19] deplores the excessive individualism of western democracy, finding it, *inter alia*, manipulated by the wealthy who excessively favor liberalism, radicalism and legality. Conversely, European societies may find it not so easy to shift into the "seamless web" model of understanding the universe and the place of humans in it without drastically overhauling the expectations of people who currently live in a less "green" world.

INTRODUCTION

There is another aspect of this book to be noted. I make no attempt to discuss all the ancient texts the Greeks produced. I have limited myself to the discussion of those that might be considered particular, rather than anything that might be called "generally human," and I have treated only those I believe to be influential. In that, I have also discussed those basic influences I judge to be deleterious.

The negative aspect of the tradition is important, perhaps as important as the good on which I focused when I began this work. Just as there are attitudes inherited from antiquity that make for admirable qualities in our society, western society is also heir to a number of attitudes either created in Hellenic times or reinforced by texts written by ancient Greeks. Just as it is important to identify the good of our heritage so that we may defend, act on, and expand it, it is essential to clarify the significance of texts that have been strongly influential in the creation and maintenance of ideas that are, in my view, harmful. It is easy to make this clear in connection with some of the texts I discuss, as in, for example, my treatment of the *Oresteia* trilogy and the Hebrew scriptures, the latter of which has been so strong a reinforcement of authoritarianism and domination that a feminist writer has thought it might be labeled "Caution! Could be dangerous to your health and survival."[20] Indeed, the effort to expose and perhaps defuse these texts by feminist writers and others in the attempt to liberate us from them underscores the effects they have had on the framing of the ways in which we think.

Some of these negative qualities go to the heart of traditional attitudes, encompassing oppression within and outside our narrow political and social groupings, and extending to one of the basic problems still afflicting modern society: the misogyny and exploitation our institutions impose on women.

Acknowledging the deleterious aspects of the texts basic to our tradition is essential to understanding ourselves and our history, but it remains impossible for me, a male writer considering my texts from the standpoint of a long tradition of masculine scholarship and – yes, mentality – to write with the full comprehension of what it means for a female to assess the impact on herself and her sisters of the insouciant dismissal of the validity of femaleness by the goddess Athena as so explicitly portrayed by the male playwright Aeschylus. The same reservation applies to the biblical texts I discuss, but I recognize the "goal of feminist criticism [that] is not to substitute female hierarchies and modes of scholarship for male ones, but to transform the system as a whole,"[21] even though as a male writer I cannot write from the female standpoint.

In all this, I have usually been able to resist the temptation to move from the delineation of attitudes to specific prescriptions of what might be done to improve the world created by those attitudes. In an excellent little book Henry Rosemont explores the difference between western ideas of the human as a rational, autonomous being with natural rights, as against a Confucian concept of the human as a being defined (and defining others) in terms of the sum total of the relationships in which that individual human operates. Based on his perceptions, he offers proposals for the future development of China, and implications for western liberal democracies as well.[22] I do not do that, but there is nothing wrong with such a venture. In looking at these texts, however, I focus on an attempt to how certain attitudes inherited from Hellenism have led to contemporary attitudes and behavior. As an individual, understanding why I think a certain way is a necessary preliminary to changing that thinking. Thus I hope that some readers, at least, will share my comprehension of the difficulty of making change, while at the same time

INTRODUCTION

acknowledging the necessity of doing so; in the matter of ecological exploitation, for example.

I have tried in this introduction to set out my own conscious assumptions and attitudes as I review what I believe to be true about the past and about the texts that not only have emerged from the past but still remain deeply influential over our attitudes as we build the future. Brief sketches of events, summaries of historical, poetic, dramatic and philosophical works, interpretations of texts, and, perhaps less common in historical work, judgments on these texts, all seem to me to be essential to provide what is, I suppose, an intuition about the meaning of the past. At the very least, all this will at least explain the basis for my conception of the past, and will offer some material for others to use in considering its effects. It is my hope that if I can generate some understanding of the origins of the unspoken assumptions of our culture, it will be possible in the future to make informed choices about what attitudes we wish to retain for the future.

---

[1] Hillman (2004) pp. 178-201.
[2] Starr (1987) p. 5
[3] Armstrong (2007) p. 218.
[4] Euben (1990) p. 16.
[5] Meier (1993) p. 205.
[6] Ober (1996) p. 3.
[7] Meier (1993) p. 211
[8] Lloyd (1990) p. 36.
[9] See Appendix.
[10] Popper (1963) p. 179
[11] Lloyd (1990) p. 126.
[12] Matteo Ricci, Letter to Martino de Fornari, 1583, quoted from Spence, J. D. (1985) *The Memory Palace of Matteo Ricci*, pp. 136-7, by Wardy (2000) p. 6.
[13] Whorf (1956).
[14] Wardy (2000), attacking the "guidance and constraint" hypothesis that Chinese thought is prevented from taking the same approaches as we find in

the West. For half his pages Wardy assaults the hypothesis, taking specific assertions about the Chinese language, and scrutinizing the hypothesis in several case studies. The second half of the book argues that a collaboration in 1631 between a Chinese literatus and a Jesuit managed a reasonably successful translation of Aristotle's *Categories*, with commentary, into literary Chinese.

[15] Two careful examinations, finding Wardy fails to establish his thesis and insisting that the attempt to translate Aristotle was unsuccessful, are in *Mind* 110, pp. 1130-33 (Jiyuan Ku) and *Philosophy East and West* 51, 2001, pp. 545-553.

[16] There are no tenses to the verb, and only the pronoun used shows the person; nothing in a word itself indicates singular or plural; many words we would consider adjectives are actually used as verbs: "day hot," = "the (or a) day is hot." Syntax is entirely a matter of word position with particles, such as those indicating question or completion. Specific words can have a wide variety of denotations, let alone connotations, and some words can be used as function words, for example, to convert what is in its position a verbal clause, into a noun-clause: words meaning "assassinates a state's ruler," become "the one who assassinates a state's ruler."

[17] For a brief summary of the changing views on the authenticity and origin of the early texts see Shaugnessy (1997) pp. 1-6.

[18] Graham (1992) p. 73.

[19] Chen (1976) p. 25.

[20] Fiorenza (2001) p. 37.

[21] Reinhartz, A., "Feminist Criticism and Biblical Studies on the Verge of the Twenty-first Century," in Brenner and Fontaine (1997) p. 35

[22] Rosemont (1991).

–Part One–
The Individual and the Self

–3–
The Pursuit of Self–Knowledge

I have a very clear memory of explaining to my young children that the person who startled them with his grimaces and jerky motions was a victim of cerebral palsy. "He is just as intelligent as you are, and maybe more, and his mind is every bit as worthwhile as yours." I told them. "It's just that part of his nervous system is damaged and his mind can't control all his muscles."

The deeper text lying beneath the surface of my words told my children about more than the misfortune of cerebral palsy, more than muscle control and brain function. It gave them a vision of my view of what made up human value, what was to be rated as desirable, and more still, what makes up a human being. "Intelligence makes value," I seemed to be saying, and in the designation of mind I was expressing my cultural attitude – and I believe of many other people as well – that makes of "mind" an entity separate and distinguishable from the rest of the human organism – a tacit attitude totally unlike the sense that lies behind the Chinese word *xin*, usually translated "heart-mind." I was speaking as a child of, and making my own children heirs of, René Descartes, whose *"Cogito me cogitare, ergo sum* – I think I think, therefore I am" has become a summarizing phrase for the cultural assumption of the duality of human existence, a duality that presumes a separation between mind and body, makes the mind more valuable than the body, and the activity of the mind more precious than the efforts of the flesh.

I don't think I challenged that cultural assumption for most of my life. Even now, I have a lot of difficulty inventing images of "mind" that makes it an integral, organic brain process. I tell myself, (and Hannah Arendt, whose book[1] wrestles with some of these issues and makes the nature of many of the problems clear) that "thinking" is just another chemical/electric brain process like calling the perception of certain light rays "green." The trouble I have doing that comes from my background, just Germanic enough to inherit the assumptions of philosophers whose works I have read with only partial understanding. Despite all the efforts I make to distance myself from the influence of ancient presumptions, I can hardly think at all without their categories and vocabulary. It is even worse, because I have been steeped in Greek literature, and the notions of "mind" and thought I struggle with in my self-examinations are the notions of Greeks persisting into modern times. To be Germanic, after all, is to be Greek in a cold climate.

These days, the idea that the mind is a separate entity is coming under increasing challenge. The tradition to which Descartes belonged is no longer accepted as the only proper understanding of human behavior. The old expression "mind over matter" is being replaced by an understanding of "mind" that makes of it an expression of the function of matter, neither independent of matter nor superior to it, but in some mysterious way an aspect of the unified organism we call human – or perhaps even, anything animate. I hope that's clear: I said I was having trouble with this. In this contemporary concept of what it is to be human, some people claim a conscious rejection of what is often designated as Cartesianism. As if poor old Descartes must be made to bear the burden of misleading philosophy into a byway that turns out to be a blind alley. "If," some writers seem to imply, "we could erase the impact Descartes has made on thought, we could get back to a proper understanding of what it is to be human."

Proper understanding. That would really be nice. But to get to a different understanding of what it is to be human seems to me to require a good deal more than the obliteration of Descartes' assertions. My understanding of human nature is based on two and a half millennia of accepted assumptions, assumptions based on teachings and writings of two of the most revered intellectual and moral thinkers in our tradition, Socrates and Plato. To have any success in modifying my understanding or concept of myself, and by extension, other humans, I will have to reexamine what I take as truth, the truth or enlightenment credited to Socrates and Plato and passed on to successive generations to be embodied in the portrait of humanness that I and at least some others now take for granted as accurate.

The first of these ancient figures, Socrates, is a culture hero so attractively painted that it is almost impossible not to embrace his attitudes with an emotional endorsement. The life of Socrates is a story that has had a huge influence on me. When I read through the speech – penned by Plato as a rendition of a defense against a charge of impiety – Socrates made before an Athenian court in the year 399 BCE, I find myself in the grip of admiration and grief for a personality I feel I know and would love to emulate in whatever way I can.

I think that the two Greeks best known to westerners are Alexander the Great and Socrates. The first grips memory and imagination for accomplishments of conquest and the success of his use of force, while the second is preserved in memory by constant reference to his dedication to thought and adherence to a moral position. The first died young after ten years of military victory spread out over ten thousand miles; the second died at seventy after a life devoted to improving the intellects and virtues of the citizens of a single city. The death of the first is mysterious, from a cause unascertained; the death of the second is perhaps the most thoroughly documented execution in history, after a trial recorded in more detail even than that of Christ, but subject as much to questions about what lay behind the desire to see the man dead.

When Socrates died in 399 BCE, whether for political, philosophical, religious or even ignorant reasons,[2] the Athenians among whom he lived made up a society familiar with the issues of right and wrong as authors treated them in the ancient works that deal with the event. Writings of three Athenians who knew him personally, Plato, Xenophon and Aristophanes, have come down to us to present often contradictory pictures of the philosopher, and of the three, modern writers most frequently use dialogues by Plato to derive an understanding of what the man said and taught during his lifetime, and the literary genius of Plato has ensured that his version, his Socrates, is not only the most memorable, but also has influenced for all time the sense of philosophy and its potential. However, the Socrates of Plato's dialogues, almost everyone agrees, is a good part of the time merely the mouthpiece for ideas Plato wishes to put forward, and therefore a confusing guide at best, for the investigation of the so-called "historical Socrates" and what he taught.[3] In what follows, I use the name Socrates as a quasi-historical figure with characteristics that may be derived from Plato, Xenophon and Aristotle, and using Aristotle's evidence to define him; later, in the treatment of Plato himself, I will use the name Socrates as the philosopher Plato devised to present ideas in dialogues. Thus Socrates becomes a character in two stories, one, about the man himself, and the other, about Plato.

In the *Apology*, the speech Plato wrote to reflect the defense Socrates made at his trial, the philosopher is made to say:

> As long as I breathe, and am able to do it, I will not stop acting as a philosopher, exhorting you and pointing out to any of you I happen to meet, saying what I usually say, "O best of men, being an Athenian, of a city that is the greatest and most reputed for wisdom and strength, are you not ashamed of your concern for money, that you may have as much as possible, and of reputation and honor too, but of wisdom and truth and the soul, that it become as good as it can be, you neither care nor occupy your mind?"[4]

Years ago, when I read this for the second time (the first time, it was an exercise in learning Greek, and went pretty slowly) I finished it with an emotion of loss, almost grief, because Plato's prose involved me deeply in the personality of Socrates, and left no space for thought about the circumstances of the trial and execution.

The circumstances are important, however. I think that Socrates' description of the Athens recently defeated in the Peloponnesian War and at the time powerless would have puzzled many of the Athenian jurors at the trial. I also believe that the description of Socratic activity challenged many of the assumptions about the good life current in his time. This concept of the philosophical life has received almost universal approbation from later philosophers, who portray it as a dedication to the attempt to attain wisdom and truth and virtue of the soul. However, if Socrates really said to the Athenians what Plato has written in this speech, and if he really behaved through all his adult life in the manner depicted by Plato and Xenophon and accepted by most modern readers of their works, he had made a revolutionary break with the norms of Athenian and most Greek societies.

Although other writings – historical, tragic and other texts that have come down to us from the period during which Socrates lived his life – explore issues of justice, truth and virtue, they take a different view of the appropriate activity for human beings. The questioning of the nature of virtue and the relationship between human and divine justice assumes that what might be called the "public goods" – wealth, reputation, honor and a happy life – are those to be used in the calculation of reward and punishment for just and unjust behavior. The poets celebrate honor as the outcome of just action, and the historians record success and prosperity as well, and when they portray an outcome which reverses expectation, they – and we – are forced to reconsider our understanding of what justice might be.

The conventional rewards, however, are precisely those rejected by Socrates as unimportant in comparison to the real values of the state of one's soul or spirit, and this completely private matter had never before been part of the equation. If then, Socrates really used the completely personal matter of the condition of one's spirit as the appropriate measure of the quality and success of life, he was changing completely the standards of behavior and the approach to the challenge of imperfectly understood justice. But it is difficult not to believe that he did this, for this portrait of Socratic teaching in the *Apology* is consistent with much of the rest of Plato's portrait of him, and with a large part of the presentation of Socratic teaching by other contemporaries and by Aristotle, who lived in the century after Socrates and serves as the most important secondary source for our understanding of the philosopher. There are, however variant traditions, and in Plato, in particular, an entire philosophy built up of many dialogues besides the *Apology*, and the discrepancies among the sources create the so-called "Socratic Problem," the matter of determining what Socrates actually did think and teach.

The issue has been tackled by many different writers using widely variant approaches to the sources to produce strikingly different versions of Socratic thought, and the solution will always escape complete agreement because Socrates himself left no writings that would confirm what the sources report. You may remember the black humor of the cartoon depicting two men looking at Jesus on the cross, saying "He was a great teacher, but he never published." The comment works for Socrates as well, and the absence of writings by Socrates himself explains the ambiguities in the sources' information about Socrates or the differences among them.[5] In full awareness of the pitfalls of using the evidence of a philosopher who uses the figure of Socrates to put forth his own ideas, modern investigators usually take Plato as the best evidence for genuine Socratic thought.[6] However, any careful reading of Plato's dialogues forces a conclusion that, as Gregory Vlastos writes, "in different sets of dialogues he [Socrates] pursues philosophies so different that they could not have been depicted as cohabiting the same brain throughout unless it had been the brain of a schizophrenic."[7] It is Vlastos' early Socrates that has so caught the imagination of later ages, and it is the thought that this Socrates presents that makes so radical a break with the ethic of life in Athens.

That "early" Socrates can, in some measure, be squared with the picture presented by Xenophon, or even that of Aristophanes, the comic playwright whose parody in *Clouds* may give some indication of the philosopher's involvement in the teaching or study of natural science and the possible evolution of his thoughts and behavior in the years between the 420s, when the play was produced and revised, and the last years of the century when Plato would have known him. Later, Aristotle distinguishes Socrates' thought from his predecessors and from his great successor, Plato, who was Aristotle's own teacher. Aristotle could be in error, of course, and in any case merely summarizes the significance of Socrates' activity, but he presents a specific, coherent statement in philosophical terms. In *Metaphysics* 1078 B 17-32 Aristotle writes:

> Socrates, dealing with ethical virtues and first seeking definition by universals for these ... reasonably enquired into the essence. He sought to infer syllogistically, and the start of syllogistic inference is the essence.... One might fairly attribute two things to Socrates, inductive reasoning and definition by universals. Both of these relate to the beginning of scientific knowledge. But Socrates did not make the universal or the definitions separate in existence. It was others who separates them, and denominated them the Ideas [Forms] of whatever exists."

Another passage, *Metaphysics* 971 B 1 ff., repeats the description of Socrates as seeking the universal and concentrating on definitions, but distinguishes Plato's approach which places the universal in a world other than that of sense perception.[8]

In examining all of Aristotle's statements about Socrates, the Aristotelian picture can fit the views Plato puts in the mouth of a so-called early Socrates, while assigning to Plato himself other views he puts into the mouth of Socrates.[9] These statements not only show Aristotle's view of the place of Socrates in the history of philosophy, they limit themselves, for the most part, to a very brief explication that shows more about the *subject* of Socratic investigation rather than the fruit of those inquiries or the elaboration of his thought. However, even if Aristotle's testimony be rejected, and the "historical Socrates" be sought only in the figure of the *Apology* and perhaps the *Crito*, even the minimal view of Socrates gives us a figure seeking for wisdom rather than teaching it and acknowledging his own ignorance, a philosopher insisting on care that the soul be as good as possible and refusal to do anything unjust.[10] Perhaps most important, Aristotle treats Socrates within a separate discipline of philosophy, not as it pertains to the overall development of Athenian or Greek thought expressed in drama, poetry and history.

This last point calls for some emphasis, for it has not received its due since Nietzsche. It is important because I want to treat issues that arise in drama, epic and other "non-philosophic" writing in a different way than philosophers usually deal with them. This is partly a matter of taste, but I do so also because before Plato, or perhaps, stretching the time, before Socrates, there was no such things as a philosopher, no such organized discipline as philosophy. The Ionian writers on the physical universe in the sixth and early fifth centuries were called, if they were given any name, *sophoi*, "wise men," and not "philosophers." The professionals who taught in Athens and elsewhere were identified as teachers of disciplines: mathematics, rhetoric, music, politics, grammar, and the like, and if they had any general name, it was that of *sophistes,* and that is how the immediate predecessors of Socrates, and perhaps

Socrates himself, were known. It is not only the case that the teachers who dealt with the usual matters we assign to the realm of philosophy were not yet identified as the practitioners of a specific and discipline; some of the topics of examinations that in the time of Aristotle were identified as clearly the concern of philosophy were treated in fifth century Athens by writers who at no time in history could conceivably have been called "philosophers." But writers did examine issues of ethics and morality, and I, being a professional historian, naturally think that treatment of these matters by writers like the historian Thucydides is a valid enterprise.

I spend as much time as I do dealing with this because the tradition established by Socrates and Plato has been the basis for ethical and even psychological reasoning by almost all thinkers who have been educated on these texts. Socrates' approach established the parameters of philosophical thought on these issues. The manner in which Plato dealt with them created a major mode of thinking in the succeeding centuries, and a mode which, as I will show in later chapters, became the dominating mentality of Christian thought and fundamentally affected what would become acceptable conceptions of the nature of human beings.

Ethics, which Aristotle states was the concern of Socrates, was important in the work of tragedians and historians and was not considered to demand specialized training or treatment for consideration, or call for any specialized techniques of investigation, although some Sophists claimed special competence in teaching it. A Socrates concerned with ethics, dealing with definitions and seeking the essence of virtue and justice, as Aristotle implies, pursued the same questions as did the historians and tragedians. Doing so by inductive reasoning and definition by universals was a difference in technique from that of the dramatists and historical writers, but the difference was only technique. Aristotle's statement thus is of great value in showing us what the successors to Socrates actually thought he did: he reformed the treatment of morality and justice and fashioned formal methods of investigation, taking the discussion of justice out of the realm of the amateur and dilettante to make it into a formal discipline.

This is quite consistent with the presentation of many statements in which Plato shows Socrates suggesting special qualification for the teaching of virtue. The idea will be familiar to every reader of the *Protagoras*; the issue goes to the heart of the controversy over the possibility of teaching *arete* and the fact that the Sophists were the first professional teachers in the experience of the Greeks. Socrates in the *Apology* brings his customary irony to the matter, congratulating a man named Euenas for teaching the qualities of good citizenship for so small a sum as five minas when he, Socrates, would have taken great pride in such a capability. The *Apology* also stresses Socrates' pursuit of virtue and his rejection of the things usually thought to be good, saying that "not from possessions does virtue arise, but that from virtue, possessions and all the other good things, both private and public, exist for men."[11] The *Apology* has Socrates insist that in this life-style he obeys the gods, guided by his divine sign, rather than working for pay, distinguishing him from the paid Sophists. The same is true for his continually repeated assertion that he has no knowledge, and only enough wisdom to make him aware of his ignorance. Furthermore, he repeatedly asserts his pursuit of knowledge with a constant urging of the same pursuit on those he encounters, to the detriment of other occupations, an acknowledgment that he followed a rule of behavior different from that of other men. In the broadest sense, this dedication to the promulgation of the pursuit of virtue was a professional pursuit, in that it was all Socrates did, and was done in a particular manner.

The particular manner of Socratic discourse was his famous method, called in Greek *elenchos*, a kind of cross-examining and refutation of those proposing a particular position. Socrates takes some general question, often one of definition, as "What is courage?" and after obtaining an answer from one of the participants in the dialogue, pursues it with a series of new questions, some of which may not have an apparent relationship to the original question. As the discussion proceeds, the answers to the subsidiary questions conflict with or lead to a contradiction with the answer to the first question. At the conclusion, Socrates urges the participants to pull together all the answers to the questions, making the contradictions clear. The conclusion to all this is that the knowledge offered in the first answer was only the presumption of knowledge, and was erroneous, and that the respondent really did not know the answer to the question, although he thought he did. With this the discussion terminates.

It is the type of inquiry described in Plato's *Apology*, when Socrates describes his questioning of all sorts of people to prove there were those who were wiser than him in order to refute the baffling reply of the Delphic Oracle that there was no one wiser than Socrates. The whole procedure Socrates describes in the *Apology* was an *elenchos*, and Socrates asserts that it was this sort of questioning of people – statesmen, poets, artisans – that generated hostility toward him. To artisans he gave credit for knowing how to do some things, but because they wrongly thought they knew higher things on the basis of their knowledge of their crafts, he chose to do without their knowledge rather than take their knowledge and their ignorance together; the poets, including the tragedians, he found able to write poetry, but unable to explain what they had written as well as bystanders could, so he concluded their poetry came as a kind of inspiration rather than knowledge or wisdom.

To this "early" Socrates the critical issue was knowledge, with *elenchos* the vital procedure by which error was purged. A more positive method of understanding the nature of things was that of definition: Justice, Temperance, Courage – each was approached with the question "What is it?" Socrates always proffered his ignorance of the answer to such questions, the famous "Socratic ignorance," and he never provides an answer to such a question, but instead subjects any answers to *elenchos*, comparing himself in this to a midwife who could not give birth to wisdom but who by conversations with others helps them give birth to it while actually teaching nothing himself. However, the conversations are not so barren, for they make it possible to learn much about the subjects even though at the end of the conversations "Justice," "Temperance," "Courage" and "Virtue" remain undefined. The discussion may delineate some aspects of the subjects, and common opinions have been evaluated and their content of truth understood. The relationships between the subject and many aspects of everyday activity have been considered and sometimes clarified. It was this search for definitions through *elenchos* that Aristotle thought important, and Socrates' innovation, as it appears in the dialogues and was pointed out by Aristotle, was the introduction of method to the study of ethics, and a fundamental aspect of this method was the attempt to define, even if the definition was not achieved and the investigator again and again asserted himself ignorant.

Aristotle did not carry his description of Socratic thought to a conclusion that the ignorance admitted was philosophical, not behavioral: no matter how often Socrates asserted his ignorance, whether of virtue, courage, justice or the like, his actions conformed to some code of behavior, an apparent contradiction that has been noted by many. It is quite clear from a number of statements Plato has him make that he based his actions and decisions on his own understanding of what made for virtuous or wicked behavior. For example, in *Apology* 32 he tells the story of his opposition to the illegal action of gathering in a single judicial trial a number of generals who were held responsible for not picking up sailors from the water after an important battle at Arginusae, on the grounds that he was acting "with law and justice on my side." There was a principle also in his refusal to participate in an execution ordered by the thirty tyrants ruling Athens at the end of the fifth century BCE; instead he simply went home, as he wanted above all not to "do anything which was unjust or unholy."

The most memorable instance of his refusal to act "contrary to justice" is recounted in Plato's *Crito*, which shows Socrates as unwilling to escape from prison and thereby avoid his execution, on the grounds that this disobedience to the *nomoi* or laws would be an act of injustice. Socrates seems to have no doubt about the rectitude of his position, and in a hypothetical dialogue between himself and the laws[12] Socrates presents the laws arguing convincingly that should Socrates escape he would be taking an action that would destroy them and the whole city. The argument asserts that in view of the fact that he accepted both the laws and his trial, it would not only be absurd to reject the requirements of the laws, it would be wrong.[13] And as the passages in the *Apology* show, Plato consistently represents Socrates refusing to do anything he considered wrong.

Xenophon reinforces this position at the beginning of his own account of Socrates' words at the trial; the philosopher claimed that his whole life had been spent in preparation for the trial, as he had always tried to avoid unjust action. In addition, the four books of his *Memorabilia of Socrates* collect the

THE PURSUIT OF SELF KNOWLEDGE

evidence to justify Xenophon's final quotation of Socrates, that "I never did wrong to any man ever, nor made anyone worse."[14] On the basis of these texts, and because of the impact Socrates made on the minds and hearts of many of his contemporaries, it is safe to believe that he lived his life according to some principles of what constituted just behavior, and that while searching for such principles as the main thrust of his philosophical inquiry, at the same time he adhered to some. And, while there remains an inevitable doubt[15] about the identification and nature of the "historical Socrates" because we have no texts and no statements that can be attributed to him with certainty, the "probably historical," or the "literary," or Vlastos' "Socrates (Early)" will do as well to recreate the Socrates of my story about him.

This is the Socrates to whom Aristotle's statements apply, a philosopher whose concern was the discovery of ethical concepts. In this version of the story, the version I accept, at that time there was debate among the professional teachers, the Sophists, about the priority of moral principles, contrasting any creature's natural effort to aggrandize the self – *physis* – with *nomos* – the imposed and unnatural restraints generated in the process of community living. By rejecting old definitions and exploring new ones, Socrates evaded that controversy, and in a sense did more than evade it: he destroyed it by uniting the antitheses in redefinition. He repeatedly argued that no one intentionally caused self-injury; that virtue was the knowledge whereby this self-injury could be avoided; that the state of the soul was the most important consideration; that injury to others harmed the soul of one who did that injury; and that the knowledge of this protected the wise person from harming others. This reasoning eliminates the *physis-nomos* antinomy, because it makes the *physis* or nature of the human require that the human seek to benefit and avoid harm to fellow creatures, precisely the object of the *nomoi* as the propounders of the controversy see them.

The difference between Socrates' position and the traditional view of the issue lies in the definition of *physis*. Those who adhered to the Sophistic discussion believed the *nomoi* were in opposition to a *physis* that seeks self-aggrandizement at the expense of others, while Socrates would presume no conflict between *nomoi* and *physis* because in his definition of *physis*, it was selfish only in seeking improvement of the soul and avoiding any material gain achieved unjustly at the expense of others.

Socrates' position, so different from the views of the Sophists, is not something he argues for or demonstrates, and it would be fair to say that this description of Socrates is my own interpretation of the story. When Socrates argues, as in *Crito* 47 and 48, that the part of the human that is improved by justice and harmed by the practice of injustice is more important than the body, he is stating an article of faith rather than a reasoned conclusion. And this conclusion, that the *psyche* or soul is more important than the body, assumes an even more fundamental characteristic of the human, that there is an aspect of the human makeup that is improved by justice and damaged by its opposite.

It is here, I think, that we find the core of the idea of two aspects of the human, the body part, and the superior, that may be designated variously as mind, or spirit, or *psyche*, "soul." There is no hint of such an idea in the admittedly fragmentary information we have about the Sophists, but it is so characteristic of Socrates as he appears in the works of Plato that we are probably safe in assuming this fundamental difference between his views and those of the Sophists and, for that matter, of the tragedians. We will see how this separation, however beneficial it may be seen to the ethics propounded by Socrates, became a feature of the thought of successive generations with monumental consequences.

The assertion of the primacy of the soul and its improvement by virtuous action helps to resolve the apparent contradiction between Socrates' assertion that he has no knowledge, and his consistent acceptance of what his contemporaries generally thought was benefit and harm, at least as applied to the body. There is a clear indication that while one may inflict greater harm on one's soul by harming another unjustly, Socrates accepts the bodily harm as such. Killing is harm; so is deceiving another, or calumniating. Extending this to other areas of action, Socrates does not challenge the norms of his society in defining just and unjust action,[16] and has no hesitation in using these norms as part of his argument for a more fundamental definition of virtue as knowledge. For example, in defining courage as knowledge, Socrates accepts society's general condemnation of cowardice in asserting that the knowing man will avoid this, even at the expense of his life, as a known evil more to be avoided than the unknown quality of death. So too, he accepts that view that belief in, respect for and obedience to the gods is right,[17] just as he accepts the validity of the laws, a position that was a social norm in Athens, and as a result he accepts and executes upon himself a judgment he believes to be in error.[18]

Logic might suggest that Socrates was pretending to a knowledge he did not have in accepting these social norms, but his *action* is quite apart from his words about knowledge, and he does not propose a definition of virtue or present an objective system for determining just behavior. Rather, as the *Crito* shows, he is accepting a kind of social contract[19] as a valid guideline for action within a society. Implicit in his behavior is a willingness to use social norms in dealing with people in a society because the issues involved therein are less important than making the care for the soul paramount.[20] Relying on the norms of his society, Socrates seems to accept most of the ethical assumptions of later fifth century Athens, and there is in his conceptualization no conflict between divine and human morality and justice because he promulgates no details for either. Even the *daimonion,* the divine voice that warns him from proceeding in a manner that would be wrong, never offered positive precepts for action, as he makes clear in *Apology* 31. The idea of "divine law" in opposition to human is inherently contradictory to this approach to virtue as knowledge, for Socrates depends on human reason alone as the path to knowledge, not only in evaluating everyday actions but in seeking the definition of the essence of virtue and morality. But, by derogating the customary ideas of good and evil in human experience, Socrates avoid the conundrum that faced so many ethical thinkers, who regarded as genuine harm the injustices suffered often by apparently good people, and sought resolution by positing a higher law.

Asserting the primacy of the soul and its improvement by adherence to justice, Socrates avoided the whole contradiction often posed by the tragedians, because the Socratic view claims that in the most important aspect of the human condition, just behavior always benefits the person acting justly. So too, unjust action could seriously wound its victim only in the lesser aspect of the body, and the harm it did was much greater for the perpetrator who thereby wounded the soul. Success and failure or reward and punishment in this life was measurable only in terms of the condition of the soul, with conventional "goods" of wealth, reputation and even family of little consequence in weighing up this fundamental gauge.[21] This is a value system quite different from that prevalent before the time of Socrates, "a new model of virtue to the Greeks who had been concerned for centuries with *arete* – excellence, valor and integrity."[22] It allowed Socrates to accept current norms while at the same time rejecting current assessments of advantage, and it gives a new direction to the study of ethics. This was really the beginning of moral philosophy. As such, by positing or even just assuming the existence of a "soul," the Socratic tradition established the concept of a divided self, a dualism inherent in human beings that became an inextricable part of philosophical thinking and investigation of ethical matters.

The efforts of Xenophon in writing of Socrates, and of Plato in presenting him in the *Apology* and the dialogues dealing with his trial and execution, aimed to defend him rather than explain his thought. In his later work, Plato so inveigled the figure of Socrates into position as expositor of Platonic ideas that Aristotle felt it necessary to disentangle the two, and later ages often thought of this Platonic Socrates when the philosopher came to mind. After Aristotle, however, there was a gap of two millennia[23] before the figure of Socrates became important either as a subject of investigation or as a symbol. As a result, Socrates, even the Socrates so admired by Montaigne, did not have much impact on thought apart from the after-effects of his separate assessments of the importance of soul and body, and it is in the modern debate over Socrates' political sentiments, democratic or anti-democratic, that thinkers can be asserted to have had any real encounter with the philosopher's thought.[24] At best, he was a symbol to express the goals of intellectual activity, as the eighteenth century used his story. Not until Kant presented his *Critique of Pure Reason* at the end of the eighteenth century do we see the formulation of ethical ideas that could be asserted to have any relation at all to the Socratic method. And at the end of the next century Nietzsche developed a completely different story about Socrates, making him the promoter of a rationalism that destroyed the vitality of earlier Hellenism with all its heroic aspects. This assertion of Socratic importance in Nietzsche's story may have been responsible for the twentieth century tendency to make Socrates "the leader of all modern enlightenment and modern philosophy, the apostle of moral liberty, bound by no dogma, fettered by no tradition, standing free on his own feet, listening only to the inner voice of conscience."[25]

Not, however, as a predecessor or mentor or even opponent of philosophers, nor even in the quarrel between democracy and its opponents, is the Socratic story so influential in the development of western ideas. It is his execution that poses issues with which thinkers and writers have struggled, particularly in the last two centuries, as the ideas of freedom of speech and conscience have been inserted among the "inalienable rights" asserted for society. Although Pericles boasted of an "open society" as the hallmark of Athenian democracy, the notions of freedom of speech, freedom of conscience and even freedom of religion were not a necessary part of the Athenian system of government. The charge of impiety Socrates faced was not exceptional; it was one of the charges brought against the philosopher Anaxagoras, and even if that accusation was an indirect attack on Pericles, it might have brought about a condemnation had Pericles not helped his friend escape from Athens.

In a certain sense Plato may be responsible for the lingering sense of injustice done in the trial of Socrates. I have already mentioned my own emotions decades ago when I closed my Oxford text once again on the last words of the *Apology* with a sense of – almost grief – at the impending departure of a man so honest and courageous. This grip on the imagination is illustrated by the place in history assigned Socrates by Karl Jaspers, the twentieth-century German philosopher who remained in Germany beside his Jewish wife to resist Nazism at considerable personal risk and cost: Socrates appears with the Buddha, Confucius and Jesus as one of the four thinkers who influenced philosophy more than even such great minds as Plato, Aristotle and St. Augustine.[26] While Jaspers' evaluation emerges from that philosopher's view of Socrates' own philosophical contribution, the literary force of the *Apology* conveys a sense of the man and the sense of oppression made by the trial that makes' Socrates' death in some way comparable to that of Jesus. As Christ's crucifixion was in subsequent centuries a paradigm for moral and religious error, the act of executing an innocent figure generally believed to be the son of God carried over into the condemnation of Socrates to make that crime, although entirely human, no less reprehensible. That is, I think, the version of the story most common today.

I think that it is clear that the majority of writers from the beginning of the enlightenment on tell the story of the trial of Socrates in a way that faults Athens and sides with Socrates in the case.[27] Beyond the question of the rightness and wrongness of the condemnation of the aged philosopher, however, lie issues that this story has planted in me and others. The grip of his personality, and the importance of the moral issues his trial raised tend, I think, to obscure the importance of assumptions he made and the impact those assumptions made on his followers – philosophers and non-philosophers alike from antiquity to today. As I see the story, however, it is a narrative of fundamental importance affecting how I see myself and other human beings, and as I think about what I have read over the years, I see how the narrative has affected others in the same way.

The idea that there is an aspect of the human that is separate and distinct from the body, a *soul*, or mind, if you will, creates a sense of dualism within the human creature that I cannot quite escape. I can see the assumption of this dualism at work in literature and philosophy of many centuries of the past. The story of Socrates is so forceful that it carries into concepts of human beings the assumptions Socrates made, as a torrent sweeps along the creatures that swim in it. Indeed, it may create so powerful an assumption, so determinative of the understanding of the nature of existence, that those who are nurtured in this tradition can not really see themselves as unitary beings, that in some way we will always live with a concept of "mind," if not "spirit" or "soul."

---

[1] Arendt, H. (1971).

[2] For a recent suggestion on the reason for Socrates' conviction, and bibliography on the matter, see Munn (2000) pp. 284–291.

[3] Two recent books illustrate what are almost extremes in the treatment of Plato's dialogues as evidence for the historical Socrates; Vlastos ed. (1971) pp. 22-49, argues that we can identify a Socrates (early) from a series of Plato's writings including the *Apology* and a dozen or so early dialogues, while Kahn (1996) accepts only the evidence from the *Apology* supplemented by a few items from the *Crito*.

[4] Plato, *Apology of Socrates* 29 d.

[5] A good starting place among modern studies of the question would be would be Brickhouse and Smith (2000) that offers a discussion of Socratic philosophy and the interpretations of current scholarship for the most part in a balanced and untendentious text. Earlier surveys are worth pursuing: Guthrie (1962-81) III, pp. 323-75; Lacey A. E., "Our Knowledge of Socrates," in Vlastos, ed. (1971) pp. 22-49. Vlastos himself has examined the sources in detail in Vlastos (1991); on which see Nehamas (1999) pp. 83-107 (and other essays there published on Socratic and Platonic questions.

[6] E.g. Santas (1979) p. x commenting "that it is only Plato's Socrates that is of major interest to the contemporary philosopher."

[7] Vlastos (1991) p. 46.

[8] It is, perhaps, worth pointing out that Kahn (1996) pp. 71-95 and esp. pp. 79-87, gives reasons to reject Aristotle's testimony if one wishes to do so.

[9] Vlastos (1991) p. 97, in reference to ten critical theses expounded in different sets of Plato's dialogues (pp. 47-49).

[10] Argued by Kahn (1996) pp. 71-95 and esp. pp. 88-93.
[11] *Apology* 30 b.
[12] *Crito* 50 ff.
[13] This passage has struck many as inconsistent with other Socratic statements on obedience to law, and I do not intend to enter the dispute over whether Socrates is inconsistent on the issue of civil disobedience. A. D. Woozley makes much of its logical contradition with *Apology* 29 d, where Socrates asserts he would continue his pursuit of philosophy, against the authority of the Athenians, in "Socrates on Disobeying the Law," in Vlastos ed. (1971 pp. 299-318. A good survey of this discussion (with bibliography) is now offered by Brickhouse and Smith (2000) pp. 200-216, although it seems to me that the attention to the described contradiction between *Crito* and *Apology* as commonly posed does not make enough of an apparent contradiction in action, whereby Socrates in *Crito* and elsewhere acts as if he has a knowledge he denies elsewhere.
[14] *Memorabilia* IV. 8. 10.
[15] Doubt, but I do not accept the extreme position of Chroust (1957) which argues that any information about Socrates is legend, deriving from one or more of the fictitious traditions that grew up from the fourth century BCE on.
[16] Cf. Xenophon, *Memorabilia* IV. 13-25, portraying Socrates as identifying what is just with what is lawful, not only in respect to law but unwritten *nomoi*.
[17] According to Xenophon, *Memorabilia* 1. 3. 1, repeated in IV. 3. 16, Socrates' behavior and advice followed that of the priestess at Delphi, who set up the "nomos of the city" as the guide to pious behavior.
[18] As evidence of the correctness of his behavior, Socrates cites the advice of the god he calls his *daimonion*, which opposed him even in small matters if he was about to go wrong, and did not impede him in his current behavior, a phenomenon he takes to establish the validity of the *nomoi* for members of society.
[19] Explicit, *inter alia*, at Xenophon, *Memorabilia* IV. 4. 13.
[20] This may help resolve the surface contradiction between *Crito* and *Apology* 29, made so much of by Woozley in Vlastos, ed. (1971).
[21] Rejecting the long-standing Greek acceptance of the moral validity of retaliation, which to Vlastos (1991) pp. 179-199, p. 195, marks "Socrates' break with the established morality." Vlastos can find anticipations of Socrates' position in fifth-century dramatic and historical writing (pp. 190-94).
[22] Hulse (1995) p. 28.
[23] Hulse (1995) Chapters 3 and 4.
[24] For Socrates in modern schools of thought, see, Lane (2001) pp. 11-51.
[25] Jaeger (1943) II, p. 13.
[26] Jaspers (1962).
[27] A notable exception in modern times is the polemic of Stone (1988).

—4—
The Knowing Self

Let me review what I am trying to do in this section of the book. I have started out with a story about Socrates, and have told it as the emergence of the notion of two partially oppositional aspects of human personality. What I have written so far, however, is just part of my narrative of a longer story telling how a concept of human beings evolved. The narrative goes on through the story of Plato, and then into that of Aristotle, Plato's most notable student. It is part of a story often referred to in histories of western philosophy, but I want to tell it as the beginning of the attitude that had me talk to my children about the cerebral palsy sufferer whose "mind" was what made the person's value. We will use the Greek word *psyche* as the name of the lead character in this story.

The long-standing use of the term psyche by Greek writers suggests the notion that the human being possesses some quality different in nature from the body. Because of the importance of "soul" to religious thought, classical and religious scholars have studied the Greek term as long as Greek and biblical studies have existed, and have made much of the fact that in its origin, psyche seems to have meant in Greek something like "breath." Thus Socrates was using an old, well-known term when he asserted the ethical primacy of the psyche. The psyche may have been intangible in Socratic thought, but it had real existence, and the insistence on its ethical importance and potential for improvement was an important inheritance Socrates left to his pupil Plato. The fundamental assumption that the human being possessed some intangible aspect that could be designated as the psyche was thus as much part of the thought of Plato as it was of Socrates. Unlike Socrates, however, Plato proposed some specific characteristics for the psyche that tended to firm up the concept of a separable aspect of being that directed the actions of the body, and was superior to the body. Plato explored questions like the ability of the psyche to know and to learn, and even proposed a theory of its immortality, giving it dimensions that could be imagined and asserted. Because Plato used the figure of Socrates as the expositor of his ideas, there will always be some doubt about the distinction between ideas that can be ascribed to Socrates himself and those first promulgated by Plato. This problem does not really effect my story, however, because the ideas themselves, once they were offered in written text, existed to frame the concepts of successive generations. In any case, there can be seen a common thread uniting "Socratic" and "Platonic" thought – the acceptance of a separable psyche in the first place. Even so, there is some value in focusing on Plato himself and the probable distinction between his ideas and those of his master.

There is probably no other single author who has affected western philosophy as much as Plato. If we attribute to Plato rather than Socrates the doctrine of the independent "Forms" – idealizations of the perfect nature of phenomena – following

Aristotle's distinction that it was Plato who separated the Forms from the entities to which they related, then the dialogues that depend upon assumptions related to the ideal Forms can rightly be termed "Platonism." This might be described as a system of thought that created assumptions about humanity and the cosmos paralleling, but often different from, older Hellenic views about the nature of reality. For me, this is the story the texts tell. Because this stream of thought has been so important to the formulation of cosmological, ethical and political ideas in the West, the Platonic corpus has been studied and restudied from the time of its first promulgation, and it is fair to say that there is still great dispute about the manner in which the dialogues are to be read and the conclusions that may properly be drawn from them.

Before I tell my story of Plato's thought or the meaning of the texts themselves, it will be worth while for me to say what I leave aside as tangential to the main theme of the narrative. I do not intend to argue chronology or development in Platonic thought; whether or not the chronology for the dialogues is now fairly well agreed, sequence is not important to what I say about the ideas presented in the text. Second, my story has nothing to do with what might be described as a kind of "intentional fallacy," like the intentional fallacy exposed by literary critics in the middle of the last century. That is, the story has nothing to do with what Plato intended to accomplish outside the realm of philosophy itself, by writing his dialogues – "saving the polis," or offering a genuine proposal for a perfect or near-perfect human society.[1] I do not know what Plato intended to achieve for his society, and reading the many books that argue that issue has not enlightened me very much. Third, the story in this chapter has nothing to do with the argument over whether Plato is pro- or anti- democratic, a supporter or opponent of totalitarianism.

Although I deeply sympathize with Karl Popper's proposals for principles of politics presented in his discussion of Plato, I am not sure that his exposé of Plato's totalitarian bias,[2] or Moses Finley's characterization of Plato as "the most powerful and most radical anti-democratic moralist the world has ever known"[3] helps to understand the manner in which Platonic ideas influenced subsequent thinkers so deeply. Finally, fourth, I am not writing a story about Plato to give an overall description of all his ideas in a general survey of the dialogues,[4] but I am writing a story about an idea as it appears in some of his work.

In what follows in this chapter, I am attempting to tell the story of some basic Platonic principles about the self and the manner in which the self knows its environment, natural or moral. I hope any reader familiar with Plato's texts will agree that my narrative can reasonably, and fairly easily, be derived by an ancient or a modern reader from a moderately careful consideration of the texts. I do not ask that the texts be considered from a new standpoint, and in fact, for my purposes, a new standpoint would be undesirable, because part of my objective in setting out these ideas is to assert that they have long been influential in the establishment of western assumptions about humanity and the universe. Furthermore, in all this I do not feel it necessary to cite overmuch of the voluminous bibliography that has grown from the Platonic field, although from time to time I may cite a later writer as an illustration of the acceptance – or rejection – of an aspect of the story as I see it.

It seems to me that Plato accepted some of the basic tenets of the teaching I have called "Socratic," at least those fundamental ideas that the earlier "aristocratic" ideals of prowess, wealth and the like should be replaced by the therapy of the psyche, and therefore adopted the Socratic notion of the existence of an educable psyche. The idea of the pursuit of virtue on principle was not new, of course, although Socrates' evaluation of personal benefit and harm and the implications of these was new. Plato wrote to carry forward the exploration of virtue, justice and the like beyond the position Socrates had reached, and in so doing found himself forced to move from the world around him to seek a more fundamental and absolute reality that would allow for the existence of a justice that could be determined by techniques better than Socrates had proposed. Plato concluded that understanding and right conduct only became possible with perception of truths higher than those of human experience and society.

Socrates, evaluating achievement in terms of the extent to which the self, and particularly the soul, was perfected, proposed a revolution in moral thought. This was the revolution that Nietzsche later perceived and condemned as the triumph of the slave mentality of the weak over the ideals of the noble and the strong: the overturning of the aristocratic ideal. Until Socrates' time, the aristocratic ideal seemed to serve well enough as a regulator of human conduct, and the world in which that ideal had set the standards of virtue seemed understandable, with its moral uncertainty and confusion examined and sometimes resolved by tragedy. People were what they were, the world was what it was, and the noblest nature was that which did the best job of making the most of it. The ethos of Homer remained basic to people who saw many of Homer's attitudes reinforced by Athenian tragedy: persistence, strength, the stubbornness to try to dominate were humanity's noblest effort and highest object. The statesmen aligned their policies with this view.

Plato's texts show quite clearly how the Socratic ideal would overturn all this, and the conflict between a new ethic and the traditional virtues praised by epic and drama played an important part in his condemnation of the poets and the interdiction of their work from the ideal society he presented in the *Republic*. His concept of reality allowed him to dismiss their work as imitative[5] and deceptive, so that he had an intellectual justification for the elimination of their seductive charm. The ideals of epic and tragedy ran so counter to the ideals he was promoting that he found these works objectionable on practical and moral, as well as theoretical and philosophical, grounds. Modern readers find reprehensible the passages in the *Republic* whereby Plato excludes the poets from his society, or allows their participation under the condition that their imitations aid in the imitation of justice.[6] Ordinary free speech is violated, and there is no notion of the later utilitarian doctrines of Mill against the prohibition of censoring ideas on the grounds that the prevention of their discussion might preclude "the clearer perception and livelier impression of truth, produced by its collision with error."[7] Plato's censorship has long roused the hostility of readers who often dismiss his ideas as totalitarian; the importance of poetry as political discourse in Athens does not necessarily alleviate the criticism.[8]

The assertions Plato makes about the world run far deeper, however, than matters of censorship or free speech. He seems to concur with Socrates' principle that gave different values in the scale of worth on the basis of each individual's potential for and actual pursuit of the soul's improvement. However, the "early" Socrates shared a willingness to accept the imperfect nature of human beings, so he posited a requirement not that perfection of virtue and knowledge be reached, but that their acquisition be attempted, just as noble values accepted effort, however unsuccessful, to impose the human will. Plato, on the other hand, proposed a concept in which perfection really existed, devising a program by which human beings could turn away from the imperfection inherent in imitation and pursue the reality of virtue. Plato could not compromise on his vision of rejecting the world as the senses perceived it in order to pursue reality; for him, perfection must exist. The occurrence of imperfect phenomena and concepts in the world around us required the notion of their perfection in form, and a concept like good, or virtue, must have a perfect form. To Plato, that perfect form was objectively real and perceptible to the mind. When perceived by the mind it becomes the standard for the many different, imperfect and changing concepts and phenomena we denote by the word "good" when we appraise them in the world of the senses.[9] It is also the existence of these perfect Forms that leads to the expansion of the notion of the independent soul, and the notion of its immortality and transmigration through which it can apprehend these Forms which exist on a different plane than everyday perception.

Plato's view of the existence of perfect "Forms" not only posited a human goal of apprehending the Forms through reason, it affected Plato's understanding of the manner in which knowledge could be achieved or even exist. The deep implications of Platonic thought may be approached by pursuing into Platonism the implications of what I have assumed as "Socratic" thought about the soul. Because Socrates focused on a program for the improvement of the soul, a stunning implication of the Socratic definition of virtue seriously undermined that traditional regard for the aristocratic notion of *arete*, – "goodness," "nobility," "prowess," or however one might translate the Greek word. If virtue is knowledge, as Socrates, even the Platonic Socrates, consistently asserted, then it is teachable,[10] and teachable to anyone who has the wit to learn. Or, if one takes the view that Socrates' wisdom consists in the awareness of his own ignorance, then the *arete* or the nobles is worth nothing against that wisdom of knowing that one does not know. Furthermore, if Socrates' daemon is a guide to virtuous action, or at least, a warning against error, the nobles are not in a superior position. And finally, if correct action is the service of one's soul to make it as good as possible, as well as the pursuit of that knowledge which is virtue, in Socrates' view all the activities on which the nobles prided themselves are of no value and little importance.

    Socrates is consistently portrayed in all the dialogues as speaking and acting in accord with these fundamental themes, whatever other ideas he might put forward in addition to them. Wherever an issue related to this concept arises, the attributes of nobility – athletic or military prowess, good family, comeliness, wealth, political position – are all rejected as measures of a good man or a good citizen. Only excellence of soul makes for a good person, and the idea is expressed in *Laws* 770 D and underlies a good part of the *Republic* as well. That dialogue is explicit in asserting that neither family, nor background, nor any characteristic other than the potential for training for virtue qualifies a person for the education that leads to the duty of philosophical kingship.[11] Plato's proposal for education to subordinate all the traditional values of the aristocrats and all the traditional aspects of Greek culture to the goal of improvement of the soul is a reasonable extension of the basic Socratic idea, although there is no reason to suppose that Socrates himself ever institutionalized the principle as Plato would do in the *Republic* and elsewhere. Nor is there any reason to lift from Plato the responsibility for proposing that in this education system, such great works as the epics of Homer and much of the lyric and even tragic tradition be excluded from education because they presented misleading guides to conduct, portraying gods who were anything but perfect, gods who were examples of behavior that distracted from rather than promoted right thought and conduct.

These Platonic proposals are consonant with Plato's goal of creating circumstances in which individual souls can be improved – what might even be seen as a practical method for producing results that Socrates had called for: producing people who would concentrate on the improvement of their souls. There are Platonic dialogues that provide the reasoned arguments to produce a full theory, and those dialogues have generally been taken to attest "genuine" Platonic thought. The theory as it appears even includes a hypothesis – some would say a demonstration – of the soul's possession of knowledge of which even the possessor is unaware, in an argument that reinforces the conceptualization of the soul as an independent entity. In the dialogue *Meno*, Socrates confronts the apparent dilemma of knowledge and the inability to teach: if one does not know something, how can one recognize knowledge obtained; if one does know, how then can one be taught? The *Meno* uses a slave boy to demonstrate that the boy knew propositions of mathematics even though he was totally unaware of the fact, and the teacher, in Socratic terms, is the "midwife" who brings to light knowledge already there. Step by step, Socrates asks the slave boy questions to lead him to correct answers to arithmetic questions. We will take up in a later chapter the implications of this demonstration to consider – as Plato did not – that if the theory of knowledge will work with a slave boy, then the theory of universal potential for improvement of the soul might have broader value, and one might propose a system of education that would allow for that, rather than provide primarily for the education of those who were to be the rulers as he proposed in the *Republic*. For the moment, however, I want to continue examining the implications of education for the understanding of the separability of the soul, its immortality, and its effect on our own understanding of ourselves and our ability to know.

Another dialogue, the *Phaedo*, makes proposals about the nature of the soul consistent with the notion in the *Meno* of the soul having preexistent knowledge. The *Phaedo* is seductive, and makes us receptive to any ideas propounded by the Socrates we meet in it because it is the drama of Socrates' last hours and death. Here, Plato presents Socrates as aiming at the demonstration of the immortality of the soul. Socrates discusses the Forms a number of times, alluding, for example, to the Forms of Beauty, Goodness and the like in contrast to imperfect copies of such concepts as they are perceived by the senses. He draws a parallel between the independent existence of the Forms and the existence of souls before people are born, and he summarizes the relationship of the Forms and the objects of sense perception. The Forms can be apprehended only by the intellect, or reason, for they are shapeless and invisible, and the imperfect copies of the world of the senses take their names from the Forms in that they partake of their characteristics.[12] These Forms exist, unchanging, models for the objects of sense perception but amenable to perception themselves only by reason. The presentation of the Forms is tied in with Plato's development of his argument for the immortality of the soul. Instead of a soul that requires attention to gain improvement, we have a new conception of a soul that has wandered, immortal, through an undefined number of prior existences, and acquiring through its encounters with the Forms of absolute reality a knowledge of them; recollection of the knowledge thus gained provides humans with the understanding they seek. However different this may be from a Socratic proposal for the primacy of the soul,[13] Plato uses the theory of the immortality of the soul in a way that obviates the problems created by a contrast with the argument for the improvement of the soul. By the time he is writing the *Phaedo*, he has developed the theory of the immortality of the soul in a way that ultimately affects our own ideas about ourselves.

Whether or not we accept the notion that the soul is immortal, or believe that it can in some way be educable or attain to absolute knowledge, Plato's argumentation has strongly influenced the acceptance of the existence of a separate, perhaps separable intangible entity that is part of the human make-up. While Socrates' argument for the improvement of the soul implies the existence of a rather ill-defined aspect of the human being, Plato's assertion of its immortality and trainability creates images that intensify the presumption that the human being can be divided in the first place. Finally, there is another aspect to Plato's ideas, implied and perhaps not even intended by him, an aspect that had great impact on philosophical and religious thought in later centuries. If the soul is an immortal receptacle for truth, and truth, in the perception of the Forms, is discoverable only by reason and the perceptions of the senses are mere apprehensions of imitation and error, then the senses are of a lower order. That much is almost explicit in Plato's treatment of them. Implied, however, is another value judgment. The body itself is of a lower order than the quality of reason, and that implication, at the outset a mind-body antinomy, became in later times a general derogation of the body and bodily activity and functions. I will not pursue this issue for the moment, but it seems to me important to note the manner in which Platonic thought could later lead to a whole series of new attitudes and new conclusions that would affect the course of western religion and frame attitudes toward the proper occupations of human beings. It is also the case that Platonic assumptions about the soul began the tradition of formal investigation about the nature of the human being that accepted some form of duality in the organism in which bodily functions were seen to be directed by an independent force within.

The sense of duality in the human organism lies at the heart of the understanding of what is valuable in human pursuits: the activity of the soul – and in later thought the mind – is deemed the highest of human activities. It is part and parcel of the continuance of the emphasis in Greek and later times on the understanding by the mind of the external reality perceived by the senses, and the sense of distinction between mind and body leads without difficulty to the approach to externals I will be discussing below. But this duality, so deeply rooted in thinking that until recently there has been little challenge to it, is not the only way to understand the human. I will be discussing below the Confucian sense of the unity of the cosmos, the unity of the individual person with all things, from a pebble to the cosmic world of the stars, that permeates a great deal of Chinese thought. In the writings of Confucians or Taoists alike, there is no soul-body or mind-body dichotomy, but the human being is assumed as an integrated entity, and prescriptions for human activity are based on that assumption.

While the Platonic-Socratic sense of division is coming under some challenge today among the inheritors of their thought, it persists in most of the tacit assumptions and attitudes about human behavior on which we base actions and prescriptions. Freudian terms like *id*, *subconscious*, *libido*, and *unconscious* are all names attached to a presumed aspect of human beings that determines actions, and until very recently, treatment of so-called "mental illness" has rested on techniques thought to influence mental processes. Only the possibility of profit from the pharmaceutical trade has impelled the investigation of the chemical potential of influencing behavior, and the application of those techniques to "criminal" behavior is still largely theoretical or confined to moralistic science fiction. Our understanding of the divided human rests on a tradition of seeking a stable, controlling element that acts upon human behavior and can be influenced by mental acts we call reason, rather than regarding the human as an arena for change and development that can be affected by simple actions, as Chinese thought tended to see the human being.[14] It thus has discouraged the treatment of the human being as a unified entity, while at the same time promoting and celebrating an aspect of human behavior that we call reason, and endorsing the acquisition by the mind of information and skills we call knowledge. Plato leads to us through Aristotle.

---

[1] Or the ironic reverse, as Leo Strauss argued.

[2] Presented in Popper (1962) Vol. 1.

[3] Finley (1991) p. 140.

[4] Nor am I concerned with why Plato reasoned as he did, or the conditions under which his development of philosophy operated, either to reinterpret in the manner of Crombie (1964) or to explain, as does Havelock (1963), that Plato worked under the constraints of the contemporary change from oral communication to literacy.

[5] Imitative of imitations, in that poetry deals with matters of sense-perception that are imitations in themselves.

[6] *Republic* 607 a-d. For a contrarian position, and a defense of Plato's position as not to be taken literally, see Shankman (1994), pp. 3-31; 295-313.

[7] Mill, J. S. (1859) *On Liberty*, in Alexander, ed. (1999) pp. 59-60.

[8] Wallach (2001) pp. 319-25 argues that in opposing the poets, Plato was fighting "the establishment" (p. 320), that the treatment of poetry is that of a form of discourse in which the contest is with "lawgivers, practitioners of the political art" (p. 323), and "Socrates suggests that because the conception of justice fostered by mimetic poets typically fails to help one deal with the misfortunes that beset human life, poetic activity requires critical supervision in a justly ordered society" (p. 324). I do not think this gets at the issues raised by the advocates of free speech.

[9] This is the case whether there is a separation between the Forms and the world of sense perception, as Aristotle asserts was Plato's position, a dualistic metaphysics, or whether the Forms are immanent, as some followers of Plato see the argument.

[10] This is the basic conclusion reached at the end of the *Protagoras*, 361 b-c; as the *logos* shows that Protagoras and Socrates reverse their original positions, with Socrates' position that virtue is knowledge implying that virtue can be taught.

[11] This selectivity is one of the characteristics that lead modern writers to judge Plato as elitist and totalitarian, but the passage has also been used by some to assert egalitarianism, in that while admitting that parents of the lower orders would not be likely to produce offspring suitable for higher things, it is not impossible, and the system must allow for this possibility; similarly, there is equal possibility for women.

[12] Cf. *Phaedo* 76 d-e; 79 a; 102 a-b.

[13] There is a qualitative difference between the approach to the soul when it is treated as part of the human makeup and more important than the body and requiring preferential treatment, and an approach that argues for its immortality, its perception of the Forms in a different existence, and as a determinative which can move into existence in a mode different from human life while at the same time preserving a record of all its experience.

[14] "This transformative aspect of ritual performance that received paramount emphasis in the early study of the *Rites* canons, mainly because early Chinese saw humans less as innately fixed natures than as loci for boundless change." Nylan (2001).

–5–
The Psychology of the Self

When Aristotle reached Athens and joined the Academy at the age of seventeen, Plato was a man in his sixties, and the Academy already about twenty years in existence. Aristotle joined the group of students and seekers after knowledge who had collected around Plato, who himself at the time of Aristotle's arrival in Athens was on his first visit to Syracuse in his reputed attempt to mold the young Dionysius II into a wise ruler. Aristotle spent about twenty years in contact with Plato and the other philosophers of the Academy, absorbing the ideas and pursuing the investigations and speculations generated by a Platonic philosophy that was fairly mature by the time Aristotle first encountered it. By the time he left Athens to sojourn with Hermeias, a ruler on the east side of the Aegean, he had already established a name for himself with the composition of dialogues (now lost except for fragments) like those of Plato, and had done some of the writing later assembled as his works. He continued his philosophical writing at Mytilene on Lesbos, in Macedonia as tutor of Alexander the Great, and in his native city of Stagira.

After returning to Athens in 334 BCE he opened his school, the Lyceum, at the edge of the city, and continued his philosophic writing and discussions with his philosophical comrades, and engaged in some teaching. After Alexander the Great died in 323, and anti-Macedonian sentiment rife at Athens was producing accusations against him, he left the city for Chalcis and died there in 322.

There is less written today about Aristotle and his ideas than there is about Plato, partly because the encyclopediac virtues of Aristotle's collection of information resulted in his data simply being incorporated into later works. His scientific texts were, however, cited repeatedly by medieval writers before the advent of modern observational science, and it was, for example, the break with Aristotle's earth-centered cosmology that led to so much trouble for Copernicus and Galileo. When it comes to Physics and Metaphysics, we use what Aristotle says about his predecessors to understand earlier philosophy rather than employ his texts to understand the physical world. Aristotle thus becomes a vital link in the history of ideas. His treatment of the Platonic theory of the independent Forms making up true reality carries forward his master's attempt to understand the nature of learning by treating sense perception as a necessary part of the acquisition of knowledge, and it is enlightening to read his rejection of Plato's assertion that the Forms as universal substances are separable and distinguishable individually:

> The people who state that the substances are universal did not make them amenable to sense perception. They considered that the individual items perceived by the senses are in flux, and none of them are stable, but that the universal stands beside them and is something other. This, as we said earlier, Socrates proposed, because of his

definitions, but he did not make them [the particulars and the universals] distinct from one another; and he understood rightly in not making the separation.[1]

Taking his position against Plato, Aristotle becomes, for all time, a hero to those who insist on empiricism, even though Aristotle's own dependence on reason excludes him from those who place complete reliance on sense perception.

These remarks about the Forms come rather late among Aristotle's compositions, if the general view of the placement of the *Metaphysics* is correct, but it seems from other writings that he was openly denying the Platonic theory of Forms within a half dozen or so years after Plato's death in 347.[2] Thus the vast amount of the Aristotelian text we have is written from a point of view opposed to the notion of the independent existence of the Forms, and Aristotle discussed both natural phenomena and ethical and political issues in terms of his own notion of the nature of form. All his writing, from that on natural history, motion and astronomy, to that of the nature of the human spirit, logic, politics and ethics, is permeated with the effects of his view that the Form determining the development of the particular is structurally integrated with it, and forms an inseparable unit with it. The Form is basic to the very existence of the entity, which can neither be what it is without the Form, nor can the Form exist without the entity to express it. This fundamental disagreement with Plato not only shaped Aristotle's thought on the physical universe of which he wrote, it created a very different approach to political and moral philosophy as well. At the same time, by his promulgation of the notion of Form contained within and controlling the development of an entity, he continued and developed the concept of some independent, if internal, aspect of the human – as any organism – that was conceptually separable from the rest of the being.

A good part of Aristotle's investigation of the nature of the human being appears in his ethical works. He readily admitted that his method in ethics would yield conclusions and results less precise than those he could expect for science.[3] Nevertheless he employed techniques of observation and comparison to establish an ethical and political system that could claim some sort of operational validity, and put his ideas forward in two major works, *Nicomachean Ethics* and *Politics*, which form a connected whole. The first work analyzes human nature and the behavior that conduces to the highest human good – happiness, and the second is an essay on governing human beings in political systems. Aristotle attempts to establish the Good in human terms, as accessible to human reason. What may be to some people truisms, frequent and often banal, his arguments proceed from the desire to establish, define and create agreement about the nature of the Good and miscellaneous virtues and goods, not as abstract definitions but as practical guidance to living.

In the *Nicomachean Ethics*, Aristotle proceeded from a standpoint completely different from that adopted by Plato in the *Republic*. The ground is familiar from the discussion of Socrates, or at least, the Socrates who can be deduced from some of Plato's texts as proposing no external, divine or human, superior form of knowledge by which to regulate human conduct. This is the Socrates Aristotle praised in his own allusions to the philosopher, rejecting Plato's assertion of separate Forms to be known through reason. In what Aristotle says about public and private virtue, he rejects almost everything Plato wrote about knowledge or the Forms of Good or any other absolute. Aristotle directly denies that knowledge is innate or developed from some higher state, and insists that scientific knowledge – perhaps better stated as "intelligized" knowledge – derives from sense perception. Perception passes into memory, and frequently repeated memory is what is understood as experience; that experience, in turn, becomes a universal – knowledge established in the soul[4] (we might say the mind). This is scientific thinking, according to Aristotle, and the only other valid thinking is that which apprehends the primary premises directly and thus originates scientific knowledge.[5]

In the reasoning for *Nicomachean Ethics* and *Politics*, sense perception produces information about the effects of actions, and memory of these effects when repeated frequently becomes experience, and this is stabilized in the soul as the universal, or standard against which to measure action in the future. Once the soul has these standards established, evaluation of the good is no more than the fixing of the objective, the end, or aim of human life, in order to establish as good just those actions which experience shows advances that end. This is an enormously influential theory of knowledge and learning, and it survives today as the model largely controlling education and the content of teaching. The soul, or what today we call the mind, is a receptacle to be filled by sense perception, and is capable of stabilizing and using what sense – or teaching – presents to it. It persists – and may be a correct understanding – even at the highest levels of thought, not only narrowly confined to the accumulation of information, but even ethical, moral and political judgments.

Assuming that knowledge is acquired through sense perception and refined through mental processes like logic, the *Nicomachean Ethics* aims to establish the proper goal of human life, allowing, however, the end of happiness to be necessary to the equation,[6] and arguing that no one pursues Happiness in order to gain some further good, but that all other goods are pursued with the objective of attaining happiness. This Happiness or Good, Aristotle calls *energeia*, or activity and occupation, of the soul in conformity to virtue; and if it is necessary to admit more than one virtue, then it is the best and most final virtue. From this point, he works through a long and comprehensive analysis of Happiness and the way it can be achieved, surveying aspects of the soul and the virtues that pertain to it.

Aristotle examines these virtues in some detail, but all of his discussion is intensely practical, just as he uses the general opinion of philosophers, and others, as support for his definition of the final Good as Happiness.[7] He does not assert that the virtues are inherent in humans (as, for example, Confucians might claim) but they develop in people from habitual repetition of proper behavior. It is a reversal, Aristotle comments, of the situation we can observe in the matter of the senses, for we see because we have eyes, while in the matter of moral virtue, we do not act in a certain way because we have virtue, but we create the virtue by acting consistently in a virtuous manner. By Aristotle's definition, "Virtue is a deliberately chosen permanent state, representing the mean between two extremes in regard to ourselves and which is ascertained by calculation, and in the manner in which a man of good sense would determine it."[8]

Aristotle's reasoning, and his practical advice on finding the mean, reappears in ethical tracts and philosophical writings for centuries, not only in antiquity but in the hundreds of years after his works became known again in Europe. Discussions of specific virtues like Courage, Soundness of Mind, Liberality, Magnificence, Greatness of Soul, Proper Concern for Honor, Easiness of Temper, and other assets of character as well as a long disquisition on the virtue of Justice, recur in the works of later writers as paraphrases, translations, or commentaries. Some of his propositions became received truth, and even those that did not molded later understanding of human moral and intellectual function. Such ideas as the division of the soul into rational and irrational parts, or the numbering of five truth-producing intellectual virtues, Technical Skill, Knowledge, Good Sense, Wisdom and Mental Capability, were accepted by many as true attributes of the soul, which continued to be conceptualized as an entity in itself. This reasoning allows Aristotle to deal with Happiness in terms of the soul to present that Happiness which is the most perfect. This is the Happiness of Contemplation, as his Greek term *theoretike* is usually translated, and accords with the highest virtue, suits the best in humans, affords the steadiest of pleasures, is sweetest, self-sustaining and suitable to the aspect of human beings closest to the divine.

    This approach works so long as virtues are regarded as attributes of the soul and Happiness its condition, and there are parallels with the Socratic or Platonic asseveration that the most important human interest is the improvement and concern for the quality of the soul. But Aristotle also takes over the idea of perfection, as in *Nicomachean Ethics* he remarks that "Happiness is a certain activity of the soul pursued in accord with perfect goodness."[9] Thus the attending to the soul, in Socratic terms the highest human activity and offsetting any potential benefit of other activities, is not an end but the process best leading to the final end of the human, the goal of the most perfect Happiness. Furthermore, rejecting the view that the Good, or anything termed good, was independent of phenomena, Aristotle regarded the Good as recognizable through experience, and therefore definable. At the same time, granting a certain validity to human consensus to establish knowledge in a scientific manner rather than by a "memory" of an immortal soul, as Plato proposed,

Aristotle was forced to include among the goods and the virtues a multitude of secondary qualities accepted as goods not only by thinkers and educated Greeks of his own time but inherited from previous generations. He was forced, in a different sense, to emulate Socrates in "bringing philosophy down from the heavens," to place it among people and propose principles of scientific inquiry that would produce knowledge of the Good as it might do for anything else.

Aristotle's impact on western thought goes far deeper than the fact that Aristotelian science was the only accepted version of physical reality allowed in Western Europe for centuries. Not only is it true that much of what he wrote about the physical world established opinion on many subjects for two millennia after his death, even where this is not the case his work was the foundation of the methodologies by which people approached the subjects, and set the parameters limiting human understanding of the self and the manner in which it learned and knew things. The range of the texts covers most of what was human knowledge in his time, or for that matter, in a broad sense, ever since, so that the influence of his thought permeated almost everything until the twentieth century. It includes a group of essays we call the *Organon* in which he presented a developed system of reasoning, not only analyzing definition and explaining valid syllogisms and fallacies, but offering a careful explication of the building of arguments and refutations thereto.[10] The modern style of analysis is often a replication of the manner in which Aristotle approached his subjects: observation must be accepted; conclusions reached through observation should attempt to maintain an economy of hypotheses. Although his explanations of how sense perception actually works are frequently wrong because observation does not always reveal basic function, his method is consistent and legitimate in depending on what seems to be observably true.[11]

A good deal of Aristotle's writing, based on careful observation as it often was, if not always,[12] is still valid today, especially in the biological and zoological sciences, where observation could generally be applied. It is limited, however, to what I call "the middle world." This is the part of the cosmos amenable to seemingly accurate perceptions by the senses, and in which "common sense," in the Einsteinian sense of the prejudices we have acquired by the age of 18, is a good guide to reason. It is the universe in which scientific theory manipulates well the treatment of external phenomena as objective, independent and unaffected in their nature by our perceptions or our understanding of these perceptions. It is the universe for which the distinction between observer and observed reality seems valid, and in which the scientific method predicated on these assumptions has produced predicted and useful results. Although this does not always work, or at least seems not to work in the domain of sub-microscopic particles or the huge domain of super-space and super-speed, where ordinary, "middle-world" concepts of matter, motion, time and mass do not apply as they do in the world of ordinary perception, this middle world is the one in which we live most of the time, and to which we have been completely limited until very recently. The mental set Aristotle established for thinking about the outside world, the world we perceive, has produced remarkable results in the manipulation of matter, and it remains very difficult to absorb the changes in the understanding of reality that have occurred in modern physics.

The standpoint from which Aristotle "did" science still controls the manner in which a great deal of thought about humans and their environment is carried on. Aristotle never challenged the confidence of the physical scientists of the fifth and fourth centuries BCE that their theories about the phenomena were theories about real objects, and that they, or Aristotle, as observers, could learn accurately about physical reality and, furthermore, treat it as objective. This permits the conceptualization of the cosmos as external and manipulable, and just as the internal, educable and comprehensible entity, the soul, or mind, can act upon, modify and even control the organism within which it exists, so the learning observer and thinker can comprehend and control the external and objective reality. While today we may deplore some of the excesses of control that this theory of reality has generated, we should not lose sight of the extent to which Aristotelian thought-processes have generated human activities that have benefited many in a world that has become much more crowded and complicated than that of Aristotle's time. Furthermore, the mental set that accepted the gap between the observer and the observed permitted a characteristic Greek attitude toward understanding the human, an attitude that was Platonic, or at least Socratic, as well as it was Aristotelian, but found its fullest expression in Aristotle's work. That characteristic attitude of Hellenism allows for the objectification of the human being by that human being itself, the idea that one can discipline oneself, by wisdom, reason or whatever, to live a kind of life that one might not otherwise choose. This discipline is imposed as a matter of individual human will, not as a characterist6ic of natural life or social interaction. And *that* attitude, for two millennia – despite the interruption of medieval times – absorbed subliminally through the works of the Greek with the most philosophical and scientific authority, had a controlling effect on the nature of western thought.

[1] *Metaphysics* 1086 a 36-b 5; cf. also 1039 a 24ff., 1078 b 30-3, 1033 b 26-1034 a 8.
[2] Rist (1989) pp. 37-9, 53.
[3] *Nicomachean Ethics* 1094 b 13 ff; 19-27.
[4] Worked out in *Posterior Analytics* 99 b-100 a.
[5] *Posterior Analytics* 100 b.
[6] *Nicomachean Ethics* 1095 b-1096 a 4.
[7] *Nicomachean Ethics* 1098 b 20-29; 1101 b 13-27.
[8] *Nicomachean Ethics* 1106 b 36-1107 a 2.
[9] *Nicomachean Ethics* 1102 a 5-6.
[10] *Sophistical Refutations* 183 b 35 ff. For his originality.
[11] Even sometimes producing error, as in *de Anima* 418 b 20 ff.
[12] Obviously, it cannot be the case that observation caused errors, such as the statement that women have fewer teeth than men, a statement more in accord with Aristotle's view of the female as the lesser of the species. Other failures, like his description of the phoenix, clearly came from reading, in this case almost surely of Herodotus, on which Aristotle also bases his description of the hippopotamus and crocodile.

–Part Two–
The Self in Community

–6–
The Harmonious Family

When I was first considering the material to be examined in this book, I had not the slightest notion that I would be including any discussions of the family. And, if I had thought the subject relevant to my concerns, I would probably have looked at it in terms of the studies with which I am familiar – sociological or anthropological considerations of family life, the importance of family connections in politics, or along the lines of the investigations of Michel Foucault into sexual, medical and penal practices of ancient and modern societies. It is only after examining the impact of ancient attitudes toward the self on my own sense of myself, as I prepared to move to the discussion of the effect of Greek ideas of political life on the attitudes I and many other people hold, that I sensed a gap. The gap is one that Aristotle, at least, did not leave as he set out his ideas of the development of society, beginning with what was to him, the basic unit, the family. But I could leave the gap because, Aristotle notwithstanding, I live in a culture that, for all its blather about "family values," sets store on objective notions of behavior, rather than on the personal values necessary for the successful operation of family life.

The world in which we live allows us to be increasingly aware of other places, other people, other traditions and ideas fundamentally different from those on which we base our lives. Among the challenges we began to take up at the end of the twentieth century is that posed by a civilization which until very recently developed quite independently of the traditions we have inherited from the Greeks. Chinese thought represents a completely different way of viewing the human being, human morality, the human and non-human environment around us, from the small group of the family to the vast scope of the starry universe. Of all the attitudes that are different from ours, the one that seems to be most attractive, to me and to many others, is that setting the patterns of interaction among members of a community. Those who have reflected on the fundamental difference between Chinese assumptions and those that drive us in the West are attracted by the other, as, for example, Roger Ames, following Angus Graham, draws a distinction between Chinese thought and the styles of argumentation familiar in the West:

> Dialectal dispute is driven by the possibility of certainty and is characteristic of people who would ask, What is the Truth? The "art of accommodation" (*jianshu*) on the other hand is driven by a sense of melioration and is characteristic of people who, recognizing the performative and perlocutionary force of communication, would ask, How do we, harmoniously and productively, make our way together?[1]

Michael Nylan expresses precisely the point I am trying to make here: "the wise person who succeeds in living in concert with his fellow humans, near and far, will induce order within not only his immediate circle, but also the microcosm of his physical person and the macrocosm of Heaven-and-Earth."[2]

There has been little attention paid, in western philosophy and ethics, at least that written by males, to the matter of harmonious living within family and village. When I think of discussions of harmony among the Greeks, I think predominantly of the discussion of the harmony of the soul explored by Plato in the *Republic*, where the desired internal harmony of the soul is exemplified by a hypothetical arrangement of the elements of a civic polity. Harmony and justice are seen primarily as questions of political organization. Even today, in the dominant tradition set out in most published work, the issue of harmony in a family is more explored in its absence, to demonstrate how a "dysfunctional" family affects the development of an individual, and the doctrine of "win-win" negotiation and communication is offered as an aid to the achievement of individual goals in a competitive environment. Among Greek writers, where there is discussion of family life, the focus is almost exclusively on the practical, the economic needs and goals of the household rather than the social accommodations leading to harmonious living. I think of Hesiod, for example, setting out advice to peasant living, suggesting that a man marry a useful woman and a young one, who can be trained to her tasks most easily. Xenophon's *Oeconomicus*, written some three centuries later, focuses on the family and the relation between husband and wife entirely as a matter of creating a profitable economic and agricultural unit. And the portrayals of family relationships in Athenian drama can hardly be called investigation of harmonious family life. Furthermore, and very significant for what I am saying here,

Aristotle's archaeology, so to speak, his history of the development of civilization, sees the organization of the family and household merely as a stage in the evolution through community and village life to the ideal of political life structured on the pattern of the Greek polis or city-state.

How, then, can we comprehend the influence of such a tradition in the formulations of our ideas about family and community? Is it purely negative, leaving many individuals on their own to create private domains to live discrete from any broad social drive for harmony? As I write this, I am struck by the thought that despite the importance of the family in organizing society in Greek as in Roman times, I can recall no ancient work, philosophical or literary, that explores the manner in which men, women and children interact well in living together. We must wait until the nineteenth and twentieth centuries for such writers as Emily and Charlotte Bronte, and works like Trollope's Palliser novels, Galsworthy's *Forsythe Saga* and Thomas Mann's *Buddenbrooks* to see the dominantly male hierarchical tradition wrestling with the issues raised by family life.

As I write this, the North American society into which I was born and in which I live is occupied by debates over what are called "family values." But what are the issues that are seen to impinge upon family values? They are largely matters of social policy, such as the question whether homosexuals should be allowed to marry in the same manner as heterosexuals, whether women should be allowed great liberty in the matter of abortion, whether scientists should be permitted to carry on research with the use of stem cells obtained from fetuses, limits on the disciplining of children and debates over the punishment of criminals. There certainly seems to be little or no examination of the concept that harmony within the family is the fundamental goal of human activity, and that it is only on this family harmony that a harmonious society can be based. It seems to me that there is nothing, in contemporary or earlier western society, to see the amicable family relationship as basic as a Chinese writer expresses the idea: "As human nature's greatest sort of love, no pleasure is more complete than that of husband and wife.... The matter is profound and subtle, dark and mysterious. This is the start of [all] right and proper relations."[3] Could our society, now or at any time in its history, see marriage and family life as an essential cornerstone of satisfactory life, as expressed in 1984 by a Chinese Confucian who had spent most of his life in the service of Chiang Kai Shek's Guomindang government: "Women who have reached marriageable age but remain single are frequently psychologically abnormal, and men of the same kind are often homeless and lead a transient life. The men and women are not only solitary and unhappy, but also a liability to social order and harmony."[4]

I offer you the last quotation as a demonstration that the emphasis on the family does not always produce ideas that I can endorse with unalloyed joy. Furthermore, I am not so naive as to believe that the Chinese expression of insistence on harmonious family life necessarily reflects the reality of everyday life – particularly for women or younger sons. But I do believe that the striking contrast between the words of Chinese writers and the absence of concomitant views in our tradition illustrates the difference between a community-based culture and one based on exaltation of the human will and rights, at the hearts of Chinese support for the government in the conflict with Tibet, not at all well understood in the West. It is also true that the search for family harmony moves in Chinese thought hand in hand with the explicit endorsement of hierarchy, which, as I will show later, insists that each member remain in a ranked position and behave in the appropriate manner, as son to father to officer to minister to emperor, albeit with a demand for reciprocity in which the senior owes obligations to the junior.

Social attitudes inherited from the Greeks and accepted by at least the male half of western society have largely determined the treatment and the derogation of women. As early as the thought behind the poetry of the *Iliad*, the dominant attitude was acceptance of a hierarchy of males, an orientation still largely influential in the structure of modern western institutions. There are those who try to find explanation for this in biology, but I wonder if such theoreticians are aware of the extent to which negative assessments of women are not based on biology, but may originate in some of the earliest texts we have.

I think first and foremost of the writing of Hesiod. The extant poems belong in the same tradition as the epics and hymns attributed to Homer and they present an organized and general history of the cosmos in terms of the generations of gods. The poems reflect attitudes contemporary with or shortly later than the society that listened to the oral poetry of the Homeric epics. This is only partially explicable by the fact that the concepts of the organization of the cosmos found in Hesiodic writing bear striking resemblances to cosmogeny and theogony in near eastern texts.[5] Such resemblances as exist must be read in light of a comparison of near eastern texts with parallel Greek texts that are strikingly different in details, giving a particularly Greek twist to narratives attested elsewhere. In general, however, implications and attitudes presented by the accounts of the generations of the gods in *Theogony* accord with attitudes apparent in earlier texts from the Near East. Overall, *Theogony* presents a tale of conflict among divinities in which genesis moves from creation out of Chaos of Gaia ("Earth") – a female concept – who generates and then mates with Ouranos ("Sky,"

"Heavens") to produce a race of Titans, whom Ouranos hid in "a secret place of Gaia" so that they would not come up into the light. Gaia then plots with one of the children, Kronos, who castrates Ouranos with a sickle (generating other deities from the blood, and from the severed flesh Aphrodite). Kronos, now told that one of his children will depose him, swallows his children as they are born, but Gaia, responding to the appeal of Kronos' wife, saves Zeus. As a result of Rhea's giving a stone to Kronos for him to swallow in place of Zeus, Kronos later vomits up the other children. There follows a ten year war of the new generation against the old Titans, which the younger wins, and as a result the younger gods dominate, under the rule of Zeus.

There have been many analyses of the significance of all this, not least the proposal that the shifts in power attest some kind of a memory of a shift in human affairs from female dominance to male. Much more significant for its impact on the future, however, is the assumption of primacy given the male ruler, Zeus, in a narrative that reflects and fixes as normal the structure of patriarchy.[6] This acceptance of patriarchy is not, however, exceptionally Greek, but what does show in Hesiodic poetry is a misogyny, a hostility to women that seems to me, as I reread and rethink the text, to be particularly Greek. The attitude shows clearly in the story of the creation of the first woman, Pandora. According to *Works and Days*, Zeus, in revenge for Prometheus' giving fire to mankind, had the god Hephaestus fashion out of earth and water a beautiful maiden, to be clothed and graced by other divinities. Zeus sent her with a jar of gifts (plagues sent by all the gods) to Epimetheus, who sent back the jar because he had been warned not to accept a gift from Zeus. But Pandora ("all gifts") opened the jar, and all the plagues flew out bringing all the miseries humans encounter. Only Hope was left in the jar. *Theogony* tells essentially the same tale, with only a brief reference to Epimetheus, omitting the account of the jar, and, more important, adding the assertion that it was from Pandora that women descend. There may be some connections between Babylonian accounts of the creation of humanity and even some parallels with Egypt,[7] but in my reading of the texts, the more striking parallel with this part of the Greek creation-story parallel is the Old Testament account of the creation of Eve. The first woman, she like Pandora is responsible, at least in major part, for the disobedience that brought on the expulsion from Eden and the burden of travails for humankind.

But Eve is merely disobedient, eating the forbidden fruit and inducing Adam to do the same. Pandora, on the other hand, is fashioned to be evil: "high-thundering Zeus gave women to mortal men as an evil, partner of painful deeds."[8] Women, the poem asserts, are of no help in sharing poverty, but only wealth; another penalty is the bereft state a bachelor finds because he is unwed, and a man wed takes miseries from his children, and in this familial state the reason for avoiding marriage is evasion of "the baneful deeds of women."[9] *Works and Days* is more specific in describing the drawbacks of Pandora: on Zeus' orders Aphrodite was to give her, with grace on her head, "painful yearning"; Hermes a "doglike mind and thieving nature."[10] It was done, and Hermes instilled in her "lies and wily words and a thieving nature."[11] A misogynist could not ask for a better paradigm for the ancestress of women; the portrait is not that of Eve.

This is more than the patriarchal concept of society, or the concept of the geneological tree with Zeus at the top, or even the fact that in *Works and Days*, "Pandora, the first woman, is created out of earth and water, she has no divine ancestry."[12] As I read the text, the words even more than the tale itself express a hatred of women, and I cannot see how the awareness of this poetry could do other than consolidate an attitude toward women already obvious in the creation of the poem. I do not know whether this attitude is to be considered characteristic of early Greek society or has resonance for the listener; it seems to me beyond parallel in other archaic texts, but even on its own, it had its afterlife when the texts were read by later Greeks. The attitude is continued in later Greek texts, and, so far as the western religious tradition is concerned, it is reinforced by Old Testament narrative. And there is an awareness of it in one of the great tragic dramas created in Athens in the fifth century. The *Oresteia*, written by the first of the fifth-century Athenian dramatists from whom complete works survive, preserves a consciousness of a struggle between male and female dominance in society. It is first and foremost a tale of the establishment of human justice, but it ties the issue of justice into the sequence of events that lead from a father's sacrifice of his daughter – Iphigeneia by her father Agamemnon to allay divine opposition to his sailing to Troy – through Agamemnon's death at the hands of his wife and on to revenge killing of the wife by their son and in the end, the trial of that son, Orestes, for the murder of his mother. The issue of justice, and the notion of its administration passing from gods to humans, I will take up in a subsequent chapter. Here, it is important to note that Aeschylus, in writing the trilogy, makes the adjudication of the murder sequence depend in great measure on the issue of the priority of male over female right. The question of Orestes' guilt or innocence of the charge of "blood" – wrongful killing – is intricately tied to the fact that in the sequence of killings, Clytemnestra, a female, killed her husband Agamemnon, a male (to whom she was not related by blood) while in turn Orestes' vengeance for that murder involved a male killing a woman, his mother, to whom he was related by blood. The conflict of the sexes as well as the ambiguity of justice is demonstrated by the support Orestes has from Apollo, a male deity, on the one hand, against the pursuit of the Furies, female deities, on the other. The goddess Athena is to decide which of the other two divine forces has the greater right, and she creates a human tribunal, the Athenian Areopagus, with whom she shares the judgment in a manner of voting which gives equal force to human and divine voting. The issues before the court include such fundamental values as male or female dominance, as well as murder itself. The ultimate decision is made in terms of the conflict between male and female, in a manner that emphasizes that aspect of the conflict.[13]

The judgment goes in favor of Orestes, to the outrage of the Furies, whom the goddess conciliates by making them into kindly, tutelary deities of Athens, with place of honor forever in Athenian ground, "negotiating a delicate reconciliation of Olympian and chthonian deities, herself an atonement for old animosities she harmonizes and integrates the sanctities of darkness and light, male and female, private and public, domestic and civic, enlightened rationality and ancient religious dread, the inventiveness of speech and the fearful restraint of chosen silence when respect calls for it."[14]

There is no doubt that the *Oresteia*, with Athena's decision in favor of the male right, going so far as to assert that there is no relationship between mother and child, has been a strong reinforcement for the tradition of patriarchy and male supremacy. Insofar as I am right to assess the trilogy as one of the central literary texts that formulate western attitudes, we must also acknowledge its influence in solidifying the tradition of male supremacy in western culture.[15] It is not just that this is one of a number of examples of derogation of the female in Greek texts. There is the rhetorical question in the justification by the king Creon in *Antigone* for his punishment of his daughter-in-law's defiance of royal command, whereby Creon asks whether he is to be defeated by a woman. In Euripides' *Medea*, the wife-betrayer Jason dismisses his wife's objections to his behavior with a sneer that women judge everything in terms of how well the life of the bed goes. And so on. The *Oresteia* has a greater impact on me than any of these because it makes such a fundamental, even sacred human tie like mother-son subsidiary to the obligation to uphold male supremacy, and the decision is presented by a deity who, though female herself, asserts that she sprang from no mother but from the brain of her father Zeus.

The fundamental message of Greek literature in the matter of family and society is that in both the male takes priority. It is also true, of course, that Chinese culture is also strongly patriarchal, perhaps even more so than Greek, and there are many aspects of Chinese life even today that demonstrate the extreme precedence given the male. There is, however, a leavening of the derogation of women by the emphasis on family harmony to be found in Confucian thought. Again, that emphasis on family is part of the characteristic of Confucian thought that sees the human individual as part of a nexus of relationships, making the family as the primary community and therefore given great attention in Confucian ethics. The absence in Hellenism to issues relating to family relationships is part of the aspect of Greek thought that sees the human individual as an autonomous entity not defined in terms of family relationships. Whether or not the misogyny of Hesiod can be seen as extreme, the message of Hellenism is clear, and has persisted to the present day. The autonomous male is the ideal human. We must be aware of that when we read these texts, and be aware also that it is because of these texts that the dominance of male over female in society is regarded as "normal." It also may be the case that the explicit formalization of this position, its endorsement in human and divine law, may be responsible for the lack of interest and attention to family harmony in Greek and successor cultures.

---

[1] In Chan, ed. (2002) p. 75.
[2] Nylan (2001) p. 145, of the sage-king.
[3] Translation after Asselin (1997) "The Lu-School of Reading of 'guanju' as Preserved in an Eastern Han fu," *Journal of the American Oriental Society*, 117, p. 435, n. 52, quoted by Nylan (2001) p. 111.
[4] Chen (1986) p. 558.
[5] For a survey, see Walcot, P. (1966). Louden (2006) connects many of the episodes in *Iliad* and *Odyssey* with near eastern and especially OT myths.
[6] A narrative Davis (1993) sees as justifying rather than reflecting attitudes as natural, so that the story of Odysseus, for example, becomes a narrative that "establishes a hierarchy of values that promote patriarchal interests and investments as "natural" and "true" (p. 71).
[7] Walcot (1966) pp. 58-79.
[8] *Theogony* 600-602.
[9] *Theogony* 604.
[10] *Works and Days* 66-67.
[11] *Works and Days*.
[12] Graziosi and Haubold (2005) p. 98.
[13] Zeitlin (1996) makes the story the conflict between male and female principles, related to a well-established myth: "From a cross-cultural perspective, the *Oresteia* can be characterized as an intricate and fascinating variant of a widely distributed myth of matriarchy, the so-called Rule of Women ... the point of the myth is ... that women are not fit to rule, only to be ruled" (p. 90), and the role of the female deity of Athens is also supported: "If the outcome of the *Oresteia* also judges and justifies Athena ... it also justifies the male citizens' endorsement of her hegemony over their affairs" (p. 118).
[14] Zak (1995) 85.
[15] A feminist reading of the trilogy makes it justify "the shift from partnership to dominator norms.... Athene ... declaring for male supremacy": Eisler (1987) p. 80.

–7–
The Knowledge of Good and Evil

It was comfortable, I suppose, to live in a world in which the knowledge of good and evil came to human beings as a result of Eve's taste for apples – "Of man's first disobedience, and the fruit," as Milton put it. It was even better to have a society that was enlightened and guided by specific rules: "I am the Lord thy God ... honor thy father and mother ... thou shalt not steal ..." and the other commandments. The Jewish ethical tradition, when it penetrated the classical world in the form of Christianity, finally put to rest the old Hellenic questions about right and wrong, about justice: What is it? How can we know it? But even the Jewish tradition had some doubts about the human capability to know. It called for a trip up Sinai, after all, for Moses to obtain the rules from God, and Job's bafflement about his misery despite his obedience to divine law is only answered by God's challenge: "Did you make the whirlwind?" It took, I suppose, the union of the Jewish omnipotent moral deity with Hellenic confidence in human ability to know to create two millennia of absolutes.

The question of the ability of people to discriminate between right and wrong, and the confusion arising in a world that no longer has confidence in its moral absolutes, were not problems likely to arise out of the Chinese tradition. There, moral discrimination is seen as an inherent quality of the human condition, as a modern commentator points out:

> All Confucian learning rests on one significant claim, however: though humans at birth are little more than squalling bundles of needs and desires, they nevertheless have a crucial basic moral endowment from Heaven, whether Heaven is defined as distant ancestors, the gods, or the cosmic workings. That basic endowment, if developed, allows humans to attain moral perfection in their lifetimes.[1]

The Greeks, without that confidence in humanity, or without the reverse biblical view of the fall from grace, but with an attitude that accepted the human possibility of knowing, wrestled with determining the distinction between mere opinion and the accurate perception of moral truths. And unlike the Chinese, whose sense of morality made it a natural human attribute and related it to people living harmoniously with one another, Greeks, or at least Athenians, intermingled issues affecting human relations with questions of observation of divine ordinances.

This is easily observable in the surviving examples of the fifth century BCE tradition of Athenian drama – although the significance of the evidence for antiquity may be distorted by the fact that we have today only about three per cent of the tragedies produced in that city in that century. Because Athenian literature, and particular drama, has been so much a part of reading and even performance in the west since the Renaissance, the ideas presented by the plays of Aeschylus, Sophocles and Euripides have been offered and absorbed by audiences for centuries. Revivals of their plays appear more often in repertory theaters than much more recent works in German, French, Spanish and English. In every western country, far more than "modern foreign literature," they are translated again and again for students in western literature courses and for collectors or readers of "great books." The conflicts between characters and ideals in Athenian tragedy are monumental; the plays present collisions between principles of behavior and concepts of humans as self-determining and responsible agents of choice or accepting them as subject to divine necessity and determinism. The world of Athenian tragedy can be described as "a world that is at once social, natural, divine, and ambiguous, rent by contradictions, in which no role appears definitively established, one god fights against another, one law against another,"[2] for we have in this Athenian world of the fifth century more than one mind at work explaining human life, and indeed, sometimes it seems, even one mind may fluctuate between opposing poles.

Athenian tragedy may be approached in a number of ways; the themes of the plays may be probed as deeply mythic, or purely literary; as political or quasi-political, and cosmological or ethical. While modern study of the tragedies runs an enormous gamut of ideas, the manner in which audiences understood the plays and the extent to which Athenians could have perceived meaning in subtleties is really quite obscure. While modern writers have used the plays or interpreted the plays often as statements of very abstruse ideas, those interpretations often vary widely, sometimes complementing one another, but often presented in contradiction. Perhaps the only aspect consistently agreed on by modern scholars is the public nature of the tragic performances. Whatever they meant to their audiences, the communication was a public one, and all would agree that "Drama was an important means by which knowledge, values, and reasoning became elements of a common culture."[3]

The performances of the plays, supported in part by prosperous Athenians designated each year to defray some of the expenses of putting plays on, were part of the annual festival of the god Dionysus, and were enacted in front of large audiences in the Theater of Dionysus at the side of the Acropolis. Each year, for three days, tragedies were performed – on each day, three tragedies and a satyr-play by a single dramatist; on a fourth day, comedies were presented. The tragedies were judged by designated juries, and we have some records of which plays and which dramatists won "firsts" over the years, although our information is incomplete about this as well as about all the names of plays performed and dramatists whose work was performed. This was popular entertainment, in that large numbers of Athenian citizens attended the festival and watched the plays, and also in the numbers of plays that were performed, and presumably, larger number that were written. If three tragedies were performed on each of three days through the fifth century, there were some nine hundred tragedies in the corpus, to which must be added the satyr plays, the comedies, and an unknown number of plays that might have been written but not performed.

We have complete tragedies from only three playwrights, Aeschylus, Sophocles and Euripides, and only a portion of the output of each. While we have only seven of the eighty or ninety plays that Aeschylus wrote, they are all fine plays and make clear statements of his thought. From Sophocles and Euripides too we have enough remaining to know some of their ideas. While we may be unable to judge how common an idea was in Athens of the time, we can know what ideas were current, and what would be understandable to an ordinary citizen of the city who went to the plays performed during the festival of Dionysus. The number of plays and other works provide some insight into the ambiance of thought in fifth century Athens, and we can certainly be confident that, whether an idea was common among Athenians and Greeks of the time, if we can find it in our texts it was available to influence subsequent thinkers as it remains influential today.

Aeschylus won his first victory in 484 BCE. The earliest extant drama is his *Persians*, produced in 472 to depict the effects of the great Greek victory at Salamis on the Persian wives, families and companions who awaited news of Xerxes' expedition. The Persians, who behave in the play like Greeks and even call their own people "the barbarians," respond with lamentation to the news of the disaster and the naming of their dead. They also continually refer to the gods of Hellas, and their words are couched in terms of the Greek pantheon and Greek theodicy. The themes treated by writers of the preceding century emerge in the words of the persons of the play, for the most part that the misfortunes of the Persians come from their evil deeds. The view that the divine order is known suffuses the words of the deceased king Darius, who speaks of judgment in the sense that the crimes for which retribution comes are crimes well known and commonly agreed to be sacrilege among Greeks: profanation of temples, altars and statues; binding the sacred channel of the Hellespont as if it were a slave, "thinking to rule the gods, even Poseidon."

There is another theme in Aeschylus' thought that suggests a different view of divinity: the gods as enemy. When the chorus ask in lines 107-8, "Will any mortal man escape the cunningly conceived deceit of god?" the speakers are touching on an issue implied also in the observation that even the swiftest are caught, that *ate* [a sort of blindness or ruin[4]] "beguiles mortal man into the net, from which he cannot emerge unharmed." This strain in Aeschylus' treatment of morality and the cosmos also surfaces in *Prometheus Bound*, a play dealing with Zeus' punishment of Prometheus, one of the Titans who ruled the earth before Zeus came to power. Although the authenticity of the play as one of Aeschylus' works has been challenged,[5] the appearance of Zeus as humanity's enemy shows that the concept of a god as enemy existed and was conceivable in performance by the middle of the century. In Prometheus' words in the play, only he opposed Zeus' hostility to humankind, and it is to Prometheus that humans owe the knowledge of all the arts that mitigate the harshness of human existence. The suffering Titan insists again and again on his concern for humanity, and the benefits he has brought – most of all the gift of fire, for the theft of which he is riveted to his crag in Scythia. Although Prometheus admits his willfulness in opposing Zeus, that willfulness is in aid of humans, clearly opposing human interests to those of Zeus. The god is again and again called a "tyrant," and with the undoubted memory that it was the expelled tyrant Hippias, the last of Peisistratus' sons, who guided the Persians to their landing place at Marathon in 490, the repetition of "tyrant" and "tyranny" can only have placed Zeus in a glaring negative light. And even more compelling, the episode with Io, remorselessly pursued by a gadfly sent by Zeus' wife Hera in her resentment of Zeus' passion for the girl, shows the god as arbitrary, harsh, unmindful of humans. Prometheus, the chorus and Io herself look to Zeus as the cause of her agony, and Prometheus (ll. 735-8) calls him *tyrannos* and violent. This is the harshest representation of Zeus as enemy of humanity, displaying violence and hostility without the slightest provocation. The moral order, if one can call it that, within which this Zeus works can have no parallel to that of humanity or any meaning to human beings. The issue of right and wrong at the human and societal level is secondary to the presentation of divine action as establishing the parameters of individual action.

This notion of divine antagonism did not spread broadly through Greek thought, perhaps because Aeschylus himself in other plays emphasized the more common Greek view that divine morality exists, that it is intelligible, and that it serves to mete out justice. The Zeus of fairness appears in the play *The Suppliant Women*, where he is called father, god of suppliants. This is the Zeus envisioned by Darius' ghost, whose rule sets the principles by which individual and community can be regulated, and this is the Zeus of Aeschylus' masterly trilogy, the only trilogy that has come down to us intact from antiquity.

The plays of the *Oresteia* trilogy, *Agamemnon*, *Choephoroe*, *Eumenides*, although couched in terms of Athenian religion, custom, and social behavior, have such universal application to human experience that we still respond to them today. It is a measure of the impact of the plays on western thought that they have so determined the parameters of thought that the *Oresteia* and its mentality has remained completely accessible to later centuries. It has established questions of divine and human justice and posed answers in a manner that has been determinative of western culture, as "in its form, content, and context of performance, tragedy provided, by example and by precept, a critical consideration of public life."[6]

The *Oresteia* treats justice in both universal and specific terms, as a force of nature, an unseen agent of the cosmos that lies behind the events of history and the motives of gods and men who are the causes and actors in history. It can be read as a presentation of justice in terms of civic life, as contributing to the city's "self-education, wisdom, and its justice."[7] The trilogy proposes the transfer of the power over judgment and retribution from gods to men, as, in the first two plays, vengeance follows murder follows vengeance, and each character in turn interprets divine law and exacts retribution for a killing deemed unjust. In the *Agamemnon*, Clytemnestra, whatever her parallel motivations of jealousy and lust, designates her husband Agamemnon's killing of their daughter Iphigeneia as her justification for killing him. Agamemnon's sacrifice of the girl to pacify the goddess Artemis so that the Greek fleet can sail to Troy is mere butchery to the mother, and she alludes to it frequently to justify her assertion that she has fulfilled divine law in killing him.

Then, in the next play, *Choephoroe*, or *Libation Bearers*, the god Apollo demands vengeance on Clytemnestra for her murder of Agamemnon. Their son, Orestes, is the god's agent, and though reluctant, he carries out Apollo's demand, and then is driven screaming from the stage as the Furies sweep down on him to avenge his mother's blood. In the final play Orestes flees first to Delphi, to seek Apollo's protection, and then proceeds to Athens, where his fate is to be decided. In setting out the manner in which the conflict was finally resolved, Aeschylus dramatizes the creation of a unique aspect of the Athenian community and explains the notion of the participation by the members of society in the rendering of justice and the discrimination of guilt and innocence. Athena, the patron goddess of Athens who is to render judgment, does so by establishing the court of the Areopagus to share in this case and take over in later times adjudication of such disputes.

The establishment of the Areopagus to adjudicate such matters[8] transfers the jurisdiction and administration of divine law from the gods themselves to human judges, and the play's balance between divine and human votes provides the link between human and divine worlds as the authority is passed from gods to humans. In a sense, as one scholar has written, "a great part of the interest of the trilogy, and particularly in *Eumenides*, is sociological, in the sense that Aeschylus has dramatized a signal advance in the advancement of human society – from the vendetta to the court of law."[9]

Each event in the plays arises from the workings of the law of retribution, understood as equally human and divine; there is no deceitful or beguiling god or *ate* behind events, and the characters in the plays carry out their vengeances in full knowledge of divine law. The principles of divine law are available to humans, and the revelation of them is accurate. Divine help is theme of the final play, and even the hostile Furies are in the end are transmogrified as Kindly Ones to bring safety to the citizens of Athens, and as such they recite the blessings they will bring to the Athenians. All this emerges as the will of Zeus, who rules all, with even the gods depending on him. Humankind has a place in the cosmos of this Zeus, and conduct is regulated by the divine order which he administers. His thunderbolt punishes and protects, but is no random assault on a helpless humanity. While Zeus rules and the other gods share that rule, they are all trusty guides to anyone who seeks their advice. The rules of conduct that humans know and apply to themselves are the same rules that gods apply to people, and divine law is human law. Zeus has made sure that humanity knows this law, and thus Athena can set up the Areopagus as a human agency of judgment. This is the Zeus of Hesiod and Solon, and it is the kind of divinity who "hastens and chastens his will to make known," as the hymn asserts human knowledge of the law of God. Although there would be Greek thinkers to challenge this confidence in human knowledge, they never erased it from the Hellenic mentality, and it survived to permeate later religion to such an extent that doctrines of a most abstruse nature could be presented as clearly enunciated by the divine.

Debates over justice, its nature, and its applicability to the human community, show themselves in many areas and genres outside tragic drama. However the nature of justice may be related to the divine regime, Greek thought carries a confidence in the potential of humans to know, a confidence that persists even today in the firm convictions of antagonists that "God is on my side." For examples there are the two great debates presented by Thucydides. One focuses on the fate of the population of the city of Mytilene who had been defeated in their attempt to leave the league that Athens dominated. The other is an actual debate with the representatives of an independent city, Melos, in which Athenian envoys are represented as arguing their case without regard to justice, especially meaningful in the context of the Sophistic arguments over justice, natural law and self-interest. In both of these, Thucydides represents the speakers as confident that they know the nature of cosmic reality.

The Mytilenean debate has two phases, first that in which the democratic politician Cleon carries the Assembly to decree execution of the male population and enslavement of females and children, on the grounds that such ruthless punishment was needed to deter future revolts by others; not an argument from justice. Nor was justice enlisted on the other side, which prevailed after second thoughts convinced the citizens that such drastic punishment would only mean that in future revolts – which were inevitable – there would never be surrender, so that rebellions would be more difficult to suppress.

An argument from justice was explicitly ruled out in the second example I cite, the long dialogue between the Melians and the Athenian representatives who convey the city's demand that the inhabitants of Melos abandon neutrality and join the Athenian side. Thucydides presents a lengthy dialogue, occupying the last fifth of his Book V, and he represents both sides arguing, in conformity to the Athenian exclusion of justice as a consideration, to reach differing conclusions. The Athenians assert that it is in the interest of the Melians to surrender to avoid destruction, while the Melians attempt to prove to the Athenians that it is to Athenian self-interest to allow the Melian neutrality to continue. When the gods are introduced into the argument by the Melians, the Athenians respond that they are acting consistently with human opinions about the gods and the principles the gods use to determine their own behavior, and they "hold, in opinion of the divine sphere but in knowledge of the human, that in every respect it is necessary by nature [*physis*] to rule where there is power to do so." In this the Athenians have something in mind different from any claim for the eternal quality of divine law, for they make the immutable law of conduct not divine law but *physis*, natural self-interest and desire, a position completely familiar to any Athenian acquainted with the *nomos-phyis* controversy of the Sophists, and the rhetorical training in which some of them specialized. Awareness of that philosophical dispute by the audience is clear from a comedy, Aristophanes' *Clouds*, where a long parody of Sophistic argument in the debate between the Just Argument and the Unjust Argument shows the extent to which a playwright could count on Athenian familiarity with the issues.

    Self-interest and practicality, the necessity to act ruthlessly to maintain an empire however unjustly acquired, are the hallmark of Athenian rhetoric throughout Thucydides' work.[10] This is, of course, only in accord with Thucydides' own judgment of human character, as he reveals in one of his rare expressions of personal opinion in Book III, Chapters 82 and 83, commenting on the slaughter of their opponents by the Corcyreans in 427, that he records as the first example of the savage civil strife that occurred in city after city as the war proceeded and pushed men into greater and greater violence. The love of power, greed and personal ambition led men to every kind of injustice, cloaking their acts in fine words but producing every sort of evil for the Greeks. It is all human action, in Thucydides, with very little reference to the gods, save for the occasional invocation by the human actors seeking divine support in general terms or the infrequent report of divine service usual before battle or the beginning of an important project. Even human justice is an unimportant consideration, and admitted injustice is subordinated to the needs of policy. Pericles himself, the "best man," acts in this way, in his noted characterization of the immoral nature of the empire in Book II, Chapter 63: "You hold your empire as a *tyrannis*, which on the one hand seems unjust to obtain, but on the other is dangerous to let go."

The blunt assessment recorded by Thucydides, as if made by Pericles, is part of an account of the war as something more than merely an accurate text; it is an instructive narrative, history that would "serve as a form of political analysis, and a way of living politically in so far as it was good history; for Thucydidean history appealed to what man is actually like, and the way the world actually is."[11] There is in Thucydides' account of the war no moving force other than that produced by the human actors, and if there is any justice at all, it is the justice that conforms to human perceptions and human needs. Imposed, if at all, for convenience or the necessity produced by the interaction of two parties who are more or less equal in power, justice, in a sense, is a substitute for power, and comes into play when one's power is not equal to one's will. Thucydides may be introducing this extreme of the *nomos-physis* controversy to suggest the implications of this kind of morality for human behavior. The force of his prose has ensured that to this day Athenian politicians or the late fifth century BCE are seen as amoral or immoral, and has invested subsequent ideas of Athenian democracy with a heavy dose of suspicion and moral condemnation.

This view that restricts the application of right and wrong to the human plane emerges in the writing of another historian, Herodotus, who came from Halicarnassus, on the southern coast of Anatolia. Working in the middle of the fifth century and producing a history of the Persian Wars, Herodotus knew Athens from visiting the city, just as he had personal familiarity with so much of the Mediterranean world from his experience of travel and from his investigations – "historiai" as he called them and his work, establishing the term for the discipline of which he has been called the father.

Despite his apparent trust in oracles and omens and his ready acceptance of what appears to be a simplistic belief in gods, Herodotus presents a highly rational sense of history and historical causation. This is evident from a careful reading of the relativism at work in human affairs, from his treatment of the oracles he reports, and from the manner in which he treats the separation between the human and divine spheres. Many readers today find in his history a rationalism that is presumed to have a debt to the pragmatic investigations of natural phenomena by the presocratic philosophers of Ionia. Although there are contradictions in Herodotus' writing that may show shifting and insecure opinions about the roles of the gods and their oracles in human affairs, those contradictions may be, as some have supposed, instances of Herodotus' willingness to lay alternative interpretations before his readers.[12] They often occur when the historian's curiosity and detailed investigation impels him to produce data on oracles, predictions, omens and dreams, with which he usually deals quite carefully in showing the manner in which they influenced their recipients.

Oracles and portents, important and multitudinous as they might be, are not the means by which divinities control human affairs; they are announcements, not causes of what is to happen, and they express, not the will of the gods or cosmic justice but divine knowledge of what is to happen.[13] Even when Herodotus reports threats from the gods, as those directed against the Persian king Xerxes' abandoning the expedition against Greece and his councilor Artabanus for advice to do so,[14] people are warned not for or against doing or planning evil, but rather standing in opposition to inevitability. What the gods know and command in portents is not human conformity to divine morality or justice, but merely accord with the state of affairs that is to unfold. To Herodotus, any historical necessity that might exist was not a cosmic rule established by supernatural power, but rather part of the nature of humanity and the world.[15] Unlike the different and multifarious presentations of Athenian tragedy, where the gods act to punish, to deceive, to enforce law, or deal with humans completely arbitrarily, they do not usually[16] impel events in Herodotus' history, but people do that, and any rule to which they are subject is deducible from human experience, and in this sense the historian's approach to his story is completely rational.

If there is any impersonal force working on the progress of history, it is Herodotus' well-known doctrine of the alternating quality of human experience, to which he alludes frequently after setting out the concept of rise and fall at the beginning of the work. This is the lesson Solon gave Croesus, that a man's good fortune cannot be asserted until his life is over, for any happiness he may have at a time of evaluation may be destroyed before he dies. Croesus absorbed the lesson well enough to repeat it to Cyrus when the Persian king stood victorious over him: "Learn this first, that there is a wheel for the affairs of men, and as it turns it does not allow always the same people to be fortunate."[17] There is no moral view to events in this view of history, and good and bad fortune are due not to human action, good or bad, but are simply part of the nature of things. There is no need to propose a solution to the problem of why just behavior seems on occasion to be rewarded with evil instead of good, or to have resort to a hypothesis that human fault lies in the inability or unwillingness to perceive the divine order. The divine order, if it can even be called that, consists merely in the alternation of good and bad, the unstable quality of human prosperity with its random appearance and endurance.

Thus oracles, important as they might be, had nothing to do with the workings of a divine providence nor with the establishment or maintenance of justice on earth. They, along with portents like dreams, show how the alternating good and bad are to emerge in the future, and Herodotus' account of them shows people responding to them in diverse ways. Some impugned their reliability, but most believed them; recipients of adverse revelations tried to evade them, but those attempts failed. Oracles could be misunderstood, their interpreters could even be bribed, but they had to be reckoned with. Herodotus declared himself quite categorically as a believer in oracles, although he shows the difficulty of accurate interpretations, as in the case of Croesus' famous misunderstanding of the oracle that "if he campaigned against the Persians, he would destroy a great dominion." It is oracles that hold Herodotus' interest in divine activity, focused on their practice of revelation[18] or their specific acts rather than a consideration of the workings of a hypothetical divine justice. Thus Herodotus tells us that Apollo saved Croesus at the last minute by sending a rainstorm to extinguish the fire of his funeral pyre, and that he had deferred by three years the end of Croesus' rule. Gods predict and they do things in Herodotus world, but the account of that world does not raise tragedy's problem of understanding divine practice.[19]

Even at the human level, human justice and the perception of it are of minor importance. The motives for human action are almost always perceived self-interest of individual actors, almost never judged in terms of law or justice. The troubles flowing from these actions are not seen by Herodotus or any of his actors as arising from the infraction of some law. Even the well-known Herodotean concept of limit, supposedly imposing restraints on human activity when natural boundaries are passed, is more a characteristic of the natural world like the cyclical nature of prosperity than it is a principle of justice and morality, and Herodotean "limit" may be more applicable to our reading of the histories than a guide to the perplexed. The exceeding of limit can only be discovered when disaster marks the excess, for not every apparent boundary is a limit in this sense, and the boundaries that do create limit are personal, not general. For Croesus, crossing the Halys River was exceeding the limit. It was not so for Cyrus.

Thus history, for Herodotus as for Thucydides, is essentially a human affair, and even if his treatment of the gods seems to be "the old, completely naïve belief,"[20] his treatment of law and justice was not the view of Pindar, whose work he quotes. He was aware of a relativism at work in establishing human behavior, a relativism operating entirely on the human plane. In a famous passage, arguing that each nation thinks its own customs best, he tells the story of Darius' contrast of the Greeks with the Indians, the former refusing to eat their deceased parents as did an Indian tribe, the Indians on the other hand horrified by the Greek practice of cremation. Herodotus is inclined to regard human law as relative, determined by custom and not any superior agency, and that is the way he understands Pindar's phrase, "nomos (law) is king of all," which he quotes.[21] Justice, when it appears in his work, is conceived only in human terms, as a practical matter and not as an abstraction, and something to be dispensed by humans, not gods.[22] Herodotus, for all his equipage of gods, oracles, portents and the like, is closer to Thucydides than to the Athenian dramatists in his evaluation of human motives and causes of historical events. Like Thucydides, he wrote history supposing that in human life, morality and justice, divine or human, played a small part if any part at all.

By the end of the fifth century, if there was any assumption about justice, divine or human, common to Greeks, it was that justice must be calculated at the human level. If justice and morality existed at the cosmic level, it might be comprehensible to humans or be subject to the limits of human understanding, but whatever understanding might be achieved, that comprehension was expressible in human terms. The broad rules of human conduct derived from human experience and the analysis of that experience. Although there might be specific enunciation of divine statements of right or wrong and judgment of particular human acts, there were no supervening principles laid down by the divine for the general guidance of human activity. In attempting to act in accordance with justice and morality, human beings were for the most part on their own in achieving rectitude. Moral law was human law, either because there was no law beyond the human, or because the human was able to know accurately nothing higher. A tragedian might draft a myth whereby the right to judge was transferred to the human by the gods; another might allege that imperfect human understanding could not fathom the divine; a historian might make law exclusively relative, a matter of nomos, custom. Whatever opinion an individual might accept, it left moral choice and moral description to the human mind, for the gods offered no Ten Commandments or Golden Rule. In a welter of conflicting opinions about the validity of morality or its nature, none were demonstrably correct, and speculation in the end must yield to action, the search for first principles less productive than programs for behavior.

---

[1] Nylan (2001) pp. 352-3.
[2] Vernant and Vidal-Naquet (1988) p. 32.
[3] Euben (1990) p. 55.
[4] This is the "deliberate deception which draws the victim on to fresh error, intellectual or moral, whereby he hastens his own ruin," which Dodds (1951) pp. 38-9, sees as one of the evil spirits truly feared in the archaic age, an aspect of popular belief from which Aeschylus was trying to lead the Athenians into a higher level of morality, from the "daemonic, as distinct from the divine," as Dodds puts it, pursuing his developmental model of Greek thought. That both meanings, blindness or "subjective" meaning, and ruin or "objective," are found from Homer on, is shown by Doyle (1984).
[5] The arguments against authenticity of Griffith (1977) have convinced many, but Conacher (1980) reviewing the argument and history of the controversy, finds the ancient inclusion of the play in the Aeschylean corpus not yet successfully challenged.
[6] Euben (1986) "Introduction," p. 29.
[7] Euben (1990) p. 91, concluding the discussion beginning on p. 67.
[8] The question of whether Aeschylus intended his treatment of the Areopagus as an expression in favor of or opposed to the reforms of that body in 462/1 is quite irrelevant to an understanding of the poet's treatment of the moral order, but that issue may be explored in Podlecki (1966) pp. 80-100.
[9] Winnington-Ingram (1983), p. 127.
[10] Even in Book I. 76, where the Athenians praise themselves in their treatment of their subjects as being more cognizant of justice than they are constrained to be, they present their regard for justice more as a matter of generosity than external morality.
[11] Farrar (1988) p. 128.

[12] As the view may be influential because of its location, I cite T. S. Brown, in *Encyclopaedia Britannica*, III, 1974, s.v. Herodotus. Dealing with alternative interpretations of fact and motive, Brown finds an ambivalence which extends more generally to divine action.

[13] It will be clear that my views on Herodotus' treatment of oracles concur with the findings of Lachenaud (1978) pp. 225-305.

[14] VII. 12 ff. The story, in which the advice comes to each in a dream, also shows Herodotus' awareness of the rationalist interpretation of dreams.

[15] Well expressed by the comment of Fornara (1971) p. 89.

[16] Exceptions, like Apollo's direct intervention to save Croesus, or the revenge taken on Cambyses for his sacrilegious treatment of the Apis bull, III. 29-30, should be read with his warning in VII. 152 in mind: "I am obliged to report what is reported to me, but I am not obliged to believe everything; let this word of mine suffice for the whole account."

[17] I. 207.

[18] The god is fond of giving prophecies: VI. 27.

[19] It is worth pointing out that, in the oracle reported in I. 13, the retribution on Gyges in the fifth generation is not expressed as justice, *dike*, but as punishment, *tisis*; and there are many dynasties terminated by royal murders for which no vengeance is asserted either by oracle or by Herodotus. The retribution falling on a later generation has been seen as important in Herodotean thought, but this passage is one of the few in which it is explicit; it is at best only implied by the troubles that fell on Periander of Corinth, V. 92, and there is a much broader morality to the story of Glaucus, VI. 86, who wished to break his oath in regard to a deposit, and in consequence for even considering such a thing was left without descendents in Sparta.

[20] Jacoby (1913) "Herodotus," *RE* Supplement II, col. 482. On the other hand, Hunter, V. (1982) p. 295, applies such terms as "scepticism, logic, rationality" to Herodotus as well as Thucydides.

[21] III. 38.

[22] For examples, the story of Deioces, (I. 96 ff.) who became king of the Medes when that people beset by lawlessness (*anomia*), finding that Deioces was the only one among them who judged rightly and that they could not do without him, made him their king. Similarly, it was Lycurgus who was responsible for changing the laws of Sparta (I. 65), and although Delphi greeted the lawgiver as perhaps a god, the oracle had nothing to do with the laws themselves.

–Part Three–
State and Society

–8–
The Possibility of Justice

For several hundred years, now, the western world has been occupied with issues that relate to the question of justice. As long as the flow of history could be understood in terms of the gods, justice as an abstraction might be seen as no more than conformity to the divine will. Indeed, the advice given to Alexander the Great, when he had murdered his close friend Cleitus, makes the action of a temporal ruler, *ipso facto* just. The seer Anaxarchus came to Alexander as he was moaning with regret over his action, and laughed at the king, asserting that in parallel to Zeus' actions always being just because they are done by him, so "whatever is done by a great king must be considered just, first by the king himself and then by other men."[1] Although the narrator of that event did not endorse the position, the idea recurred many times in the form "the king can do no wrong." So long as God's justice was paramount, it was assumed to lie in some way behind the misfortunes of the world. By extension, the justice of kings could be challenged only when royal authority itself was no longer completely accepted.

–Part Three–
State and Society

–8–
The Possibility of Justice

For several hundred years, now, the western world has been occupied with issues that relate to the question of justice. As long as the flow of history could be understood in terms of the gods, justice as an abstraction might be seen as no more than conformity to the divine will. Indeed, the advice given to Alexander the Great, when he had murdered his close friend Cleitus, makes the action of a temporal ruler, *ipso facto* just. The seer Anaxarchus came to Alexander as he was moaning with regret over his action, and laughed at the king, asserting that in parallel to Zeus' actions always being just because they are done by him, so "whatever is done by a great king must be considered just, first by the king himself and then by other men."[1] Although the narrator of that event did not endorse the position, the idea recurred many times in the form "the king can do no wrong." So long as God's justice was paramount, it was assumed to lie in some way behind the misfortunes of the world. By extension, the justice of kings could be challenged only when royal authority itself was no longer completely accepted.

Nevertheless, the idea that there is such a phenomenon as justice and that it ought to be implemented in human affairs has, for the most part, been accepted in the modern world. But this justice needs definition, and the effort to do that goes back at least as far as the fifth century BCE. In modern times, the renewed pursuit of justice, "the first virtue of social institutions,"[2] probably relates to the fact that it is only again in this period that people have been able materially to affect their social institutions and alter them in response to principles they perceive as valid. And it has been a matter of a good deal of philosophical effort to propose and sometimes establish the attributes of justice.

In the earliest Greek epics, nothing that the heroes did or suffered was evaluated in terms of justice. It would be fair to say that the issue of justice did not occur to the bards who sang the *Iliad* or *Odyssey*. The Homeric uses of the Greek words that are related to the root of *dikaiosune*, which probably comes closest to our word justice in its connotations, cannot well be translated "justice." Yet by the time Greek society presents the texts that follow closest in time to the epics, the issue of justice is important, and in some of them it is paramount, establishing for western thought a basic insistence on adherence to justice.

The movement toward determining the meaning of justice and pursuing it accompanied a dramatic change in social and political patterns in Greece. Apart from peripheral areas like Macedon, kings were supplanted by broader-based forms of government, by aristocracies and oligarchy, and later, in some cities, by democracies. By the sixth century, the small class of wealthy landowners who provided military power no longer controlled Athens. The noble warrior, with his chariot, brilliant armor and fine horses was not the deciding factor on the battlefield, and with the loss of that importance went some of his authority over his society. The combat style of the individual noble warrior gave way to massed power of large numbers of heavy-armed citizens who marched in ranks against equally disciplined lines of the enemy. It was in this environment that the assertion of justice emerged, and the concept of its importance became inextricably entwined with those occasions in western history when more than the most limited numbers of members of the community became involved in its affairs.

It is interesting to compare this Greek experience with the impact of history on Chinese philosophy. Many students of China draw parallels between the Greek experience in these centuries and the Chinese period when the old unitary central government had broken down and the political structure was one of competing warring states, not unlike, claim these historians, that of early Greece. This disintegration of central power began with the "Spring and Autumn" period (from the division of chronicles into periods designated as spring and autumn) lasting from 722 to 481 BCE and marked by the decline and eventual collapse of the feudal-like system of the dynasty of the Zhou. The next centuries, beginning with 481 BCE and continuing until the reunification in 221 BCE of China under the centralized imperial control of the Qin dynasty, were a time of continual warfare, the "Warring States" period, in which a number of competing rulers fought to increase the extent of their own states and to solidify monarchical power. This "Warring States" period saw the rise of a bureaucratic, educated professional class, with notable members offering themselves as ministers and advisers to the competing kings, and among whom emerged the great intellectual figures of ancient China, Confucius (551-479 BCE), Mo-Tzu, dated to the fifth century BCE, Mencius (371-289 BCE),[3] and Hsün-Tzu (298-230 BCE). One result of the interchange of people and ideas in the period was the development of a common culture in all the states, so that, political conflict or no, there developed a unified culture which, characteristic of China in general, continued to dominate Chinese thought for millennia.

In Greece, however, developments did not move towards the establishment of bureaucratic monarchical states. In a few cities the aristocrats seem to have been able to maintain their control in the turbulent centuries that followed the collapse of the great Bronze Age centers. Some cities dealt with the changing times by promulgating formal law that by its very existence undermined the power of clan leaders who hitherto had settled issues in a self-serving or arbitrary way in the "crooked judgments of the corrupt rulers" assailed by their contemporary, Hesiod.[4] Some cities emerged into the light of history with institutions in place that vested control of affairs in a fairly broad body of male members of the community, in a system of demos-rule (control by the male citizenry as a whole), or democracy.

This unique Greek idea of government can be traced best, even if still imperfectly, at Athens, its paramount exemplar. Developing in the first place as a polis – a city-state structure exceptional in itself among human political institutions – Athens became a democracy in a series of steps in a transition long studied by historians and philosophers.[5] In more recent decades, the importance of material factors to the development of societies has led to a supposition that democracy arose to meet the demands of the newly important military class for a greater role in political decision-making: as Greece recovered from the destruction of the late Bronze Age, populations grew and the needs of increasing numbers led to more warfare among neighboring communities struggling to add to their exiguous agricultural lands, and that warfare called on more and more soldiers to defend or occupy the valued lands. As the cities came more and more to depend on the increased number of militarized citizens, the outnumbered nobles lost power as the requirements of warfare generated attitudes that in turn pushed society to a reformation of its structure. It is a reasonable, although not a necessary, hypothesis,[6] and the emergence of this form of warfare has been seen as emerging out of cultural attitudes rather than the attitudes coming from the background of circumstances.[7]

The kind of institution that emerged from all this was the polis. Kings and aristocrats were supplanted by magistrates and councils. Law was formalized and became publicly known to preclude the old patterns of paternalistic dispensation. Disputes no longer were settled privately, but were adjudicated in popularly constituted courts. Family and clan loyalty, while still important to many, gradually yielded to a sense of civic loyalty. Eventually, in almost all centers, a sense of community focusing on the physical city and its surrounding terrain dominated the Greek social ethos.

By the time the fundamental nature of the Greek polis had emerged in many communities on the Greek peninsula, Greeks were moving from their homeland cities in the great colonizing movement of the eighth to sixth centuries. Some later Greeks tried to reconstruct the process that developed this polis-society that spread across the Mediterranean.[8] The philosopher Aristotle posited an organic development, human institutions evolving from family to village to city, and his concept at least fits the shift from monarchy through oligarchy and aristocracy to the broader-based citizen involvement characteristic of a number of important cities. The Athenian tradition reports that power passed from kings to archons, or magistrates, who were first elected for life, then served for ten-year periods, and later changed annually. At Corinth the family of Bacchiadae first provided the city's kings, and then controlled affairs as a tight oligarchy. At Sparta, two families provided concurrently serving kings, but over the years their power yielded to that of magistrates and councils, although individual kings with exceptional political or military talents might aggrandize themselves.

It is clear from our texts that the fundamental characteristic of the polis in maturity was the sense that those who belonged to it had a status denied to any outsider, a status of real, practical importance. Only a member of the group had legal standing, could own property in the territory the group controlled, shared in the worship of the group's gods, and in general, only through marriage with another member of the group could children's status as citizens be achieved. The very concepts of citizen and citizenship derive from these institutions, and citizenship was so important that it filled all the social and spiritual needs of most people, while at the same time it created close ties with other members in the mutual obligations it entailed. By the time of the fifth century BCE, at least in Athens, this concept of the "citizen" as an individual constitutive of and enjoying privileges of participation had developed fully. The concept of participation, recorded as it was by so much literature that has come down to modern times, has recurred in western political thinking in opposition to traditions that saw individual members of society as subjects of a sovereign, and has generated repeated demands for "rights" that often baffle leaders of modern states who consider themselves to be regulated by democratic elections.

By the fifth century BCE the Greek concept of citizenship had survived difficult times. At the beginning of the sixth century the Athenians called on one of their prominent men, Solon, to draft laws that would alleviate the domestic turmoil, while a little to the west, the Boeotian Hesiod elucidated the wrongs done to peasant farmers. From Megara, to the south, came the response of aristocratic notions, in the poetry of Theognis deploring the rising power of the *nouveau riche* who were acquiring greater power in the state.

In some cities the continuing trouble provided opportunity for dominion by a single man, the *tyrannos* in Greek, a man who held monarchical power by force or unconstitutional means rather than inheritance of royal position. Thucydides, one of the few who offered a general explanation, explained that tyranny arose as Greece "acquired more wealth than before.[9] Alcaeus of Mytilene remarked that "money is the man, and no poor man is noble or good,[10] while Theognis complained about base marriages, "money mingles family,"[11] indicating that the wealth Thucydides reports was not always in the hands of the aristocrats. Thucydides' text suggests that the increase in wealth created stresses that opportunists exploited to seize power, and according to Aristotle, in oligarchies the pursuit of wealth generated strife that destabilized them. Herodotus wrote that factionalism was inherent in oligarchy, producing strife and bloodshed that ultimately issue in tyranny. Solon portrayed a situation in which people turned in ignorance to a tyrant when the city was overturned by the destruction caused by its great men, and at Megara, Theognis wrote that "factions, and kindred slaughters of men, and sole rulers"[12] emerged when leaders turned to wrong.

Whether with tyrants or without, few cities came through these troubles without being touched by the concept of "justice." Its appearance in literature with connotations like the modern English word justice shows the idea coming to the forefront in Greek thought, and it emerged in a number of separate places. "Justice" and "injustice" more and more denoted political and economic relationships, and with time, the need to define justice would become one of the driving forces behind the development of Greek philosophy. It would inspire some of the most far-reaching explorations of the nature of humanity and its place in the cosmos and create a fundamental influence on the development of values that would ultimately define the nature of western society.

When early Greek writers use the term justice, they simply assume its existence, just as they assumed the necessity of membership in the group for eligibility for certain privileges. These basic, unargued principles of social organization existed for political thought in later times, often being explicitly stated, as in the U.S. Declaration of Independence. The late 18th-century colonists asserted "We hold these truths to be self-evident, that all men are created equal, that they are endowed by their Creator with certain inalienable Rights...." The 18th-century Christian writers interposed a creator as source of the rights, and the equality they assert is a matter we will discuss in later chapters, but for them as for the Greeks, who assumed the rights without attributing them to a creator, the truth of their existence was self-evident. For modern political thinkers endorsing the existence of inalienable rights, observing them was a matter of the justice that had been asserted as a factor in the cosmos by the original Greek writers.

The issue of justice as a major concern appears first in the writings of the eighth-century Boeotian poet Hesiod, the earliest Greek poet of whose life and character we have any real indication.[13] Hesiod has left us two long works full of ideas that show the state of Greek thought in the early period, the *Theogony* and the *Works and Days*. The first of these, with the *Eoiae* and the *Catalogues* that explain the genealogy of the Greeks, presents a coherent account of the generations of the gods and the sequence of the progressive ages of humanity. I have already pointed to ideas in Hesiod's poetry that take back to his time some of the basic ideas of the nature of men and women. Much more obvious in Hesiod's writing is a concern with social relations.

The principles of justice emerge in everyday detail in Hesiod's *Works and Days*, advice to Hesiod's brother, Perses, in a poem of homely peasant moralizing attached to an agricultural calendar drawn up according to numerological superstition. *Works and Days* is the earliest surviving example of the poetry that also produced personal and love lyrics characteristic of the early period. Writers like Archilochus, Sappho, and Alcaeus wrote of individual happiness and satisfaction at the time of the struggle of the old aristocracies to hold their position against the pressure of demands by members of classes they regarded as lower orders. Even when the theme of ethical conduct was stressed, as it was by Hesiod, it focused on individual virtue, not the problems of justice and lawfulness that arise in social contexts. Justice was the maintenance of the old order, and it would take an urban environment to shift it to the broader significance it had for later ages.

The change is apparent in early sixth-century Athens. The lawgiver Solon produced ethical and political thought affected by the full impact of the transformation. The most famous of all the lawgivers of Greece, Solon became almost a code-word for democratic advance in Athens and stood for western thinkers as an example of progressive and liberal evolution that started Athens off on a path later writers approved.[14]

While we have some of Solon's poetry to throw light on his thought, the man and his times are so obscure to history that the actual details of what he did remain doubtful and the subject of dispute among Greek historians. Later Athenians designated

Solon as the creator of many of their laws, assuming without any real evidence that he was the author of each and every one of the provisions eventually summed up in the first century of our era by the writer Plutarch in his *Life of Solon*. The tradition asserts that Solon shaped a thorough reform of the Athenian political system, as the *Life* recounts his activity, and this, according to Aristotle's *Constitution of Athens*, established Athenian democracy. Great achievements like the "shaking off of debts," the prohibition of debt slavery, division of the citizenry into property classes, establishment of councils and regulation of their size, recognition of certain legal rights in lawsuits and the creation of courts were all gathered to the lawgiver's credit and given the imprimatur of antiquity and virtue of the name "Solon."

Of a different nature, and a different importance, a whole series of measures affect testamentary procedure, marriage and family affairs, commerce, agriculture, funeral and sexual matters. Although all these measures were attributed to Solon, many or most probably came into effect over the period before Solon himself enacted some of them, and they represent a far-reaching change in the relationship between individual and state in Athens, whereby the society for the first time intervened in and controlled many private matters. This great alteration was not recognized in antiquity because of the long-standing acceptance of state involvement in private matters, as I have argued elsewhere,[15] and it demonstrates the manner in which ideas become established as institutions and then later are accepted as tacit assumptions about the nature of life and society. The turmoil Solon alludes to before his time emerged out of and was undoubtedly responsible for the shift that saw so much that had hitherto been unregulated fall under the jurisdiction of public rules and institutions. But once those institutions were accepted and their authority over the aspects of life they regulated became part of the customary state of human affairs, the fact of change was forgotten and the new dispensation continued into the future without challenge. Established at the dawn of civic history, the authority of citizens to regulate the private lives of one another is a fundamental aspect of western culture.

Solon's poetry and his political ideas emerged from a background of reform and the whole panorama of the movement from a clan-oriented society to a political state. The history is a thin web made by constructing a few dots of evidence, but it is certainly clear from the poetry, if not also from what we can reconstruct from archaeological evidence, that "Solon presents *dike* [Justice] as the objective measure of what is politically right and wrong.[16] Whatever may have been the actual events of the early part of the sixth century, the poetry established a number of themes in response to civic turmoil, and created an appreciation for civic leaders who use their judgment and their authority to benefit their fellow citizens. Solon refers to some of his own specific acts like eliminating mortgages on the land and liberating those who had fallen into slavery for debt, and focuses on his creation of law, "fitting together," as he says, "force and *dike*" – justice.[17] He claims that his laws applied to all citizens, well-born or lower class, to whom he refers by the Greek words that may be translated merely "good" and "bad." Thus we have a concept of all-encompassing law without which a political state cannot exist, and furthermore, law that admits legitimacy to claims by underclasses and adjusts power in society to some extent to avoid civil war. Indeed, inherent in this is the very concept of political government, explicit for the first time in Greek literature. The control over this is Justice, rebuking the excesses of greedy and grasping evil leaders who steal from the people and the gods until Justice arrives to exact her punishment, and when she does, she often brings disaster on an entire city.[18] This Justice is not a metaphysical abstraction; she is a real power, and acts on human beings. As Solon presents the case, misfortune falls on people not by whim of the gods or as the accidental by-product of divine activity, but results from human misbehavior. Furthermore, in this retribution for wickedness, a whole society may be made to suffer for the actions of a part, so that in ethical terms too, a polis is a unit, an organic whole. Justice does not just single out individual wrongdoers, as does Zeus in Hesiod's scheme; she may impose her punishment on the whole society, a notion that helps explain why at times the innocent seem to suffer.

There are also poems in which Solon shows something of more general political and ethical ideas, even though the poems were written as justification of his actions rather than an explication of abstract ideals. Some of this poetry appears quoted in Aristotle's *Constitution of Athens* with repetitions and additions in Plutarch's *Life of Solon* and elsewhere, and the popularity of Plutarch over the centuries assured continuity to many of the ideas of justice and government in Solon's poetry. Some of the concepts lend themselves to an understanding of why Solon was seen to have pushed Athens along the road to democracy, such as "I gave the populace just so much privilege as was fitting,"[19] while others provide evidence for his decision not to redistribute land, his cancellation of debts, and his freeing of the debt slaves. And beyond the political explanations there are poems of a more general nature, like the *Song to the Muses* which reveals Solon's views on human prosperity, wrongdoing and retribution, and on human misfortune, and which seems in some of its ideas not to be so far from the views of Hesiod in attributing the punishment of wrongdoing to Zeus, who may wait, and then strike suddenly, so that "one man pays immediately, another in the future."[20]

Turmoil, conflict and development over several centuries ultimately produced the unique Greek polis with ideas of citizenship providing the groundwork for modern national states. By the time this formative period was over a constellation of ideas came to the fore and then slid into the background of thought as "self-evident" truths about people and their societies. The ideas not only molded the thoughts and actions of successor generations in antiquity, as might be expected, but they became such basic assumptions that they continued into the future, sometimes subliminally, carried by the writings that remained significant in later centuries, to burst forth as rediscovered when opportunities presented themselves. It is hard to imagine that Voltaire, Rousseau, Tom Paine, or for that matter, Franklin Roosevelt, could have written and thought as they did if they had not assumed that statesmanship called for a dedication to justice, and in particular, a justice that endorsed "rights" of individual citizens who were entitled to those rights purely on the basis of their membership in the society with which they were concerned.

I think it is important to recognize that the direction the Greek thinkers and statesmen took in their approach to justice and "rights" of citizens is not necessarily a natural progression of attitudes that might be expected to emerge in any human society.[21] The notion that a number of historians of China have offered of a parallel between Greece and China in these centuries, in which turmoil and conflict engendered intellectual and philosophical activity,[22] should stress that whatever the parallels in history (doubtful, in my view, in this case), the two societies produced very different sets of philosophical and political attitudes, and widely diverging value systems. For the Chinese thinkers, an abstract "Justice" was not at issue.

Confucius and Mencius, for example, were concerned with behavior correct for a hierarchical society in which obligations up and down should be understood and followed. We read in their texts of righteousness (*yi*), a quality that comprehends, for the most part, fulfillment of one's duties to parents, elder siblings in the family, and then on the pattern of family relations, to superior officials and ultimately to the sovereign. The same basic concepts can be found in the words attributed to Confucius, and they persist even in the rare challenges by other ancient Chinese philosophical writers and texts.

The path that Solon and Hesiod took to the establishment of a concept of an overriding Justice demands that one find an answer to the question "What is Justice?" and runs in a straight line from Plato to Rawls, as if only by answering that question can one expect to produce a satisfactory society. The Chinese took a different route. Very early in that tradition we can see at work a focus on the development of a pragmatic humanism, repeatedly expressed in advices to rulers or so-called "charges" to ministers quoted in China's earliest written work of history, the *Shu Ching*, or *Book of History*. Among the counsels of the great Yu, a minister, later sovereign, advising the sovereign Shun, traditionally dated in the 23rd century BCE, is the advice: "The virtue of the ruler is seen in good government, and government is tested in nourishing of the people," and the advice continues in practical detail.[23] The pragmatic character of advice, rather than concern with abstract Justice, continues through the following centuries, as in the "Great Plan" presented to King Wu (1122-15 BCE), listing "the eight objects of government: the first is food; the second, wealth and articles of convenience; the third, sacrifices; the fourth, the business of the minister of Works; the fifth, that of the minister of Instruction; sixth, that of the minister of Crime; the seventh, the courtesy to be paid to guests; the eighth, the army."[24]

By the time we get to the late sixth and early fifth centuries BCE, we see the ideas formulated in the program of Confucius, whose "primary concern was a good society based on good government and harmonious human relations."[25] In Confucius' statements, or those of Mencius, his successor and follower, there is no attempt to discover the nature of justice or define it as an objective reality; the effort is to establish patterns of behavior that lead to harmony of activity within the family in the first instance and then by extrapolation of the rules of familial piety, into government, thus rectifying the instruments of government: "A ruler should employ his ministers according to the rules of propriety, and ministers should serve their ruler with loyalty."[26]

The attitudes inherent in these quotations from the Chinese tradition are quite alien to the thought of the early Greek writers. They bespeak a confidence in the order and harmony of the universe, remote from human affairs and moving to express heavenly order only when a dynasty violates the mandate of heaven, which by the time of Confucius is an abstraction, not a figure with personality like Zeus or the other Greek gods. Dealing with virtue and morality in this tradition is a matter of following established paths of propriety, family piety and official loyalty and the like, rather than hypothesizing a principle called Justice. The absence of a preoccupation with an abstraction "Justice" in moral thought is characteristic of whatever I have read of the Chinese philosophers. Even so modern a Confucian as Chen Li-fu, whose career as a government official stretched from the days of Sun Yat-sen down to Chiang Kai-shek, deplores both capitalist and communist materialist focus on competition: "In the Confucian concept, governing of the state and pacification of the world should be based on sincerity in order to bring about universal peace."[27] Among the nine Confucian rules Chen gives, rules like cultivation of one's own character, honoring of men of virtue and talent, affection toward relatives, respect toward great ministers, consideration for the body of officers, treatment of the populace as children, there is no mention of "Justice."

The concept of justice we have inherited from the Greeks is a concept that depends, for us just as much as for them, on a sense of the desirability of individual autonomy. As the Chinese seek propriety of behavior for the creation of a harmonious society, the Greeks and we seek an order in society that protects the individual from mistreatment in a competitive environment. Justice becomes the maintenance or reestablishment of balance, and the concept is symbolized for us by the representation of the goddess carrying a set of balanced scales. It is not a concept called for by a society that aims to follow changeless patterns of relationship. It is needed in one in which individuals are encouraged to maximize their wealth, power and reputation, and in doing so may exceed the tolerance of those who are weaker. It is not a concept needed by a society that agrees to and values a hierarchical arrangement with agreed responsibilities up and down the line, but is called for when political and social structures readily tend toward abuse of power and individuals feel no obligation towards lesser people. I am not referring here to the notion of "individualism" often decried today as an ideology of selfishness and disregard of others. I mean the assumption that the individual is in some measure sacrosanct, in the words of Gletkin in Arthur Koestler's *Darkness at Noon*. It is for the benefit of this individual that we demand the imposition of justice.

We will return a number of times to the theme of the individual in a value system, and we will see both the benefits it brings to people and society and the difficulties it presents in the organization of life in the world as it is. We must acknowledge both, for both are present, and we must also acknowledge that the search for justice, an effort on which we pride ourselves and our tradition, is valuable primarily to a society which values the individual, in particular against the collective. This focus on the justice needed by the individual is part of the characteristic of Hellenic thought and society that today is so regularly cited as agonistic – occupied with rivalry and contest – and it called forth that equally cited Greek preoccupation with the need for and the manner of verbal persuasion, even extending to a contrast between Chinese and the Greek concept of poetry, which "seeks to account for poetry not in terms of a process or phenomenon based on incitement as in China, but in terms of *persuasion*, through which poetry tries to make us believe the things described, give us a *convincing* impression of the truth."[28] Our society requires a concept of justice and demands an effort at persuasion, to allow a necessary scope and flexibility of action to the individual actor whose role in life is seen as the primary element of civilization. On this does all our attention to egalitarianism and democratic government depend, and in addition, to our concern with autocracy.

---

[1] Arrian, *Anabasis of Alexander* IV, 8.7.
[2] Rawls (1971) p. 3.
[3] Apparently, scholars are divided between this traditional date and the placement between 390 and 305 BCE; see Chan, ed. (2002) p. 3.
[4] Hesiod, *Works and Days*, 250, etc.
[5] For the invocation of archaeological data in pursuit of an understanding of the development of the polis in Archaic Greece, see, *inter alia* Snodgrass (1987) and Morris (1987) who differ in their interpretation of the evidence, and whose subsequent discussions illustrate the tenuous nature of the evidence on which any understanding of the archaic period rests.

[6] It is worth noting that in this period in China, the same movement toward the use of massed foot soldiers in their thousands and ten thousands had no implications for the assumption of power or influence by the soldiers, but shows rather the tight control the new monarchs were able to maintain over their states.

[7] The idea is turned on its head by Jullien (2000) pp. 35-44, arguing that the Greek method of frontal clash in war shows a "direct link between the phalanx and the organization of the city ... the foot soldiers were reduced to 'interchangeable elements' that corresponded exactly to their positions in the egalitarian framework of political life. It therefore appears that the phalanx, and with it the logic of a frontal approach, could indicate a choice of Greek culture" (p. 44).

[8] Not only Greeks; the period has been a breeding-ground for reconstructions of society and its development, because the absence of reliable literary evidence and the plethora of variously interpreted material artifacts challenges the human desire to integrate evidence into a coherent and significant history. More recent works dealing with the period, and adding to their interpretations offering useful bibliographies, are Osborne (1996) and Murray (1993).

[9] Thucydides I, 13.1.

[10] Alcaeus, Muller 59.

[11] Theognis, 183-90.

[12] Theognis, 39-52.

[13] See Nagy (1990) pp. 36-61 for the treatment of Hesiod as oral poet in the tradition of "Homer."

[14] In a clear recent example, Saul (2001) p. 33: "Solon released the energy and creativity of a large part of the citizenry ... gave a kick-start to their society, including its economy ... imposed a salutary slimming on a rather lazy business class which was living off interest and other people's labour."

[15] Samuel (1963) pp. 231–36.

[16] As in Almeida (2003) p. 220, also providing a valuable and up-to-date survey of writing on Solon's political and philosophical stance along with an account of recent theorization about the emergence of the polis on the basis of the analysis of archaeological data.

[17] Solon, fr. 24 Diehl = Lattimore, R. (1960) fr. 4.

[18] Solon, fr. 3 Diehl = Lattimore 2

[19] Solon, fr. 5 Diehl = Lattimore 3; Aristotle, *Constitution of Athens* 12; Plutarch's version of the verse (Solon 18) has Solon giving "power" to the populace.

[20] Solon, fr. 1 Diehl = Lattimore 1.

[21] Although it is often assumed as in Almeida (2003) p. 71: "Justice, however, is a universal reality of all human activity."

[22] Graham (1989) pp. 1-9, focusing attention on the period, referring to Karl Jaspers' designation of it as the "Axial Age," summarizes differences, while

suggesting some parallels; I will, obviously, not agree with his assertion (p. 5) of the essential disjunction in modern times and that "the idea of a "Western civilization,' pushed back beyond AD 1600 to incorporate at each fork the culture more directly ancestral to ours, is no more than a restrospective fiction by which we claim for ourselves most of the genius we have heard of since Homer." Of Graham's emphasis on the "alien climate" of the medieval period – a legitimate view, in many way, although neglecting its very real influence on our attitudes – I will note that the sense of alienation in Graham's treatment of the period is suggestive of an acknowledgement of connection with the centuries before the medieval era.

[23] Waltham (1971) p. 21. Yu continues: "There are water, fire, metal, wood, earth and grain; these must be duly regulated. There are the rectification of the people's virtue, tools and other things that supply the conveniences of life, and securing abundant means of sustenance."

[24] Waltham (1971) p. 127.

[25] Chan (1963) p. 15.

[26] Chan (1963) p. 25.

[27] Chen (1976) p. 41.

[28] Jullien (2000) p. 163.

–9–
Autocracy

Herodotus, the so-called "father of history," gives an account of the war the Greeks fought against Persia, and his manner of telling the story provides a narrative basis for many Greek – and modern – attitudes towards the nature and differences between monarchical and pluralistic forms of political organization. Among the stories he tells about men who arrogated power to themselves is an account of the second attempt of Peisistratus of Athens to establish himself as an autocrat in Athens, when he had a woman dressed as the goddess Athena lead him into the city. The account of the sixth century BCE events is one of the earliest stories creating the attitudes we have towards government. Herodotus, as well as other sources, makes it clear that the eventual success of Peisistratus was not due to simple-minded ruses; in his second period of tyranny he resorted to a political combination with a powerful Athenian family, and in his the third and final assault, military power was his weapon. Yet there was more even than that to a tyrant's success, not only in Athens but in other cities, like Corinth, that experienced this kind of government in their early history. When we take into account what we know from writers who followed Herodotus, and combine it with modern insights into the fragmentary bits of information about the period, we create a story in which tyranny seems to have been, in many if not all cases, a seizure of the state by an autocrat who wrests power from the hitherto existing aristocratic power group. Aristotle explains the circumstances giving rise to a successful seizure as a kind of populism, in which a tyranny "is set up from among the people and the mob against the notables, so that the people may suffer no wrong from them."[1] He asserts that the greater number of tyrants originated as popular leaders, and that their establishment responded to kings or other leaders abusing their power. In this philosopher's mind then, tyranny, which in Greek tradition eventuated in abuse of power, also arose from it.

The Greek term *tyrannos* is not in itself one of opprobrium, nor one indicating moral or even political judgment. It rather is a matter of law, indicating that the man who is so designated seized power and held it outside the law, assuming a position that does not exist within the traditional or constitutional structure of government. Yet, despite the potentially neutral meaning of the term in moral terms, Greek tradition and history renders a negative judgment on tyranny as an institution and on the tyrants themselves. Ancient accounts of the Peisistratid tyranny at Athens, offering the people good government during the life of its founder as it appears from Herodotus, portray it as deteriorated under the regime of Peisistratus' sons, who used arbitrary and excessive force to preserve their power. Similar patterns are reported for other cities: individual tyrants might account for some beneficial actions, but overall, Greek writers almost universally condemned individuals who held control of cities forcefully and illegally by military might. Two millennia of historical writing perpetuated a consistent Greek tradition rendering a negative judgment on such regimes, and sets the attitudes of today.

As early as the *Iliad*, Greek texts derogated the abuse of power. That story opens when Agamemnon, the leader of the Hellenic army, begins a series of events by his exercise of royal power. Told that he was expected to return a prize of war, he reacts in anger and seizes the captive of another of the Greek kings, Achilles, in retaliation for his own loss. There is no suggestion that Agamemnon exceeded his rights; neither Achilles nor any of the other warriors protest that Agamemnon has overstepped his authority, but Achilles is ready to resist the senior king with his sword, only to be held back by the goddess Athena's hand. And Achilles' peers do not condemn his incipient assault on the senior king. Resistance to power is as legitimate as its exercise. This episode precipitates the story of Achilles, and it shows how epic society saw the exercise of power. Even later in the story, when Agamemnon proposes to recompense Achilles, he does not say he abused his power, but simply refers to the action as a mistake, blaming divinity for his actions, madness, he says, brought on him by some god.

But this use of power by an autocrat was, in the *Iliad*, undesirable for practical reasons. Agamemnon's actions led to Achilles' withdrawal from combat and the consequent success of the Trojans. The aura of condemnation of this exercise of power attracts is based on this, rather than some moral or ethical principles laid down for the behavior of rulers. It was only later, in the period of democracies and citizen-oligarchies after the experience of the tyrannies, that Greek attitudes treated autocracy as reprehensible, culturally undesirable in its interference with the proper operation of the polis system by the group of citizens sovereign in each city. It was not until the collapse of the polis system after Alexander that Greeks began composing the essays of advice to kings that were addressed to the rulers of the fragmented empire Alexander left behind.

Although there was some rudimentary theory of kingship in Herodotus' account of the debate among the Persian followers of Darius, mooting the benefits of monarchy, aristocracy and democracy, we do not have the enunciation of political analysis of monarchical institutions until the fourth century BCE, in the writings of Plato and Aristotle. Even then, government by a single man, when seen as appropriate, is deemed monarchy, a form of constitutional government, and it is the degenerate form of monarchy that is designated as tyranny. For the most part, Greek writers deplored autocracy in its sense of unrestrained and unconstitutional power, whether in Greek cities or established over the hordes of barbarian "slaves." Greek texts established a tradition followed by the famous dictum of Lord Acton, "Power tends to corrupt, and absolute power tends to corrupt absolutely."

Since antiquity, autocracy in western societies has been regarded, for the most part, as a practical mechanism: "Mussolini made the trains run on time." For the thousand years in which the Church dominated politics, political theory was based on the mythical "Donation of Constantine," the alleged grant of secular power by the Roman Emperor Constantine to the bishop of Rome, later known as the pope. The concept made the autocracy of kings secondary to the authority of the pope, and the kings, theoretically, held their thrones at the discretion of the religious authority; the theory led to repeated conflict between holders of religious and secular thrones. And even with the asserted divine endorsement of both, history is replete with resistance and opposition to secular and theological power of religious and secular leaders, so much so that it seems that the exercise of autocracy carries with it constant dissension and the threat of dissolution from internal rebellion.

That is, however, not necessarily a universal experience. It may be part of the inheritance of the Greek resistance to authority, for the experience of absolute rule is different in other parts of the world, as is abundantly clear from the Chinese experience. As early as the Zhou dynasty (1045-256 BCE) and perhaps before, the rulers of the parts of the east Asian land mass subject to the Chinese had established centralized, bureaucratic control of their territory. Records were kept in a system that may have been somewhat analogous to the empires of the Greek Bronze Age and the Near East. The great difference in the Chinese pattern is the formulation before and during the period of the warring states (475-221 BCE) of an ideology of hierarchy, discipline, moderation and obligation on the part of authority and submission to it by the populace. Even as the central control of the Zhou dynasty weakened and China slipped into a situation of separate states at war with one another, Chinese sages were developing an ideology aimed at ratifying and promoting an authoritarian, hierarchical state with authority founded on its moral and ethical leadership. Confucius, 551-479 BCE, established the dominant tradition in Chinese political thought, based on exercise of and obedience to authority. Early Confucian thought insisted that the success of this authoritarianism required that it be prosecuted in a moral and ethical manner, while some later political theorists stressed force and law as the means of securing the stability of power.

Western reactions to Chinese philosophy have varied from an assessment in the late sixteenth century in which Matteo Ricci saw China as a nation of philosophers, to modern western philosophic dismissal of the tradition as banal at best. Conversely, there has recently been a more popular seizing upon superficial aspects to make a kind of hippie jumble of eastern thought and religion. It is only in the later twentieth century as the deteriorating condition of the environment produced doubts about the direction in which western traditions were leading that the Chinese emphasis on harmony of humanity with nature led philosophers and others to make the Confucian tradition a welcome contrast with the philosophical tradition inherited from the Greeks:

> Rather than a vocabulary of truth and falsity, right and wrong, good and evil – terms that speak to the 'whatness' of things, we find pervasively the language of harmony and disorder, genuineness and hypocrisy, trust and dissimulation, adeptness and ineptness – terms that reflect the priority of the continuity that obtains among things.[2]

Chinese philosophers characterizing their tradition for westerners emphasize some of the same aspects of Chinese thought, using terms like "Intrinsic Humanism," "Concrete Rationalism," "Organic Naturalism," and "Pragmatism of Self-Cultivation," with observations that "Chinese philosophy is generally oriented toward action and practice in society and government, and aims at the reform and perfection of man and the world. It stresses, furthermore, that theory must be applied to practice or be considered empty words."[3] The endorsement and support of authority presented so clearly and firmly in Confucian writings must be seen in the context of this overarching concern with fitting the human into the natural and social environment. Abstract justice, individual rights, equality, and all the other matters traditionally of concern to western thinkers yield, in Confucius' thought, to an even-handed reciprocation of obedience for nurture between populace and ruler. For example, when asked about government, "Confucius replied, saying 'Government: correctness. If the sage leads according to correctness, who would dare not to be correct?'"[4] A similar laconic description of government proposes the requirements for rule: "Master Kong queried government. Master [Confucius] said: sufficient food, weapons, and the people's faith in it. That's all."[5] All of Confucius' precepts about government are based on the assumption that the ruler is rightly in place, and that the task of the sage is not evaluating the absoluteness of his rule, but in advising how it is to be applied for the benefit of the people and the ruler both. The full extent of the morality and ethics involved is a matter of reciprocation, the ruler looking after the welfare of the people, and the people returning the same concern for the ruler: "With sufficiency for the hundred surnames [= the people], who would allow there not to be sufficiency for the ruler? With no sufficiency for the hundred surnames, who would allow sufficiency to the ruler?"[6]

The reciprocal nature of the relationship between ruler and ruled, and the obligation of the sovereign to look after his population, is emphasized by texts designated as those of Mencius, who according to tradition, studied at the school of Confucius' grandson and was himself active in the latter part of the fourth century BCE. Mencius' writing, often addressed to a ruler as advice, deals more explicitly and extensively with matters of government, and, like the *Analects* of Confucius, offers no objection to the absolutism of the system of government in the various Chinese states of his time.[7] The position of the ruler and the direct connection with the people is delineated quite clearly:

When all those about you say, – "This man deserves death," don't listen to them. When all your great officers say, – "this man deserves death," don't listen to them. When the people all say, – "This man deserves death," then enquire into the case, and when you see that the man deserves death, put him to death. In accordance with this we have the saying, "The people killed him." You must act in this way in order to be the parent of the people.[8]

The nature of Chinese absolutism is seen as parallel to the family, with the obligations of family relations extrapolated to the organization of the state:

If your Majesty will *indeed* dispense a benevolent government to the people, being sparing in the use of punishments, and making the taxes and levies light, so causing that the fields shall be ploughed deep, and the weeding of them be carefully attended to, and that the strong-bodied, during their days of leisure, shall cultivate their filial piety, fraternal respectfulness, sincerity, and truthfulness, serving thereby, at home, their fathers and elder brothers, and abroad, their elders and superiors, – you will then have a people who can be employed, with sticks they have prepared, to oppose the strong mail and sharp weapons of the troops of Ch'in and Ch'u.[9]

The ideas of the sovereign's organization of his rule in the manner of a parent,[10] the sovereign's success as a ruler depending on his application of benevolence (the Chinese word (*ren*),[11] emerge from Mencius' explicit assertion of familial obligations in the operation of political life: "People have this common saying, – The kingdom, the state, the family. The root of the kingdom is in the state. The root of the state is in the family. The root of the family is in the person *of its head*,"[12] and the concept was enunciated well before the time of Mencius in the very early *Shijing* or *Book of Songs*.[13] In the earliest stage of Confucian thought, the family took precedence over every other principle of morality, even to Confucius' advocating protection of a parent guilty of crime. As the theory of the paternalistic government progressed with time, the hierarchy of bureaucracy and the requirement of absolute obedience to superiors emerged out of the insistence on filial piety and subordination of the younger to the elder, son to father, sibling to elder brother. Morality and ethics were matters of relationships, and the Greek preoccupation with abstract justice was not at issue.

Everyone who has written about Chinese society, past or present, has referred to the authoritarian character of the imperial government and the fact that "one of the constant assumptions of early Chinese political thought is that government is by its nature authoritarian, and that the only alternative to absolutism is the reduction or abolition of government."[14] However much individuals, inside or outside the bureaucracy, may have managed to evade regulations and achieve personal advantage, the theoretical judgment of Chinese political commentators insisted on adherence to imperial commands and obedience to superiors.

In the idealization of admirable rulers, it is the moral stance of the ruler that justifies his possession of the mandate of heaven, according to the Chinese view of government, and not his military ability or capacity as a warrior, or cleverness, or wealth. In describing the much-admired King Wen, of the early Zhou dynasty, for example, the early Chinese historian Sima Qian (ca. 145-86 BCE) writes: "He was resolute in his kindness, reverent to the old, and compassionate to the young. He paid homage to and humbled himself before worthy people. In midday he did not take time to eat, in order to receive the patricians."[15] Throughout the very early literary classic, the *Shang Shu* or *Book of Documents*,[16] speeches by or addressed to the "good" emperors emphasize their humility, filial piety, and devotion to the welfare of the people, while conversely, throughout the tradition from the *Shang Shu* on, accounts of the ends of dynasties make the final king a villain with faults the reverse of the virtues of the idealized rulers.[17] One can even trace the operation of the convention, as a final emperor of a dynasty may be praised in his own lifetime, but condemned by subsequent judgment when it was known that a dynastic change followed the reign. Autocracy is never challenged, and miscreant rulers are blamed for misdeeds, rather than the system itself.

Greek attitudes toward absolute rulers are quite different. Figures of Athenian drama like Oedipus or Creon of the *Antigone* exhibit many virtues – perspicacity, martial ability, rhetorical skill, for example – and their disastrous ends come at least in part from causes beyond their control, but their misfortunes owe something to the fact that they act with the absolutism of autocrats. Indeed, it is Creon's defense of the obligation of obedience in *Antigone*, a speech that would have been endorsed by Chinese thinkers, that presents him as an autocrat in the unfavorable light that such a portrayal elicits in fifth century Athenian thought. The image of autocracy in the Greek historians of the fifth century BCE is negative: it is a characteristic of the barbarians, who are slaves to the Great King in Herodotus' account; the dire effects of the authoritarianism and autocracy of one polis, Athens, over others, is at the heart of Thucydides' account of the Peloponnesian War. In Chinese historiography the approach is quite different. In the work of the most notable of the early historians, Sima Qian, autocracy is never questioned, but what a Greek might allege as the deleterious effects of such rule are attributed to the faults of the holders of power. The idealization of the good emperor found in the philosophical comments of Confucius and Mencius are even illustrated by the occasional ideal ruler, such as Wen, who (like Shakespeare's Julius Caesar) three times put aside the power, and whose reign was summed up briefly and affirmatively: "The King was invited to ascend the throne, and people of the world submitted to him wholeheartedly. [The emperor] abolished corporal punishment, and opened up the passes and bridges. He extensively spread favor and kindness, thus he was called the Grand Patriarch."[18]

There are, however, realities of history that demonstrate that the authoritarianism in practice was not always so benevolent, nor a gentle demonstration of virtue adequate to lead the populace to proper behavior. Historical annals are replete with rebellion, savage repression, cruelty and stories of dissolute behavior. Later consideration might attribute the collapses of reigns or dynasties to rulers' misbehavior, but in fact, events of the tumultuous centuries before the establishment of the first Empire under the Qin (221-206 BCE) and Han (202 BCE – 220 CE) dynasties amply demonstrate what Hellenism would designate as the negative aspects of absolute rule. Some streams of writing, such as that of the so-called Legalists, not only endorse authoritarianism but propose means of control that have little or no ethical content.

In the Greek tradition of political theory. autocracy is not a theory to be fulfilled in accordance with the will of heaven, as Chinese writers often put it, nor is it the natural form of government in a hierarchical universe. At best, it is one possible form of government, and it is usually seen as carrying with it all sorts of evils and disadvantages. We have already noted the negative assessment of wicked rulers made by Hesiod, and there are other early writers who join the poet in the citation of the misdeeds of tyrants. In Herodotus' presentation of the debate among the Persian conspirators after their disposal of the (supposedly) false king, the first proposal for the future government of Persia is an endorsement of democracy and a concomitant condemnation of monarchy. For the monarch, the Persian Otanes is given to say, "it is possible to do whatever he wants without any accountability. For if the best of all men achieve this, he would lose his accustomed mental state."[19] Herodotus goes on to present, from Otanes' mouth, a series of malefactions deriving from monarchy. In the debate as it progresses, the proposer of oligarchy denigrates democracy as government by an ignorant mob, whose wrongdoing does not even have the benefit of the knowledge the *tyrannos* has when he acts. Finally, Darius himself gives his opinion in favor of monarchy, a view that prevails, although as Darius propounds it, he does not refute any of the disadvantages cited by Otanes. He points out disadvantages of the alternatives, oligarchy and democracy, but his support of monarchy is based on the completely unsupported statement that "nothing would appear better than the rule of the one best man, for using judgment that is like himself he would govern the population blamelessly."[20] The only supporting proposition invoked by Darius is the allegation that the freedom from the magi recently gained came at the behest of a single man, justifying the continuance of monarchy among the Persians. A Greek reader, certainly an Athenian reader, and probably most modern readers, would come away from these passages with the sense of the dangers implicit in autocracy, and it is more than likely that Herodotus constructed his narrative to achieve that end. Herodotus' text accords with the common Greek view that the Persian people were no more than slaves of the Persian king.[21]

The theoretical assessment of democracy is even stronger in a speech of the Athenian leader Pericles, in Thucydides' rendition of the funeral oration for the Athenians who died in the first year of the war against Sparta. Pericles' praise for the Athenian government made it an example of an open society in which citizens are regulated by respect for their own laws, and the text has been quoted and repeated by democrats for centuries. Yet, despite the favorable account of the democracy in this and a few other passages, Thucydides ultimately pictures the democracy as a whole exercising an autocracy that the reader condemns.

In the fourth century we find a somewhat different view of the Persian monarchy. Xenophon, writing his fictionalized account of the sixth century BCE Persian king Cyrus, observes first that "as a human being has evolved, it is easier to rule over all other forms of life than human,"[22] and then goes on to designate Cyrus as one who achieved the task and was obeyed willingly by his populace. In the work as a whole Xenophon details Cyrus' good qualities, and while they are not all those particularly characteristic of the Chinese rulers, they do, in the end, parallel them, as is clear from some of the remarks Cyrus is made to utter on his deathbed. He notes that he had been able to maintain all his conquests, justifies the passing of the throne to the older son on the grounds that he had been "educated to yield to elders, not only brothers but also fellow citizens on the roads, in seats and in conversation,"[23] and advises his son that he will maintain himself by faithful friends but that he should know that all men are not faithful by nature. Cyrus continues his advice with an exhortation of the younger to love and obey the elder in power, urges service to the gods and respect for human beings and adverts again to warning against strife between the brothers.

However much Xenophon might have admired Cyrus, he does not make him a ruler whose power comes as the "mandate of heaven," nor does he represent the Persian king in any way as the parent of the people. That autocracy, in fact, seen even by Cyrus' admirer, is still the difficult matter of ruling over people, and in the concepts elucidated by Xenophon, it is Cyrus' exceptional qualities that permitted that king to exercise his power without resistance, when resistance is the norm to be expected.

Resistance to a Hellenic autocrat was certainly the watchword of Demosthenes in the speeches he formulated all through his life to encourage his fellow Athenians to oppose the growing strength of the Macedonian king, Philip II. Attitudes of opposition to royal power went far beyond just a mere Athenian desire to maintain the democracy's power in Greece against the increasing power Philip created for the Macedonian monarchy. Anecdotes about Philip's son Alexander – the conqueror so admired today that millions of dollars are spent to produce movies extolling him – show that at least some of those who lived in his time faced him as an autocrat to be detested. When word came back to Greece that Alexander wished to be worshipped as a god, a sneering enemy remarked "Let him be Poseidon, if he wishes," and another denied a report that Alexander had died by asserting "He cannot be dead, for the world would stink of his corpse."

Among the reasons Greek writers tended to derogate monarchy, as they did until the monarchic principle became entrenched in society after the time of Alexander the Great and his military successor-kings, was a sense that monarchs and law were antithetical. The point emerges in the story about about Alexander's remorse for killing his friend Cleitus, as the philosopher Anaxarchus told him that he was beyond law and morality. This anecdote comes from texts composed three hundred years or more after the death of the conqueror, in a Roman world accepting of autocracy and educated by centuries of philosophical justification and prescription for autocracy.

The great shift in attitudes towards monarchy and autocracy came in the centuries after Alexander's generals established themselves in the regions conquered during the famed campaign. These new monarchs were different from the rulers Greeks had known in the past. They were not the kings of Homer, nor the warrior kings of Macedonia, Thrace and Illyria. They did not serve as quasi-magistrates, like the kings of Sparta, but neither were they tyrants, unconstitutional autocrats who had seized power illegally. They ruled over Greeks, but in many cases, the Greeks and Macedonians were only a small ethnic element among millions of Asiatics. As a result of the new situation, political writers rethought Hellenic ideas of kingship, and built on earlier ideas, of Aristotle in particular, to present an ideal of kingship that formed the basis for ideas of monarchy for the future. It was to replace the earlier suspicion of autocracy, and had some analogies to the Chinese exhortations of morality addressed to sovereigns. The period spawned a plethora of tracts *Peri Basileias*, "On Kingship," much as the "Advice to the Prince" of Macchiavelli emerged in later times. Theophrastus, Aristotle's student, wrote one, and he was followed by many who outlined their ideas of the kind of rule that was appropriate for the new kings.

These tracts, most of them probably banal, have been lost over time, but there are works that can tell us what sorts of advice they contained. The seventeenth *Idyll* of Theocritus, addressed to Ptolemy Philadelphus, who ruled in Egypt from 285 to 247 BCE, gives a clear indication of what a Greek poet thought appropriate to say about and to a king in a poem that was intended as a panegyric: Ptolemy's remote ancestry was divine, tracing back to Heracles, just as Alexander could claim descent from the gods. The poem is a traditional song of praise, and many of Ptolemy's attributes are as suitable for Homeric heroes as they are for this king in Egypt.

One hundred years or so later, a tract composed by a Hellenized Alexandrian Jew calling himself Aristeas tells a tale of Ptolemy Philadelphus interviewing at a banquet the emissaries from the high priest at Jerusalem who have come to Jerusalem at the king's behest to translate the holy law of the Hebrews. The author assumes the guise of a courtier of Phildelphus writing of the events a century or so before the actual time of composition,[24] but the content shows what could be suggested as appropriate kingly behavior in their responses to the questions the king poses, and gives us a good idea of the ideals of Hellenistic kingship. With allowances for the fact that the Jewish milieu from which the tract emerged called for the regular insertion of God's help or approval as part of each answer, the observations are firmly in the Hellenic ethical tradition: the king should be patient, and deal with malefactors with more gentleness than they deserve; his best course in all activity was to observe justice; he will keep his friends by taking care for the well-being of the people he rules; in legal affairs he should be impartial, and not arrogant or tyrannical in regard to offenders. Among the many items of advice, Philadelphus is told to observe truth, that the standard of kingship is to rule himself well, that he should not be attracted by wealth or fame. On one day a Socratic question comes from the king, asking if wisdom can be taught, producing the response that the soul has the power to accept all good and turn away the opposite. Many practical observations of Greek philosophers emerge in this account of the banquet, a portion of the text more than a third of its length and hardly necessary to the asserted theme of accounting for and describing the process of translation of the Hebrew scriptures into the Greek Bible we call the Septuagint.[25] The ideal of kingship could easily emerge out of a tradition that included Aristotle's idea that good monarchy is the rule by the man or family best suited to the task in moral terms. The ideas are quite consonant with Theocritus' text praising Ptolemy.

The tradition of advice to monarchs emerges in the period after Alexander, and culminated, in a way, with the *Meditations* of the second-century CE Roman Emperor Marcus Aurelius. It suppressed for a time the traditional early Hellenic suspicion of monarchy and autocracy, and is parallel to the Confucian ideal. But while the Confucian texts remained central to Chinese thought, in Europe the texts endorsing autocracy disappeared from libraries and reader's shelves, The attitudes of earlier texts prevailed in memory and in the conceptualization of ideal government, so that the idealized principles seen as Greek and Roman were revived to justify opposition to the rule of individual autocrats. They were carried forward from the justifications of independent republics in the Renaissance to the formulation of republican and egalitarian principles in the eighteenth century. The anti-authoritarian traditions of fifth-century BCE Hellenism reappeared in the eighteenth and nineteenth centuries to give impetus to the development of the libertarian, competitive, self-aggrandizing societies that today call themselves democracies. Inherent in the personal liberty some of today's democratic citizens enjoy is the distrust of authority inherited from this early period of Greek writing, along with Greek competitiveness and impulse to maximize power, reputation, and wealth.

The challenge to authority has similar effects. No one writing at the beginning of the 21st century would deny the value to our society of the tradition that refuses automatic acquiescence to received opinion or constituted authority. This attitude has led to many of the political qualities I and many others value and endorse in modern life, and has generated advances in social, scientific and artistic realms. While traditionalists would argue that it has undermined many religious beliefs, others would point to that undermining as liberating. Still, the failure to accept authority does have some negative effects. The loss of authority granted to religious beliefs and texts has meant the destruction of absolutism in ethics and morality, increasing the impact of relativism and making it difficult to assert with confidence the mores on which human interaction in society has been built for centuries. One of the motives for writing this book is the sense of need for some touchstone, some authority to which people can resort as validation of ethical and moral positions. In the absence of authority, everything seems relative, pragmatic, even self-serving for the individual; there seems nothing to regulate action other than perceived advantage.

When it comes to matters of authority and tradition, the Chinese approach emphasizes tradition, with deference to authority not only expected, but required as appropriate behavior. One of the most famous statements in the Confucian *Analects* illustrates the position at a number of levels: when asked about government, Confucius gave an often-quoted response. "Let the ruler *be* a ruler, the minister *be* a minister, the father *be* a father, and the son *be* a son."[26] Each is to fulfill the roles of the position he holds, and that fulfillment includes respect for the superior. The extent of deference to authority runs so deep in the Chinese tradition that there is virtually no open criticism of superiors, and what has been taken by Chinese commentators as advice to rulers is distinguished by its qualities of indirection and allusion. Even rhetoric is indirect, not confrontational like Greek political statement, just as Chinese military strategy favors the oblique, rather than the direct clash of Greek phalanx warfare. In interpreting poetry of the Chinese *Book of Songs*, for example, the Chinese commentators value the indirect, the indeterminate allusion, as an aesthetic quality; the explication of meaning is turned into political commentary because one cannot be direct with the ruler or the high official. Advice or complaint is couched in poetry that has no direct connection with the issue interpreted by the commentator, and there is a plethora of commentators to show the characteristic. The more difficult poems have "meaning" only in this interpreted way, although all of them are indefinite, and have "an allusive structure ... which gives it its implicit depth."[27]

It is not only the case that among Chinese philosophers, "no one questions that government is by nature authoritarian;"[28] authority is accepted as appropriate, and resistance to it, verbal as well as physical, is seen as falling away from "righteousness." The authority to be accepted is not only the mundane and political; the "Way" of Heaven – *Dao* – is the way of accommodation. The heroes of Homer and Athenian drama would be inconceivable in China, and that may account for the absence from Chinese literature of the sort of great personal epic found in the early literatures of so many other peoples. The Chinese attitude accounts in some measure, for the absence of the extreme competitiveness characteristic of the West, but it also contributes, I think, to the absence of the development of political attitudes westerners prize so highly.

---

[1] Aristotle, *Politics* 5.1310 b.
[2] Ames R. T, "Thinking Through Comparisons: Analytical and Narrative Methods for Cultural Understanding," in Shankman and Durrant, eds. (2002) p. 99. It is worth adding other comments by Hall to show both the contemporary approval of the Chinese tradition, and the manner in which that

tradition is becoming understood in the West: "The classical Chinese tradition begins with the assumption that the human being (or better, the human 'becoming') is something that one does rather than what one is; it is how one behaves within the context of the human community rather than some essential endowment that resides within one as a potential to be actualized." (p. 100) and "Morality, then, is the effort to get the most out of one's circumstances, where one's own interests and those of one's natural, social, and cultural environments must all be considered." (p. 107).

[3] Cheng, C-Y., "Chinese philosophy: a characterization," in Naess and Hannay, eds., (1972) p. 161. See also, similar comments and characterizations, by Wu, J. S., "Western Philosophy and the Search for Chinese Wisdom," in the same volume, pp. 1-18.

[4] Confucius, *Analects* XII, xvii, in Legge (1960) I, p. 258. The translation given is minimalist, to offer a sense of the language. Legge translates the passage as: "Chi K'ang asked Confucius about government. Confucius replied, 'To govern means to rectify. If you lead on *the people* [supplied by Legge] with correctness, who will dare not to be correct?'"

[5] Confucius, *Analects XII, vii*, 1, the "it" being government, or "him," the ruler. Legge (1960) p. 254, translates: "The master said, '*The requisites of government are* that there be sufficiency of food, sufficiency of military equipment, and the confidence of the people in their ruler.'"

[6] *Analects* XII, ix, 4. Legge (1960) p. 255 translates: "If the people have plenty, their prince will not be left to want alone. If the people are in want, their prince cannot enjoy plenty alone."

[7] Even if E. B. and A. T. Brooks are right in "The Nature and Historical Context of the Mencius," Chan (2002), that the Mencius text shows divisions between the original sayings of the philosopher and those later produced and introduced into the text as his by two schools of followers, the basic acceptance of autocracy underlies all the ideas. The so-called Mencian populism with the assertion of the right of the people to revolt or to confirm the ruler (p. 262) does not challenge the idea of imperial government itself, nor does the assertion of "responses to, and in some cases protests against, the same trend toward autocracy in the state" (p. 266) alter this, for the trends in the text, if they are truly there, still deal with the manner of exercise of autocracy, not the institution itself.

[8] Mencius I, 2, ix, 5, 6, tr. Legge (1960) II, p. 166.

[9] Mencius I, 1, v, 3, tr. Legge (1960) II, p. 135

[10] E.g. Mencius II. 1. v, 6, tr. Legge (1960) II, p. 206: "If *a ruler* can truly practice these five things [honor to men of talents; ground-rent on shops in markets without taxing goods, or eliminating ground-rent by enforcing proper regulations; charging no taxes at frontier passes; in agriculture, no taxes beyond mutual cultivation of common field; no fines for idlers or failure of

quotas in the shops], then the people in the neighbouring kingdoms will look up to him as a parent."

[11] E.g. Mencius IV 1. 1, iii, 1, tr. Legge (1960) II, p. 293: "It was by benevolence that the three dynasties gained the throne, and not being benevolent that they lost it."

[12] Mencius IV, 1, v, tr. Legge (1960) II, p. 295.

[13] Karlgren (1950) p. 116, no. 172; p. 208, no. 250, both with the ruler as "people's father and mother." Bodde (1991) p. 195 points out the extension of the concept: "The magistrates of the thirteen hundred and more districts into which imperial China was divided – men who, among the emperor's surrogates, had closest contact with the ordinary people – were known in popular parlance as fu-mu kuan, ('father-and-mother officials')."

[14] Graham (1989) p. 298.

[15] Ssu-ma Ch'ien, tr. 1995, Nienhauser, W. H. Jr. ed. (1995) p. 57.

[16] Karlgren (1950).

[17] The crimes conventionally attributed to final rulers are summarized in Bodde (1991) p. 244, as: "1. Tyranny (neglect of upright officials, favoritism toward sycophants, callousness toward the masses 2. Self-indulgence (drunkenness, passion for expensive products, elaborate palaces and gardens, etc.) 3. Licentiousness (lust, sex orgies, sadism, etc.) 4. Lack of personal virtue (unfilial or otherwise improper behavior to family members, disrespect to Heaven and ancestors, etc.).

[18] Sima Qian (2002) p. 185; regarding the conventional stance of reluctance of taking the overall rule (p. 66): "The King of Han renounced it three times, before he was unable to put it to an end, and said, 'If you lords insist that doing this would be advantageous, then it must be advantageous for the state.'"

[19] Herodotus, *Histories* III, 80.

[20] Herodotus, *Histories* III, 82.

[21] Even officials could be designated slaves, as in the fourth century Philip of Macedon describes the satrap of Caria as a slave.

[22] Xenophon, *Cyropaedia* I, 1, 3.

[23] Xenophon, *Cyropaedia* VIII, 7, 8.

[24] There have been many studies and arguments about the date. One would not be likely to be wrong setting it in the last half of the second century BCE. See text and translation, and the discussion citing earlier studies, of Hadas (1951).

[25] There is no doubt that the translation was made in Egypt, and the linguistic evidence is perfectly compatible with a date in the third century BCE, although the attribution to the desire of the king to include a Greek text in the Alexandrian Library is generally taken to be imaginative.

[26] Transl. Chan (1963) p. 39.

[27] Jullien (2000) p. 184. My discussion follows Jullien's for the most part.

[28] Graham (1989) p. 3.

–10–
Democracy

If I were to ask a random collection of people in the modern western world what they would designate as the most important political concept left to them by the ancient Greeks, I have no doubt that the majority would answer, "democracy." Not only is the concept important in the modern world, its implementation is asserted around the globe, and by the twenty-first century most nations claim that they are governed as democracies. What government by democracy actually means varies greatly of course, and "democracies" differ greatly in structure and in the extent to which control over the body politic is extended widely, freely, and with the potential of choice. And to some extent, the styles of democracy are affected by the extent to which their adherents have been influenced by European and American democracies and the traditions and ideas about the democracy of ancient Greece.

The assumption stands that democracy is a good thing. "Undemocratic" is a word of political insult. Analysts of our contemporary situation generally treat democracy as an advanced stage of political development, extending even to Eli Sagan's argument that the single greatest threat to the existence of democracy is a mental set he describes as paranoid, with regressions from democracy involving "the reassertion of the fundamental paranoid position."[1] That sort of thinking reveals the strength of the unstated assumption that democracy is "good" and psychologically healthy, and allows for the hypothesis of progress in the linear advance of society from

> the traditional, authoritarian, classically paranoid society wherein sovereignty is exercised either by a monarch (Louis XIV, Frederick the Great) or by an aristocracy of a small group of noble families (the ancient Roman Republic, Venice in modern times). The second stage, democratic society, always arises out of this authoritarian stage, and is made possible only by overcoming the paranoid position sufficiently that the most extreme defenses against paranoia itself are no longer necessary.[2]

I quote at such length to show the strength with which the underlying value is held, in an argument that goes on to assert that "our present liberal, bourgeois, capitalist society" is a second stage democracy, and that one looks to the future for the third stage, in which such paranoid manifestations as racism, imperialism and the like can be overcome.

Remembering that this book you are reading proposes the thesis, among other ideas, that contemporary values are validated for structuring western society because the operational decisions in that society have been and are determined by the acceptance of certain specific values as they emerged over a long history, you may find that designating the opposition to those values as paranoid overstates the case. But Sagan's argumentation, whether I accept its conclusion or not, puts the issue in precisely the arena in which I believe it belongs, an arena in which ideas and their consequences can be judged in terms of their effect on the health of one another. Insofar as a society retreats from the intellectual diet that has provided its growth and health, choosing instead to absorb ideas to which its digestive system is unfamiliar, it may sicken, may even die, and at the very least will suffer a terrible bellyache. The idea of democracy is one of those vital intellectual nourishments that have made my culture what it is, and the endorsement of democracy is a value essential to the existence of the western culture as I know it. However, to judge the validity of conceptions of democracy, I am led to try to understand the nature of the democracy on which I think this society depends, and trace the views and attitudes toward it over the centuries.

An understanding of the nature of Athenian democracy[3] and the attitudes that framed later thought must begin with the fundamental assumptions about the polis shared by almost all Greeks: the polis was an organism, not a social contract, and the organism functioned with a citizen body of which every member was obliged to support the whole, and in which every member was entitled to share the profits of success in some manner acceptable to the group. This might seem a definition of democracy in itself, and democracy of course is a means of determining shares both of obligation and reward, but in fact this description of the polis can fit oligarchies and aristocracies as well. Perhaps the difference is well presented in a single sentence by a comment on the state of Athens in the fifth century: "Democracy had created a sphere of privilege, equality and freedom based solely on membership in the polity, not on personal or social qualities."[4]

Not all the city states of Greece functioned as democracies, and of those that did, little is known specifically about their structure and constitutions. Many nominal democracies were actually operated by a very circumscribed number of active participants. Athens was the broadest–based, and is known best, but for most of the centuries after the close of antiquity, what was known came from indirect sources: references to actions by the populace in historians and other writers, allusions of affairs of the day in drama and comedy, and conclusions that were derived from the words of orators, political pamphleteers and incidental writers. In the centuries of modern times, as political thinkers and writers used Athenian democracy as a touchstone against which they related their own efforts to create democracy in new nations or old, they operated with extraordinarily incomplete and very general knowledge. It is only with the discovery in the late nineteenth century of a papyrus roll containing the text of the Aristotelian *Constitution of Athens* that we have had specific information about the Athenian constitution or its development over the centuries. In the papyrus we have an ancient, if not necessarily completely accurate, account of the phases through which the political structures of the Athenians passed, and can see the formal procedures by which the city was governed in the fourth century BCE, the time when the document was actually composed.

Aristotle[5] describes the specific institutions and political bodies, councils, assemblies, boards and commissions of Athens in the fourth century when the city had reached the fullest scope of the democratic constitution, but after the heyday of Athenian imperial power in the fifth century.[6] He recounts the progress of Athens to democracy as the growth of an organism fulfilling its inherent form, making political development the same kind of progress toward completion of form that he posits for plant and animal life. Although details of the beginning of the history of Athenian political life in the time of Draco are lost with the parts of the papyrus at the beginning of the roll, we can trace most of the changes in a progression towards increased democracy – that is, more and more power over affairs exercised by the demos, or male citizens, until that widening of control reached its greatest extent in the fifth century BCE.

The great impetus toward democracy, as Aristotle reports the history, came from the reforms of Solon, not only the economic reforms affecting land and debt slavery, but the creation of political councils and courts. In particular, the establishment of courts put in the hands of the body of citizens powers of judgment that increasingly tended to reinforce the power of suffrage and decision-making in the assembly. As Aristotle tells the story, after passing through a period of control by the tyrant Peisistratus, the Athenians returned to the course of democracy with the reforms of Cleisthenes at the end of the sixth-century, which has been seen, rightly, I think, as a revolution.[7] Then in the fifth century came institutions like the use of ostracism – the exile for ten years by the "winner" of an "election" by the populace designating a politician who was by the vote ordered to leave the territories of Athens (without loss of citizenship or property) for ten years. Other reforms of the early fifth century, the election of strategoi – generals who exercised important political as well as military leadership, and the selection of archons – magistrates – by lot, have been variously interpreted by modern scholars.[8]

The great power of the demos, or body of male Athenian citizens, came not from their designation as electors of magistrates, although the constitution[9] did accord them this role, but from their ability to control policy in votes in the assembly from day-to-day in what we call direct democracy. Athenian citizens gathered in the assembly to vote not only on specific laws, but on policy: war and peace, expenditure of money, the treatment of defeated enemies, specific strategies in war as the dispatch of expeditions, diplomatic matters like the acceptance of petitions for alliance. Outside the assembly itself, they exercised this form of direct democracy in the court system, where large juries made up of citizens not only decided issues of life and death, as in the case of Socrates at the beginning of the fourth century, but regularly judged the performance of magistrates and decided charges against them when complaints arose, a power that inevitably forced officials to be wary of opposing the will of the majority of citizens. Although there were laws that in theory curtailed the authority of the citizens to do what they pleased, in fact the decision of an assembly was supreme, and the Athenian citizens decided as they chose or even altered their decisions when better arguments came forward.[10] There is a contradiction between the notion of a completely sovereign and supreme citizen Assembly and that of laws that were sovereign, especially since the citizens decided any conflict between the two principles. The Athenians, however, were willing to live with that philosophical problem, just as they were not concerned to resolve the conflict between their much-vaunted freedom of speech and a desire for consensus.[11]

Although the Assembly, or Ecclesia, was not free to discuss any issue that might be proposed to it, but was limited to examining only such matters as had hitherto been considered by the council of 400, later 500, known as the Boulé, dispositions by the Ecclesia were not subject to any restraint, and might reach into any aspect of Athenian life. Furthermore, the Boulé, for all the requirement that it consider matters prior to their introduction to the Ecclesia, was in a sense, the creature of the citizen assembly. Required to summon the assembly at least four times in each tenth part of the year, the Boulé could be ordered by the assembly to consider an issue for the assembly to treat at its next meeting. In debate in the assembly, any citizen could speak, vote by show of hands, and on most matters make decisions by a simple majority. It was the assembly that elected those magistrates who held their offices by election. In debate, the subjects ranged the whole gamut of issues that require a decision in a state.

The extent to which every male citizen had his voice in the governance of Athens is illustrated not only by the role of the Boulé as a servant of the assembly rather than as a parallel chamber or possible constraint, but by the manner in which the members of the Boulé were chosen: all citizens over thirty years of age might serve, but no one more than twice in his lifetime, nor ever two years in a row. These were no "senators" creating a locus of power as in Rome (or the United States), for it was impossible for such a body to carry a long term program or counterbalance the magistrates, even though it met every day that was not a festival. The power of the citizen extended to his role in the court system, and the quality of the law courts as intensifying democracy is apparent in Aristotle's observation tha "the demos being in control of the vote [in juries], it was in control of the polis."[12] Finally, as the fifth century advanced and payment was made to citizens who fulfilled their duties as citizens in attending assemblies or filling magistracies, the democracy widened its base by making it possible for the less prosperous to obtain some income by participation in public activity, a practice expanded in the next century. In its fulfillment of its form, to use Aristotle's mode of thinking, the democracy of Athens and its "exercise of collective power by the Athenian demos prevented elite political domination – and was intended to do so."[13]

All this was seen, even at the apogee of the democracy, as deleterious by most Athenian writers who commented on events, although their views may be somewhat suspect since all those writers were part of the aristocratic class. Thucydides, who described the course of the great war between Athens and Sparta in the last third of the fifth century, went so far as to assert that when Athens was well governed, what was democracy in name was in reality government by the best man, Pericles, and Thucydides' account of the war is rife with implications that bad decisions were repeatedly made by the demos. His portrayal of the decisions involving the dispatch in 415 BCE and later destruction of the great expedition against the city of Syracuse in Sicily draws a picture of the populace as excitable, easy to stampede by rhetoric, greedy, impetuous and without sense of long-range consequences of acts. This was just one instance of the "repeated indictment of the volatile Athenian demos [that] was to play a large role in molding the opinion of later thinkers, and Thucydides is also the first source for the notion that Athens declined steadily after Pericles' death – that her post-Periclean leaders were made of sorry stuff and that the demos itself became progressively coarser and more callous under the strains of war."[14] The comedies of Aristophanes, another aristocrat, cast derision on the "ordinary" citizen, and the political thought of the philosophers Plato and Aristotle tend to be negative in their assessment of democracy as it was practiced in Athens.

Virtually all writers who deal with the Athenian democracy, both primary sources contemporary with the activities of the democracy and those who wrote in the following centuries, produced an account of the democracy heavily influenced by their class bias. The hostility to Athenian democracy first evinced by the Athenian sources continued into Roman times, recurred in fourteenth-century Italy with the interest in creating societies that had the republican quality of ancient societies, and went on into Elizabethan times and persisted through the neoclassicism of eighteenth century Europe. Even in revolutionary America, as Jennifer Roberts points out, attitudes were hostile, as illustrated by Madison's "distinguishing the American republics from the 'turbulent democracies of ancient Greece and modern Italy,'"[15] and it is only with the liberal interpretation of Greek history produced by George Grote in the nineteenth century that the perspective changed. Essentially, up to Grote's time, statesmen and political thinkers alike who looked favorably upon the "liberté" they saw in ancient cities, and tolerated the "fraternité," were horrified by the "égalité," just as most liberal thinkers joined monarchists and aristocrats in condemnation of the French Revolution.

I will deal later with the question of equality. At this juncture it is necessary to recognize that Athenian democracy was not accepted as a paradigm for modern nation states except insofar as it – and they – were constrained by institutions that prevented governance by mob rule. Mob rule is the degeneration of democracy, as the historian-philosopher-statesman Polybius saw it in Roman times, and his proposition fits the Aristotelian notion of a proper *politeia* that had not yet degenerated into Athens' extreme democracy. But that democracy, functioning to provide a role in government for free men, as it did under the benevolent regime of Pericles, more and more became the aim of constitution makers and politicians who modified the institutions of government over the course of eighteenth and nineteenth centuries.

Of course the kind of direct democracy practiced in Athens was inappropriate for the larger nation state of modern times, a view pronounced by Thomas Paine, as we shall shortly see, but this practical circumstance made it possible to create representative institutions that also served to curtail the strength of the voters. The eighteenth century ideal of representative government did not expect the representatives to conform to the will of the great unwashed who put them in office:

> It ought to be the happiness and glory of the Representative, to live in the strictest union, the closest correspondence, and the most unreserved communication with his constituents.... But his unbiased opinion, his mature judgment, his enlightened conscience he ought not to sacrifice to you.... Your Representative owes to you, not his industry only, but his judgment, and he betrays, instead of serving you, if he sacrifices it to your opinion.[16]

It is a modern day version of Solon's "I gave to the populace just so much privilege as was fitting," fashioning out of representative government the kind of democracy Athens had enjoyed before, as these modern political writers might say, the demagogues of the fifth century hurled her over the cliff to the disposition of the fickle and ignorant mob.

Although in the latter part of the twentieth century a large number of commentators on Athenian democracy criticized the Athenians for their failure to extend the privileges enjoyed by the limited suffrage of male citizens, the impact of the Athenian structure for most of modern history was to encourage a cautious, if liberal, effort to establish or increase the liberty of the members of the society. To them, this liberty produced the grand effect presented in the words Thucydides gave Pericles in praise of Athens. The historian not only reveals his view of patriotic rhetoric, he creates a myth of Athenian life before it was perverted by excessive democracy, and establishes a goal of political life that became a fundamental goal of the generations that tried to recreate the wonders of that society. Athenians, according to Pericles-Thucydides, ought to be lovers of their city, dedicated to preserving the glory and power their ancestors had achieved. The speech puts forth ideals that became commonplace in the thought of liberals of the modern world, praising the openness and lively debate of Athenian political life:

> We do not think that discussion is in any way harmful in action, but that damage comes from not considering in advance in words what is needed in action ... each person is concerned for public as well as personal affairs, and even those primarily occupied with business are not uninformed in political matters, and we do not, like others, consider a person who takes no part in politics to be minding his own business, but we consider him useless.

It is a value that permeated political thought and surfaced in political rhetoric like the challenge of John F. Kennedy: "Ask what you can do for your country."

The ideal is one of participation and involvement, and the breadth of the base of action is enhanced by an absence of restrictions based on wealth or social position:

> The name we have given our government is democracy, because it is at the disposition of the many, not the few, and under the law everyone has an equal standing in private disputes. In public, a man gains standing by his ability, not his social position, nor does poverty hold him in obscurity if he has anything to do for the public.

This passage, if not the whole speech, has long been quoted with approval by liberal political thinkers, and it is still a valid ideal for those who think of human worth primarily in political and social terms. One of the fundamental values of Athenian society, and a value arising from the assumed good of membership and participation in benefits, it substitutes public aims and a value system based on public service for personal and private gratification of aristocratic honor and glory or harmonious cooperation.

The benefits brought by an adherence to this ideal also appear in the speech. Athens allowed for a more relaxed attitude toward war, eschewed censorship and repression, promoted culture and a love of beauty, and endorsed philosophy. Athens became, in the minds of idealistic historians and statesmen, the great exemplar of the glory that was Greece, with her drama, philosophy, architecture and sculpture. And all this, as modern writers and speakers often explicitly stated in their pursuit of a replication of the Athenian accomplishment, was taken to show what could be accomplished by free men.

The value established by Athens and similar societies to eighteenth-century thinkers was the value of individual liberty, the catchword held in common by American and French revolutions, and the basis for the upheavals that swept Europe in 1848 and after. That individual men – perhaps I should say white males, to make the emphasis clear – were entitled to liberty was an unquestioned assumption from the eighteenth century on. A theoretician of government like Rousseau formulated his Social Contract starting with the assumption that liberty was the state of nature, and explaining state institutions as the contractual ceding of that liberty to make possible social and political existence. Rousseau's assumptions, like the assumptions of many of his contemporaries and successors, were based on their reading of the experience of the ancient world and particularly Athens. They accepted democracy – a certain kind of democracy – as the necessary feature of government that would provide the liberty and wherewithal to recreate an idealized society two thousand years and more after the earlier effort had gone to smash on the rocks of greed and excess. The catchword was often "republican government," meaning representative government, seen as the assurance of liberty by creating government, in Madison's terms, "sufficiently neutral between different parts of the Society to controul one part from invading the rights of another, and at the same time sufficiently controuled itself, from setting up an interest adverse to the entire Society."[17]

Republican or representative government, however, could be seen as the necessary concomitant of size in the grander eighteenth century nations that far exceeded Athens in size. As Thomas Paine put it:

> Simple democracy was no other than the common hall of the ancients.... As these democracies increased in population, and the territory extended, the simple democratic form became unwieldy and impracticable; and as the system of representation was not known, the consequence was, they either degenerated convulsively into monarchies, or became absorbed into such as then existed. Had the system of representation been then understood, as it now is, there is no reason to believe that those forms of government, now called monarchical or aristocratical, would ever have taken place. It was the want of some method to consolidate the parts of society, after it became too populous, and too extensive for the simple democratic form, and also the lax and solitary condition of shepherds and herdsmen in other parts of the world, that afforded opportunities to those unnatural modes of government to begin.[18]

We may suppress a shudder at the inaccuracies in history that a quick reading of Aristotle on Paine's part might have avoided, to focus on the assumption that the democracy of Greece was a forerunner to the yet unknown republican form of representative government, and that the democracy of antiquity was a more natural form of government. Working from the argument that "Republican government is no other than government established and conducted for the interest of the public, as well individually as collectively," Paine proceeds to assert the "original simple democracy ... the true data from which government on a large scale can begin.... By ingrafting representation upon democracy, we arrive at a system of government capable of embracing and confederating all the various interests and every extent of territory and population."[19]

What Paine and others found in Athenian democracy or other ancient republics was not the democracy we understand as the structuring of society to provide the greatest equality (although, as we shall see below, the Athenians were concerned with equality) but the form of government that provided the greatest and most secure liberty. They had little detailed knowledge of Athens of antiquity and depended for the most part on translations, often poor, and contemporary histories of antiquity, handbooks and encyclopedias.[20] And as Jennifer Roberts has pointed out, Paine's enthusiasm for Athens is the best-known example of a favorable assessment in an environment and at a time when "the Athenian example was one from which the founding fathers wished to dissociate themselves."[21]

Still, with all the provisos and qualifications that one may want to introduce in assessing the impact of Athenian democracy on the constitution makers and political theorists responsible for the creation of the governmental structures of eighteenth- and nineteenth-century western Europe, these writers and thinkers imported with their poorly understood historical precedents the basic assumptions about human beings and government that determined the Athenian structure. This, I think, goes deeper than the complaints and demurrers seen by modern commentators on the subject. It may seem patently obvious when expressed, but it is fundamentally important to stress that eighteenth-century political theorists shared with Athenians the conviction that government and the state existed for the people who lived in it, not the converse, nor to aid in the service of God, nor any other purpose, good or bad. If Pericles urged on the Athenians of his day the doctrine that they should exert themselves on behalf of their polis, and not pass it on to their descendants lesser than they had received it from their fathers, his demand carried weight because of his assertion that their lives would be better when their city prospered. The American version of this is perhaps best expressed in the preamble to the Constitution, asserting that it is "the People of the United States" who establish the constitution, to "form a more perfect Union, establish Justice, insure domestic Tranquillity, provide for the common defence, promote the general Welfare, and secure the blessings of Liberty."

The concept is expressed succinctly by Rousseau, in describing the evidence of good government in meeting the aim of political association: "It is the preservation and prosperity of its members."[22] Rousseau accepted direct democracy in what might be called the Athenian sense in which "no better constitution could be found than the one in which executive and legislative power are combined," although "taking the term in the strict sense, true democracy has never existed."[23] His whole concept of social contract is predicated on the fundamental Greek sense of participation, in that "the social pact establishes such an equality among the citizens that they all commit themselves under the same conditions and should all enjoy the same rights."[24] That the goal of political government should be "the preservation and prosperity" of the citizens may seem obvious to us, children of the eighteenth century as we are, and perhaps excuses me from multiplying examples of its statement by eighteenth-century writers.[25] However, it does not necessarily imply the level of participation of effort and reward demanded by Rousseau and left unchallenged by Greek democratic society.

When I consider the development of democracy, even the limited, representative form of democracy I have been describing, I find I cannot escape the inheritance of millennia; I recall with approval my memory of a comment attributed to Winston Churchill: "Democracy is the worst form of government, apart from all the others." I am prepared to accept the disadvantages of this form of government in order to maintain what I see as its advantages. Still, mindful of what I am attempting to do in this book, I turn to the Chinese experience to give me some perspective on alternate cultural assumptions. There I find among modern Chinese writers examining the question of the emergence of democracy in China a broad consensus, at least among those "overseas Chinese" writing in English. That consensus sees the current mainland Chinese regime as oppressive, its harshness (now softening) illustrated by the 1989 repression and massacre of the students gathered in Tienanmen Square. Perhaps even more important, these writers agree on the desirability of replacing the current regime with a western-style, rights-based democracy, and in many instances, raise the question whether the tradition of Confucianism, firmly implanted in Chinese culture, precludes a shift to the desired western-style democracy, or whether the long Chinese tradition of Confucianism can be used to adapt western-style democracy to make a better amalgam of ideas. The issue is well defined by the words of Lee Teng-hui, president of the Republic of China, Taiwan:

> Confucianism can ... serve to correct the deficiencies of a democratic system. While the advantages of democracy are appparent, like every other system, it is not without flaws. The democratic system guarantees and emphasizes the rights of the individual. But individualism can go to extremes, even degenerating into egotism and hedonism ... Individual perfection develops alongside the enhanced welfare of the group. Confucian doctrine includes a sophisticated set of theories that can balance the excesses of individualism. Confucianists remind us to emphasize neither institutions nor the individual at the expense of the other.[26]

There is here both an acceptance of western democracy as offering benefits, and the desire to maintain traditional qualities of Chinese thought. Among theorists, however, the benefits are often stressed, seeing the modern aspects of the western democratic tradition as essential to good social life, with "the humanistic values of freedom and equality as the basic elements of modern identity."[27] The adoption of what may be called "enlightenment" ideology seems to permeate the demands and the rhetoric of the opponents of the mainland regime, with, for example, repeated demands by the students of 1989 for what we would call personal rights and freedoms, human rights, as: "everyone is born free and equal ... everyone has freedom of speech, writing, publication, and advocacy ... the right to privacy ... freedom of marriage ... the power of government comes from the people."[28] The widely viewed and very popular (mainland!) television series, *River Elegy* (*He Shang*) explicitly looks back at the success of Hellenic civilization as part of its criticism of contemporary China: "Only the civilization of the ancient Greeks developed into an industrial civilization and swept across the entire world."[29]

All that I read suggests to me that the awareness of government in the European tradition is having the effect of raising questions about the value of long-standing Chinese views of society, much as after the establishment of the Chinese Republic at the beginning of the twentieth century there was an attempt to eradicate Confucianism in order to promote western ideas. At the same time, the social difficulties of early twenty-first century mainland China are seen as rooted in moral decline:

> manifested in corruption of Party and government officials, in unrestricted greediness of the professional elites such as actors, artists, writers, teachers, doctors, and in the contagious obsession with moneymaking and philistinism of the public.... Many humanist intellectuals are either unable or unwilling to recognize that it is the erosion of the constitutional fabric and the disintegration of the triad fusion of party-state-people after 1989 that fundamentally underscore the cultural and moral crises that they fear.[30]

I have read many similar comments about the society in which I myself live, and the "moral malaise" is usually seen in the West as a matter of extreme "individualism, but the Chinese author, Ben Xu, sees this in Chinese terms as a matter of people-state relationship – I suggest because he inherits the Confucian attitude without really being aware of it. It may be the same Confucian attitude that lies behind the rallying by Chinese all over the world supporting the governmental "parent" in the conflict over the treatment of Tibet.

At the beginning of this chapter I noted that the word "democracy" is used in contemporary writing as a favorable term. This is certainly true of China, both mainland and Taiwan, and in Taiwan in particular, the democracy envisioned is tied to traditional Confucianism. The Taiwanese government, as it first became established on the island after the Guomindang leaders fled from the mainland in 1949, could resort to the most violent repression of dissidence; it later became open to greater and greater acceptance of the rights-based democracy I and many others in western societies value. Still, throughout the Guomindang period on the mainland and on into its development on Taiwan, Confucian principles were part of political thinking, as one commentator has noted:

> Throughout his political career, Chiang Kai-shek had used Confucian rhetoric and values to appeal to the nation to reform its ways, as in the New Life Movement that he launched in early 1934 but that sputtered out for lack of popular support. In Taiwan his followers, numbering only a few, took seriously his moral message of living virtuous lives by practicing [Confucian virtues like] benevolence, sincerity, tolerance and mutual respect. Taiwan's new moral society should also distribute wealth equally so that it might resemble that ideal Confucian moral order (*datong*) of humaneness, benevolence, and virtue that the sages of the past had envisioned for China.[31]

And after Chiang Kai Shek's's death, when his son initiated great reforms, Confucianism was part of the political thinking, as "Chiang Ching-kuo's Confucian-style democracy on Taiwan meant having his party members practice high moral principles."[32]

I am not concerned here to participate in the speculation about the future of the mainland government, although it is worth noting that most commentators see an expansion of what western observers call democratic rights, arguing that "China is moving at a fair pace along the continuum from an 'authoritarian' to a 'democratic' regime, and its leaders appear determined to make China into a fairer and more just society."[33] Rather, I find that even in a society with such deep-rooted and long established political and social traditions as the Chinese, rhetoric, if not practice itself, seems bent on incorporating aspects of democratic government that I associate with the Hellenic tradition. These are the very aspects of social organization suspected by many Chinese leaders and intellectuals, and they may be, as some have asserted in the West, intricately involved with the individualism some claim as excessive in contemporary life.

---

[1] Sagan (1991) p. 22.

[2] Sagan (1991) p. 21.

[3] See Stockton (1990) for a summary of the actual workings of the democracy, with a survey of its development from Solon to the reforms of Ephialtes, and a discussion of political activity and the political actors, with a survey of democracy's opposition as well as those who criticized or supported it. For discussion of the workings of the system, see Sinclair (1988); Ober (1989); and Stockton (1990); for the assembly itself, Starr (1990); Hansen of Athenian democracy down to Aristotle, including some social considerations.

[175] Ober (1989) pp. 295-304.

[4] Farrar (1988) p. 122

[5] There remains doubt whether Aristotle himself was the author of the treatise, but that issue is not relevant to our discussion; the writer was certainly a member of the Aristotelian school, and the text deals with fourth-century Athens.

[6] Ober (1996) p. 29-31, arguing the vitality of fourth-century democracy and citing Aristotle's view of "fourth-century Athens as an example of the most extreme form of democracy" (p. 29).

[7] Ober (1996) p. 43: "The Athenian siege of the Acropolis in 508/7 is best seen as riot – a violent and more or less spontaneous uprising by a large number of Athenian citizens." The reforms of Cleisthenes were made by "a highly skilled interpreter of statements made in a revolutionary context and of revolutionary

action itself" (p. 52). The four family or tribal groups of all Athenians were now divided into ten; the council, or boulé was reconstituted to 500 members, 50 from each of the new tribes; individual citizens were identified by geographic districts rather than fathers' names; and ostracism (perhaps then) was introduced. There has been a great deal of writing on this reform, many of the conclusions speculative, such as my own, that this aspect of reform was aimed at solidifying the status of Athenians who had only recently been made citizens during the reign of Peisistratus and his sons: Samuel (1992) pp. 24-27.

[8] For some bibliography and scholarship, with my argument on the issues, see Samuel (1984) pp. 287-309, esp. pp. 296-7.

[9] The functioning of the Athenian Constitution is presented in detail in Aristotle, *Constitution of Athens*, chapters 42 ff.

[10] As, for the first instance, when they voted to judge (and condemn) en masse the generals who had failed to pick up the dead after the victorious battle of Arginusae, or in the second instance, the decree and then rapid reversal of the decision to destroy the populace of the defeated Mytilene.

[11] Ober (1989) pp. 295-304

[12] Aristotle, *Constitution of Athens*.

[13] This is J. Ober's phrase, with which I agree, in Ober (1996) p. 19, and arguing for the conclusion "that the ordinary citizens really did rule in Athens," p. 21. See the main argument, Ober (1989).

[14] Roberts (1994) p. 57.

[15] Roberts (1994) p. 181.

[16] Burke (1774).

[17] Madison J. "To Thomas Jefferson, October 24, 1787," in Madison (1999) p. 152, also arguing, pp. 164-7, that representative government is a means of avoiding the disadvantages of pure, or direct democracies, which "have ever been spectacles of turbulence and contention; have ever been found incompatible with personal security, or the rights of property; and in general have been as short in their lives, as they have been violent in their deaths.

[18] Paine, T. (1792) *Rights of Man*, Part II, in Paine (1942) p. 168.

[19] Paine (1942) pp. 169, 171. The concept is by no means Paine's alone. Madison expressed it concisely, Madison (1999) p. 168: "...in a democracy, the people meet and exercise the government in person; in a republic they assemble and administer it by their representatives and agents. A democracy consequently must be confined to a small spot. A republic may be extended over a large region."

[20] Reinhold (1984) p. 96. Reinhold points out (p. 102) the assumption of unsuitability of direct democracy by the American Founding Fathers because of the perceived "instability and capriciousness of decisions in ancient republics," the difficulty of such direct democracy governing so large a territory, so that they had resort to representative government, which they took to be a major advance over the ancient republics. It is important to note with

Reinhold (p. 100) that the ancient republics provided the best precedents for republican government.

[21] Roberts (1994) p. 181.
[22] Rousseau, J-J. (1762) *On Social Contract*, in (1988) p. 137.
[23] Rousseau (1988) p. 125,
[24] Rousseau (1988) p. 103; all of Chapter 4 of Book II of *On Social Contract* deals with this issue.
[25] Or even Rousseau's predecessors, as Hobbes (1651), whose argument for the institution of government to secure for people the ability to feed themselves and live in contentment is made in Chapter XVII of *Leviathan*.
[26] Quoted from "Confucian Democracy: Modernization, Culture, and the State in East Asia," *Harvard International Review* 1999, p. 18, in Ogden (2002) p. 58.
[27] Xu (1999 p. 33.
[28] Ogden et. al. (1992) p. 280.
[29] Translated in Wakeman (1989) reprinted in Ogden et. al. (1992) p. 37.
[30] Xu (1999) p. 36.
[31] Chau and Nyers (1998) p. 37.
[32] Chau and Nyers (1998) p. 114.
[33] Ogden et. al. (1992), p. 379

STATE AND SOCIETY

–11–
Equality

Among the characteristics of Athenian democracy deplored by ancient writers and modern alike – qualities like excitability, gullibility, ignorance, instability of policy and the like – one tendency comes in for a great deal of condemnation. The Athenians were seen to be carried to error and ruin by far too much endorsement of equality. Assertions and condemnations of "mobocracy" abound, and many writers would have their readers believe that Athens moved from the legitimate principles of equal treatment under the law and equal rights of participation in the political process to a pursuit of raw equality with a pandering to the masses that produced bad policy and eventually the destruction of Athenian power. Most of the "bad policy" so envisaged from Thucydides' text is accepted as such with little critical assessment,[1] so that the degeneration of rule after Pericles, Thucydides' "best man," is portrayed as a flaw in the Athenian system that gained the upper hand in the operation of the democracy.

It is quite true that in the last quarter of the fifth century Athens had been moving toward an equality wider than legal and political. After Pericles' death, the dominance of aristocrats over the political process waned, and it was less essential for a politician to have credentials of family and clan to gain office or become prominent in political leadership.[2] Pericles' claim in the Funeral Oration of insouciance for good family or wealth when a man could serve the state was emerging as a real characteristic of political life. The career of Cleon, the son of a tanner, illustrates the point. Admittedly, he had wealth, but no distinction of family to boast of, and his ability to sway the Assembly in a new, cruder style allowed him to take the most prominent position of leadership after Pericles died. And he could win battles.[3] While there were still many instances of political leaders after Cleon's pre-eminence who came from families of wealth and reputation, there were others who did not. There was Hyperbolus, of alleged low origin, who maintained Cleon's policy of continuing the war with Sparta, and who would undoubtedly have continued to play a prominent part in politics had he not been ostracized in 417 BCE as part of a secret deal between the rivals Alcibiades and Nicias. Leadership could even be accorded a man admittedly poor, who had a reputation for honesty and who was reported to have died in poverty. Even for the sober and conservative Nicias we cannot trace ancestry back beyond his father. His family may well have been a newcomer on the scene, as was that of Theramenes, who was active during the last ten years of the war, and whose family first appears in politics with the activity of his father Hagnon, and disappears from our view with Theramenes himself. The diminution in the importance of class is well attested by the ability of such men to rise to major office, let alone prominence in public activity, and there were now fewer bars to restrain those who would not have been accepted in a leadership role a generation or two earlier.

This was the political and social environment in which the traveling philosophers and teachers known as Sophists found themselves when they came to Athens to practice their profession. Requiring a clientele of some wealth, and at the same time coming themselves from families who shared the traditions of aristocrats, the Sophists' reputations and livelihood depended on the support of the noble and wealthy Athenians who were their hosts, patrons and paymasters. There was every reason for the Sophists to try to fill the needs of these Athenians, to teach their aspiring young the skills they would need to climb the political ladder to achieve the glory and prominence they sought, in an environment in which the mere membership in an old and great family was no longer enough to assure success in public life. Thus rhetoric was taught to develop the forensic skills needed in the Assembly, and the verbal, grammatical and dialectical techniques of some of the Sophists were valuable in the disputation that was so much part of political life. Even the *physis-nomos* controversy positing the ethical dilemma of following nature or law, that we associate with the Sophistic movement, came naturally to thinkers involved with the problems of the upper class. Those aristocrats, with their freedom to act and impose their wills, had come under increasing restraint as the century progressed.

As the desires and successes of the poorer classes steadily chopped away the prerogatives of aristocrats and even cut into their resources, members of the upper class could fully sympathize with the relativism aroused by the controversy and with the designation as artificial the social restraints imposed by *nomos*, or law and custom. In the financial structure that supported the democracy of Athens, a great deal of expenditure for public purposes came not from a public treasury but the willing contribution of citizens to defray expenses of public activities like religious festivals, the training of choruses for dramatic performances, the construction of military equipment such as warships, Any allocation of public funds to the broader citizenry inevitably laid more of the burden of expense on the richer citizens. For example, when, after 410 BCE, the city determined on the *diobelia*, an allotment of two obols a day to needy citizens as a guaranteed living income, the moneyed class would see that as a further progression in directing public funds to the consumption of the masses and thus maintain or increase the liability of the rich for public expenditure. Although some Sophistic theorization might promote ideas of political equality like those attributed to Pericles in the Funeral Oration, it did not extend to what we might call "radical share the wealth" concepts.

Democracy as a political system does not necessarily include a requirement of social or economic egalitarianism, nor for that matter, does equality denote democracy. Spartan institutions maintained an economic and social equality among the small number of Spartan citizens, the "equals," and no one would have dreamed of calling Sparta a democracy, not least because of the limits placed on debate and policy control by the assembly. The Athenians certainly did not call for anything like the economic equality the Spartans imposed on themselves, although in the progression toward the complete democracy Aristotle described in the *Constitution of Athens*, the advance of democracy was measured by an increase in equality among the citizens in the prosecution of their public life. There was, in the fifth century, some measure of economic implication in the operation of the democracy, as by the middle of the century, jurors were paid for their service on the courts. An idea first suggested by Aristides early in the century, the proposal was carried in mid century by Pericles in a measure that is seen generally as providing the possibility to poorer citizens to serve on juries. It doubtless had that effect, but it should be noted that the large number of citizens who sat on courts meant not only a considerable expenditure, but also a considerable distribution of funds among the citizenry at large. This form of distribution increased after the fifth century, when participation in the Assembly earned pay, initially one obol but increasing to six or even nine for a limited number of specific meetings.

This is little enough economic equality, and even with the institution of the *diobelia* payment to needy citizens in 410 it seems hardly to justify the intensity with which the Athenian democracy is attacked for excessive equality. There were, however, other aspects of fifth century Athens besides institutional and constitutional that promoted a broader distribution of wealth. Ancient and modern writers point to the growth of the navy of imperial Athens as a cornerstone of support for democracy among the citizens. With large numbers of citizens serving in the fleet, the poorer citizens, paid as they were for a service that might stretch over considerable periods of time, had a real stake in the continuance of the policies of expansion. Even more, with Athens' power now dependent on a large and effective fleet, the poorer sailor-citizen saw himself as forming with his fellows on the ships the mainstay of the city's power, much more, at least, than the more prosperous heavy armed infantry hoplite with enough resources to outfit himself in expensive equipment. Then too, there was some financial support for those who served on land. The converse of this, of course, is that the maintenance of the navy was not only a large public expense, it was also financial support to those in the fleet and represented a public defrayment of living costs to many who might otherwise have no income at all. The effect might well not have been intended, but it nevertheless added to the impression of democracy promoting equality, at least at the lowest levels of society. And the Athenians were aware that, as Mark Munn points out, "The empowerment of the less affluent majority of citizens was the most remarkable achievement of fifth–century Athens."[4]

With all we can invoke to show the democracy and the empire providing income to Athenian citizens in the fifth century, we come far short of anything that might be deemed "communistic" society in which practice or theory called for a redistribution of wealth in any way at all. However much the wealthy citizens of ancient Athens (or of any other place or time) might have feared the loss of their riches as a result of democratic politics, nothing in the actions of the Athenian *demos* justified such nervousness. This goes a long way to explaining the stability of the democracy through most of the fourth century after the debilitating defeat of the Peloponnesian War, as well as the willingness of the wealthy elite to shoulder the limited cost of liturgies and struggle for preeminence in a society they could not necessarily control.

The acceptance by the democracy of many of the perquisites of wealth and class also solidified a willingness to endorse the aspects of equality that made up democracy and were, in later times, accepted as the concomitants of liberty in a republican state: equality of citizens under the law, and equality of citizens in the weight given each in the making of public decisions.[5] While it is clear that public discussion was usually carried on by those experienced and well enough educated to prevail in debate, decisions were made by the mass of those present in the Assembly on a given day, and the thousands of citizens who might be present carried motions by a majority, with one man, one vote. Even that made modern observers of the scene nervous when planning the constitutions of new republics, for they assumed that such broad authority of the mass produced bad policy. To the American founding fathers, the ideals of liberty they found in the Athenian experience were those they hoped the new republic would achieve, best done by avoiding the pernicious practices which the Athenians favored, so that "they had to reject the ancient democracy not in the name of an opposing political ideal, not in the name of oligarchy, but in the name of democracy itself."[6]

Across the Atlantic, a very different political scene made for a very different attitude toward the Athenian commitment to a broad political equality and participation. The attitude could almost be summed up in the career of George Grote, whose liberal version of Greek and Athenian history began to appear with the first volume of his *History of Greece* in 1846, after the passage of the First Reform Bill and Grote's own election to Parliament in 1832. The British liberals, much more than the American revolutionaries, could see parallels between British expansionism and the growth of Athenian power, and could use the universal franchise of Athens as an ideal that brought continued accessions to the voting rolls as the Reform Bill of 1867 added nearly a million in a franchise, almost doubling it in size and including many of the urban workers. The existence of the universal equal voting rights among Athenian male citizens and the advance in democracy was prosecuted in support of the extension of the franchise in Britain by politicians and theorists, as for, example, Grote "portrayed the reforms of Cleisthenes as having in effect vindicated the wisdom of the kind of radical reform program that he had proposed in 1831.[7] The focus on reform in England, concentrating as it did on the issues like the franchise and the ballot, allowed the British liberals to remain content with the lack of voting rights by women, and bypassed the discrepancy between the existence of slavery in Athens on the one hand and on the other its illegality in England and its banning in 1833 from any of the British colonies.

Evidence for the value of equality in political life came from the brilliance of Athenian culture in the fifth century, a syllogism easily defended in a culture steeped in Benthamite utilitarianism. Macaulay prefaced his notable description of life in "that glorious city" of Athens with an alignment of the high level of intelligence to the competence of the citizen: "There seems to be ... every reason to believe that, in general intelligence, the Athenian population far surpassed the lower orders of any community that has ever existed. It must be considered, that to be a citizen was to be a legislator – a soldier – a judge – one upon whose voice might depend the fate of the wealthiest tributary state, of the most eminent public man."[8]

The situation on the continent was quite different. The slogan of the revolution was "liberté, égalité, fraternité," but the issues of equality as against liberty were mediated through non-Athenian writers. In France, those who were to become revolutionaries studied Latin writers almost exclusively, and "in their maturity, and as a group, they cited, apart from Plutarch, who lived when Greece belonged to Rome, only the classics of Rome, not of Greece."[9] Although Plutarch's picture of Greece and antiquity in general was idealized because of Plutarch's deliberate plan to present heroes for emulation, the French also had Rousseau to mediate their interpretation of Athens' democracy and equality, and it was not a friendly mediation. "Athens was not really a democracy," the *philosophe* wrote,[10] "but a very tyrannical aristocracy, governed by learned men and orators."[11]

In *Social Contract*, the revolutionaries pondering the future could read Rousseau's assertion that "true democracy never existed," that it presupposes "a very small state where the people can easily assemble and where each citizen can easily know all the others," and confront his conclusion ruling out the possibility of achieving such a state: "If there were a people of gods, it would govern itself democratically. So perfect a government is not suited to men." [12] In Germany, where revolution was avoided until the middle of the nineteenth century, Athens was a cultural, literary and artistic icon, not a society providing example and ideas with which to struggle in the formulation of a new society. Burckhardt, who probably more than any other writer is responsible for understanding the individuality of the Greeks in creating the polis, saw Pericles' praise for Athens in the Funeral Oration as "based on equality, by which privilege in the state depended entirely on merit," and Burckhardt, himself conservative in outlook, in assessing Pericles' words found it "hard to resist this optimism." [13] Although Burckhardt's efforts were bent to characterize Greece, not to reform his own time, his assessment of the Athenian devotion to equality is nevertheless apparent in his conclusion to the chapter on the fifth century, asserting his own judgment of what he calls "some of the bitter complaints heard from various writers. They are based on facts."

Modern observers of the scene have often been careful to resist a facile assumption that similarities between ancient texts and more recent ideas have a causal relationship. Mogens Hanson suggests that similar ideals emerge from "a somewhat similar development" and asserts his view that "the Athenian example was of little or no importance for those who in the nineteenth century developed the liberal view of democratic freedom, and there is no evidence of any *direct* tradition transmitted from Athens to Western Europe and America in the eighteenth century."[14] Frank Turner saw the "rediscovery of the

Greek heritage" by British intellectuals leading to "the projection of their own concerns and problems onto the Greek experience,"[15] rather than finding in the examination of antiquity a determinant of their ideas. However, without resorting to the simplistic *post quam ergo propter quam*, there exists enough of a direct line of basic assumptions about humanity from Hellenism to the Roman period and on through medieval Christianity to the renaissance and the enlightenment to suggest that ancient assumptions were in fact carried into the modern period.

The eighteenth-century version of equality was just one part of that period's reversion to what it saw as its historical roots, and could not have been maintained as successfully as it was without its juncture to other assumptions carried over from antiquity – the value of human reason, of learning, and the possibility of knowing the will and purposes of the divine. The presumption of the validity of human reason maintained by Sophists or their opponent Plato, or by Aristotle and his successors, continued through the church fathers and appeared in full strength in the work of the scholasticists, showing that "the mediaevalists had believed God's attributes to be discoverable by reason."[16] With faith in human reason as an unquestioned basis of thought, the liberal enlightenment and nineteenth-century readers or their opponents could not have understood their texts very differently from the way they did. The liberals sat with Protagoras every day, and accepted without question the Hellenic assumption that the social structure existed for the human being, and that there was a truth to be reached and that human reason was of value in achieving it. The nineteenth-century thinkers in particular were confident of human capability of learning, not only old truths but new, and the advances of science and technology in their recent past assured them of the potential of experience in gaining knowledge.

A second characteristic of Greek thought that continued into the middle ages was the attempt to understand the divine, a divinity that was ultimately rational, even if the divine purpose and actions remained unclear to ordinary humans. The position is not very different from that we have seen in the examination of some of Sophocles' plays. The important aspect of this approach to understanding, or attempting, in Milton's words, to "justify the ways of God to men," is the assumption that it is even possible, that human beings exist on a continuum with the divine that allows the human mentality to assert rationality for the ways of God, and to remain "uncertain," rather than fundamentally ignorant of the divine order. It is a rejection of that part of the Hebrew tradition expressed in the Book of Job, where Job's response to God's challenge of human knowledge is "I have been holding forth on matters I cannot understand, on marvels beyond me and my knowledge."[17] Yet even in the early seventeenth century, before the shift to observation and experimentation, researchers like Galileo insisted on the human capacity for knowledge, the reasoning power having a capability that experiment lacks: "we will work more with reasoning than example, for what we seek is the cause of phenomena which experimentation does not provide."[18] The pursuit of causes ran in direct line back to antiquity, and was allowed as legitimate by Newton even though he could neither find a cause or frame a hypothesis for the cause of gravity,[19] although he asserted that the system was established by God in such a way that it would survive and operate under the laws of gravity.[20]

The rationalist liberals of the eighteenth and nineteenth centuries regarded the achievements of Galileo and Newton as a demonstration of the potential of the freedom to be allowed the human mind in inquiry, just as the repression of Galileo was an example of tyrannical oppression. They were moving, they thought, into a golden age that might be analogous to the golden age of Athens they regarded so highly, and accordingly, they accepted, in particular from Athens, ancient characteristics of thought and social structure. The fundamental characteristics of Greek thought – the primacy of human beings and the potential of human reason, they probably never even considered, since these same assumptions were their basis of thought. The notion of equality, however, and particularly equality under the law and equality of participating in governing society, was sufficiently different from the history of the immediate past to be recognized as a principle that might be arguable, and it was accepted as a basis for society in the future not least because it seemed to have served so well as a basis for Athenian society in the past. And, because human reason could find truth, and the will of the divine could be known, it was a truth that could be held "self-evident that all men are created equal, and are endowed by their creator with certain inalienable rights."

So far I have been discussing equality primarily in terms that fit modern debates about equality – equality before the law, equality of political participation and economic equality. These issues could be, and sometimes were, debated by Greek political and philosophical writers, and they remained part of the vocabulary of political discussion from the eighteenth century on. These concepts of equality ignore, however, another possible notion of equality that emerged, however briefly, in Hellenism, one that was largely eliminated from any discussions of equality in later times. When Socrates proposed that the proper objective of human beings was to make the soul as good as it could be, he offered an ideal of human life that allowed to anyone, slave or free person, rich or poor, aristocrat or not, a position of equal moral potential. The Socratic ideal not only evaded the controversy over the relative values of *physis*, nature, over *nomos*, custom, it also consigned to unimportance the normal values of the aristocratic society of his own time. Although Plato recognized, I believe, the implications of the Socratic ideal, his understanding of the nature of Athenian society impelled him to posit a higher order of existence in which such ideals could be implemented, and removed the Socratic ideal from the realm of everyday life. However, I think that afterwards, the aristocratic ideals inculcated in the minds of educated men – men – steeped in texts like the *Iliad* and the works of the Greek tragedians, prevailed. Moral authority and political authority came, in future centuries and millennia, not from successful improvement of the soul, but rather the continuance of the ideals of the *aristoi* – the "best men," and the nature of equality would be debated in terms of politics, economics and law.

Alternatives exist, at least in philosophical discussion. It is striking to see that the Socratic approach can be a basis for a different tradition. Confucian thought emphasizes the desirability of full development of individual moral nature, and for all the authoritarianism inherent in the reality of Chinese history and thought, the authoritarianism is justified by a concept of the human not unlike that of Socrates. As Michael Nylan argues,

> Citations from the *Rites* canons, taken out of context, are often used to prove the inegalitarian nature of early Chinese society, especially in the spheres of gender and politics.... It is equally possible, however, to employ the three texts to prove quite the opposite, that they promote a kind of egalitarianism in several senses; they assume that everyone can be perfected; they stipulate that a code of manners, aristocratic in origin, be learned by and applied to all humans; they advocate the assignment of social rank according to virtue and merit, defining both in terms of

relative merit, defining both in terms of relative contribution to the larger society; and they aim to school each person, through theory and praxis, in the very skills that facilitate effective interaction.[21]

I am not proposing that the Confucian concept of the equality available through moral perfection in any way denied the strictures imposed on Chinese society by the firm acceptance of authority and hierarchy, or alleviated the oppression often experienced by the Chinese. Rather, I suggest, the Confucian texts focus on a goal for humans rather like that of Aristotle's good, happiness, asserting that "as humans are equal in having the capacity to be moral and as morality alone makes for true and lasting human happiness, humans have an equal potential for happiness, notwithstanding patent inequalities in intelligence, talent, wealth, social station, beauty, strength, and health."[22] The effect of this underlying concept of human life and happiness makes for a society in which people in quite varying ranks acquiesce in accepting the guidance or rule of their superiors, and for the most part deny the validity of the kind of self-assertion I will sketch later in my account of Achilles and the traditions established by the Homeric epics:

> Echoes of this inform the classrooms of East Asia, which tend to emphasize achievements won through diligent cooperation while downplaying the special circumstances – inequality of money or brains – that divide one classmate from another. Self-esteem in those classrooms derives from doing one's best consistently; it in no way depends on being protected from an awareness of one's failures. Failure, repeated failure, is in fact presented as a necessary and accepted part of the process of striving for excellence.[23]

In short, the kinds of inequality attacked in fifth century BCE Athens are given short shrift in Chinese tradition, and the issues at the forefront of contemporary political thought are secondary. In its best manifestation, this attitude will make for harmony, and the fulfilment of its precepts will make for government in which the ruler serves the populace and the hierarchical authority is balanced by a reciprocity in which the ruler truly attends to the welfare of the ruled. It allows for revolution only when morality is not observed, with oppression in which the superiors do not return the submission of the inferiors with a concern for them.

This peaceable acquiescence and stable reciprocity is not, I suggest, characteristic of attitudes inherited from the Greeks. Rather, Hellenic goals lead to a belief in equality as self-assertion, that each person is as good as the next, and that equality in itself is a valid goal for society. This fits into a pattern in which authority itself is questioned, creating attitudes that lead to change and what is approvingly called growth. A modern Chinese writer familiar with both government and Confucianism seizes on this difference in attitudes to comment on what he sees as an explanation for a deficiency in science and industry in modern China: "the great scholars down through the ages have emphasized only the completion of the nature of man, while neglecting the completion of the nature of things."[24] It is, as I will argue in subsequent pages, the self-assertion focusing on the completion of things that is characteristic of attitudes inherited from the Greeks, and this self-assertion is part of the different sense of equality that marks a great deal of Hellenic and modern political organization, and moves the goals of that organization in a direction radically different from the goals of harmony and equality in the potential of moral self-development.

[1] Take, for example, the disaster of the Sicilian expedition, which itself is seen by modern writers as wrongly launched to become a major cause of Athens' ultimate defeat. The expedition might well have succeeded – arguably, should have, and is not condemned in concept by Thucydides, who writes that it "was not so much a mistake in judgment," (II. 65. 11); Kallet (2001) p. 144, "Thus Athenians made decisions that caused enormous damage that Thucydides at least implies were mistakes that should and could have been avoided with proper judgment, knowledge, and guidance."

[2] Connor (1971) p. 155: "Our evidence points to the conclusion that many of the politicians of the last three decades of the century were *agoraioi* or *nouveaux riches*, and that they met in many quarters that prejudice so frequently accorded the newly prosperous; Cleon, Cleophon, Hyperbolus and their like were surely not the old arisocracy of Athens."

[3] For all Thucydides' negative portrayal of Cleon's boast that he would defeat the Spartans on Pylos and his alleged embarrassed reluctance to lead when the Assembly voted him the command, he did the job!

[4] Munn (2000) p. 46.

[5] For discussion of ancient and modern connections of democracy and equality, see the discussions by Hanson, Roberts, Wood in Ober and Hedrick, eds. (1996).

[6] Wood (1996) "Demos vs. 'We the People,'" in Ober and Hedrick, eds. (1996) p. 132.

[7] Turner (1981) p. 220. The difficulty of reaching an understanding of Cleisthenes' intentions is stressed by Osborne (1996) p. 299-304, in discussing the "revolution" of the period.

[8] Macaulay (1860) p. 146; the idealization of the glorious city, pp. 147-8.

[9] Parker (1937) p. 17

[10] Rousseau (1755) p. 63.

[11] The denigration of learning is consistent with the *Discourse on the Sciences and Arts*, asserting that "the vices which accompany the fine arts entered Athens together with them," in Rousseau (1964) p. 43.

[12] Rousseau (1762) *On Social Contract*, in (1988), pp. 125-6.

[13] Burckhardt (1998) pp. 224 and 225.

[14] Hansen (1996) "Liberty: Athenian vs. Modern Views," in Ober and Hedrick, eds. (1996) pp. 99-100.

[15] Turner (1981), pp. 450-1.

[16] Martin (1962) p. 41. Martin also concedes the notion of Whitehead's referred to by Martin, that scientific theory was "an unconscious derivative from mediaeval theology," expresses the same kind of inheritance of ideas I am arguing here.

[17] The translation is that of *The Jerusalem Bible*.

[18] Quoted by Del Veccio in his introduction to Newton, (1962) pp. 5-6.

[19] Newton, (1962) p. 446: "But hitherto I have not been able to discover the cause of these properties of gravity from phaenomena, and I frame no hypothesis; for whatever is not deduced from the phaenomena is to be called an hypothesis, and hypotheses, whether metaphysical or physical, whether of occult qualities or mechanical, have no place in experimental philosophy."
[20] Newton (1962) p. 444.
[21] Nylan (2001) p. 188.
[22] Nylan (2001) p. 352.
[23] Nylan (2001) p. 353.
[24] Chen (1986) p. 446.

–Part Four–
"You Are Not Alone"

–12–
The Human Condition and Cosmic Justice

I remember arguing politics with my father in the nineteen- fifties. Somehow, I had a Republican for a father, and I was continually challenged in my support of the "liberal" Adlai Stevenson. Liberals, my father told me, are so aware of different sides of a question that their ability to act is paralyzed. My father, although not a religious man, had a great confidence in the ability of people to know the nature of things – particularly, the nature of the moral universe, the distinctions between right and wrong. It is the confidence I later saw in the *Oresteia*, a confidence in the human ability to know what the gods decree, and a confidence in human statements about the divine. I, on the other hand, seem to have spent my life in a morass of relativism and doubt, and as I write this, I think of the power exerted by the assurance of knowledge of the cosmic order.

My contrary position seems to have been attractive to many in the same period that Aeschylus was writing, to the

Sophists, for example, who dealt with some of these concerns: whether the gods were just, whether the gods concerned themselves at all with humanity, and whether human justice is an earthly version of the divine. Many have seen traces of the teachings of the Sophists in Aeschylus' last plays, and there certainly is evidence of their phraseology in *Prometheus Bound*, where Prometheus not only speaks of the education he has brought to people, but even terms himself as a *sophistes*.[1] But the Sophists, like most Athenian or Greek thinkers, dealt with the inexplicable misfortunes which seem to come upon people who are apparently just, in terms of error, misperception or irrelevance, rather than in the terms of the contemporary Persian dualism.[2] Instead of explaining misfortune in the face of virtuous action by the existence of an independent force in the cosmos that sought and generated evil, Athenian thinkers tended to attribute human experience of evil either to a misunderstanding of the divine order or, in the worst circumstances, to the irrelevance of humanity to the workings of the universe. This is true even of Protagoras, who might well have known the Persian approach to ethics and the alternation between good and evil in human experience. Rather than dualism, Protagoras pursued the definition of virtue and its perception in human activity which, from Aeschylus' time on, dominated ethical speculation, at least in Athens. Protagoras could deal with the issues within the parameters of thought established by his famous statement, "Of all things, a man is the measure; of things that are, how they are; of things that are not, how they are not."[3] In this, at least as Plato presents him, Protagoras is arguing that an individual's perception of phenomena is accurate for that individual, so that, to whom a wind appears cool, it is cool, and for whom it seems warm, it is warm.

The relativism of this position extended to morality, but with important modifications. First, as Plato shows in the *Theatetus*, the Sophists' own doctrine and activity force one to admit that there can be some people who are wiser than others in judging the benefits of different courses of action. Second (if Plato's *Protagoras* is a genuine reflection of the original's thought), not all humans are equal in their ability to make moral judgments correctly. This ability is created and refined by teaching – and this teaching, as it is differentially absorbed, itself is better done by some. Thus behavior is unequal, and the observed disparity between good parents and bad offspring, *inter alia*, can be explained.

These Protagorean doctrines were recorded by Plato fifty years after their enunciation, and they attempt to deal with the problem of human knowledge: essentially, whichever of Aeschylus' two formulations of cosmic justice is correct – either divinity is hostile to humanity or offers true understanding of the moral order – a person can only work within the framework of the "Oresteian" conclusion that human knowledge is the means of understanding the divine order. Human beings can only understand the universe in human terms, and such divine justice as exists can only be understood in a human context. This sentiment, explicit in some of the tragic plays of the later fifth century and implicit in others, is inherent also in the *nomos-physis* controversy, which the Sophists of the fifth century put forward to dispute the antithesis of social norms versus the pursuit of "natural" inclinations. An individual chooses the *nomoi* – rules, customs, laws, norms – set up by society, or instead pursues personal self-interest and advantage. There is no question of a divine law, understood partially, fully or not at all, to direct human conduct. "Man is the measure of all things," because "man" is the measurer of all things.

Protagorean relativism was one response by the Sophists to the dilemma posed by unexpected outcomes of virtue or vice in the face of the assumption that the divine order was knowable. For the most part, however, the fundamental attitude of the trilogy of Aeschylus remained the most influential interpretation of humanity's moral position in the universe. There was a divine order, and it was knowable, and human beings could order their lives in accordance with it. This knowledge was not conveyed directly and completely by the gods, as, for example, the Golden Rule is given by God in Leviticus or by Jesus in the Gospels. It can be worked out by reason, somewhat in the manner of a Kantian categorical imperative, and it is doubtless the complexity of understanding the moral order with mere human intelligence that has allowed for the development of the vast philosophical literature dealing with ethics, justice and morality. We inherit questions from the Greeks, as well as any answers we think we have achieved.

The relationship between divine and human justice impels the action of many Athenian plays of the fifth century, such as the tragedies of Sophocles and Euripides, playwrights of the generation after Aeschylus. Again, the issues raised and the manner in which they are treated become touchstones in western thought. The gods may be challenged, as in Euripides' play *Heracles*, where Amphitryon says of Zeus (l. 347) "If you are a god you are ignorant,[4] or in your nature you are not just," and elsewhere in the play (ll. 655 ff.) the chorus challenges: "If the gods had understanding or wisdom as men do, they would give people a second life as a distinction between good and evil, but there is no clear landmark for the worthy or the wicked."[5] It is not very far from this to the assertion in Euripides' *Orestes*, first by Electra, (ll. 162-3) and then by her brother Orestes (l. 285) that a god is directly responsible for an evil human action. In that play the divine is exonerated only by what may be the most extraordinary epiphany in Euripidean dramaturgy, as Apollo puts an end to the on-stage chaos of murder and destruction by appointing a future for each participant in which each will fulfill the standard mythic role, imposing a solution that makes no sense at all.[6] In these texts, injustice comes from the gods, who are either themselves evil or disregarding or ignorant of justice; humans, who are perfectly capable of seeing and understanding the good, are impelled to evil action by gods in a universe in which human moral judgment is correct but human will is not supreme.

There were those Athenians who would not accept this, just as there are moralists in the modern world who insist on a metaphysical endorsement of standards of conduct, and we find expressions of the view that the gods are good and enforce justice, a position often taken up to defend an action or opinion. Sophocles, in his *Antigone*, often offers an invocation of divine law in defense of Antigone, such as her own assertion of divine prescription to justify her burial of her brother Polyneices (ll. 450 ff.), and there are many instances of a suppliant calling on the gods in aid of his or her just cause. It is a common characteristic of religiosity to assume divine endorsement of human actions, but it may be fair to say that the prevalence of this attitude in western history owes much to the Greek presumption of knowing the right, assuming human ethics to be in accord with divine law, and the expectation of seeing the divine endorsement. It recurs in western thought so influentially that Max Weber can see in the Calvinist mentality the creation of capitalism as a demonstration of human virtue and coincidence with God's law.[7]

Any investigation of the question of good and evil faces far more complexity than either of the simple answers, that evil exists because the gods are evil or stupid or that the gods are good and make things come out all right. There is, for example, the notion that the citation "will of the gods" can be almost a charade, as Philoctetes in line 992 of the play named after him accuses Odysseus of making the gods liars in order to use them as cover for his own actions. Both Sophocles and Euripides often propose the theme that human beings do not know what the gods intend, or why they do what they do. The heroes of Sophocles' plays suffer almost unspeakable abuse from above, almost always unmerited in human terms, and rarely understood by anyone.[8] Although Sophocles' texts occasionally offer us the commonplace notion that the gods bring down those who reach too high, there is precious little in them to justify the observation offered in classes for generations: that the hero fails because of *hubris* – arrogance. Moral understanding comes much harder than this, as we agree that Oedipus in the *Tyrannus*, Philoctetes, Antigone act as they do firmly believing they are right, and we may agree that they are right, but neither our approval or their conviction is worth much. Certainly in *Antigone* Sophocles presents forcefully the case for believing that being right in human terms – whether correctly asserting the rule of law or rightly interpreting the will of the gods – does not produce a result that any would call happy, so disjunctive are human and cosmic moralities. This is not to say that Sophocles is presenting the idea that the gods are immoral, or non-moral, or that their will can never be perceived by humans; rather it is the case that human understanding of the moral order in the cosmos is incomplete, so that adherence to perceived human justice is not necessarily a reliable tool to reach human prosperity.

In the *Antigone*, Sophocles presents his most explicit examinations of these issues, though intermixed with many other issues like the antagonism between male force and female will, the antithesis between the law of the state and the so-called "unwritten laws" of the gods, questions of filial obedience and similar issues, but they all are subsidiary to the matter of the determination of true justice and the human cost of achieving knowledge of justice. *Antigone* leaves no doubt about the conflict between human perceptions of justice and the truth about justice in the cosmic order, for, despite Antigone's conforming to what the play shows as the justice of the gods, she does not come out well, nor does her fiancé Haemon, who took her side. Both die as a result of their actions, and no Greek, at least at this stage of Greek thought, would regard death as a justifying outcome of decisions. They are, therefore, not rewarded for perceptions that are revealed as correct, either by mortal prosperity or by some indication of divine favor. If there is any satisfaction to be had, it is the negative posthumous reward of the destruction of the happiness of their opponents. The perception of the divine order or of the justice of the cosmos on the part of Antigone is at best imperfect: she buried her brother in violation of the king's order, and was right to do so, for she acted in accordance with divine law, a moral imperative higher than that of conformity to human law, but still, something has gone wrong. What that is, Sophocles does not tell us, nor does he even suggest an answer, but the notion of *hubris* is either simplistic or entirely inappropriate.

The answer must lie in the limitation of human ability to understand the divine, the problem of almost every Sophoclean hero. The Sophoclean hero is dedicated to justice, and divine justice at that, but human nature prevents the hero from achieving knowledge of the course to be followed and the normal goal of human prosperity. The hero may gain an intermediate goal, but ultimate failure is inevitable, for the divine will brings the universe to an order humans cannot thoroughly perceive, and "human life retains an opacity immune to the greatest minds and most decisive actors."[9]

Euripides brings something of this theme to a number of his plays. In the *Hippolytus*, the hero complains bitterly as he dies that his virtue has done him no good; even more chaotic seems the moral purpose elsewhere, with the brutality of the sacrifice to Artemis in *Iphigeneia in Tauris*, the madness and slaughter of the children in *Heracles*, or the sociopathic crimes of Orestes, which call out no apparent interest or intervention by the gods. Often the action has plunged into such a morass of personal disaster and moral confusion that no reasonable way out can be imagined, and in fact none is found, for some god, some hero, or some human figure simply intervenes to stop the action and bring the play to an end. Readers of Euripides have often objected to these blatant intrusions of a device, and whether or not they reflect badly on the playwright's dramaturgy, they do illustrate his attitude toward the relationship between the gods and human conduct. Euripides seems to credit human beings with an enormous capacity for evil, wickedness little restrained either by divine intervention or human fear or respect for divine law. The universe Euripides portrays has forces that affect human beings, but these cannot be calculated and there is no means of assessing the outcome of actions.

It can be safe in this world to indulge one's worst – worst in conventional morality – impulses, as safe, at least, as to hold to a perception of virtue. Medea acts without impediment from the divine, and practically without a mention of the gods, as she plans and executes the murders of the king of Corinth, his daughter, and even her own children without a hint of concern that the gods might punish her for her acts. Only human retribution is a concern to her, and when an escape route opens she proceeds with her plans. Even the chorus, so often in drama the voice of conventional wisdom, fails to threaten Medea with divine retribution, but only cites human law, in lines 812-13, to support its position.

Although at times Euripidean characters betray some idea that there might be an absolute quality to some aspects of human law, some absolute right and wrong beyond the *nomoi* of a given community, the notion appears only vaguely and in any case operates at the human level rather than as a divine prescription. This may be the most characteristic Euripidean idea of evil and justice, that any universal law supposed for humanity remains solidly in the human realm alone, and may be overridden or obscured by non-human forces in the cosmos, the rationale of which remains unknown. This position differs from that we find in Sophocles' plays, in that the morality begins and ends with humanity, rather than being a human morality modeled after an imperfectly understood cosmic justice. Nor are cosmic forces beneficial if imperfectly understood, as they seem to be in the mind of Sophocles; there is no order and the cosmos is not cognizant of human attempts to create order.

In later centuries, these are concepts found in the realm of philosophy or religious thought more than they are in drama, and it is not likely that Athenian audiences were much concerned about evaluating performances in terms of their presentation of one or another of these ideas, or, in fact, were any more patient with long discourses on such subjects than are modern churchgoers.[10] But it is likely that in any audience on any given day there would have been some people who would recognize these concepts, or have been familiar with discussions of them. Certainly some educated Athenians – those who had studied with or encountered the ideas of the Sophists or had heard them dispute different views of justice, *nomos* and *physis*, and their import for human conduct – would have recognized presentations of the relationship of cosmic justice with the human world. In fact, the frequency of treatment of many of these concepts by Sophocles and Euripides would have made references to them as familiar as Jesus' parables are to moderns who may never go to church. If the dialogues of Plato and the Socratic discourses written by Xenophon have any validity in their portrayal of the intellectual concerns of Socrates' younger companions in the latter years of the fifth century when these plays were being written, then the identification of justice and framing of attitudes to it must have been in the forefront. The drama itself, with its constant reference to these themes, played a very large part in heightening Athenian consciousness of these issues. And, to repeat the point that lies behind this whole discussion, the preservation of the plays to modern times and their familiarity to modern audiences had its usual double-sided effect: it kept the debate about the relationship between divine and human justice alive, and ensured that the Greek treatment of it would remain understandable and influential.

That later generations read Thucydides rather than the mundane arguments of orators in the law courts of the fourth century has influenced heavily the picture we have of the attitudes toward divine justice among the Athenians. He gives a completely different picture from the one that emerges from the work of the orators. The Athenians who supposedly listened to the speeches of Pericles, Cleon, Nicias and Alcibiades, secular and coldly rational in approach and with hardly a reference to the gods according to the text of the historian, were the same Athenians who heard the gods called on repeatedly in the courtroom speeches of Lysias, Antiphon and Andocides. The courtroom picture is closer to the world of tragedy than it is to Thucydides' world of the Assembly. In all the court speeches dealing with murder, for example, the fundamentally religious attitude toward pollution is prominent, and the prohibition of association with the accused, who is supposed to carry the miasma of impurity created by killing, is unchallenged. All parties agree on the necessity to satisfy the spirit of the dead and cleanse the city by the identification and punishment of anyone responsible for killing. Justice, often cited in the speeches, is part of this, but even more important is the religious significance achieved by this punishment, and in its aid, the gods below and catharsis are invoked in ways reminiscent of tragedy.[11]

In one of his speeches, *On the Choreutes*, Antiphon the orator, of Rhamnous as he is called by Thucydides, a man of strong oligarchic views who was one of those who in 411 seized power and established a short-lived oligarchy, presents a defense against a murder charge which had been laid against an official. In a very complex presentation of procedural matters, probably written in the last decade of his life before his death in 411, Antiphon makes much of the fact that the accused had been allowed to carry on his official duties when, had he been charged promptly, he would have been excluded from public places as polluted by the charge of murder. The argument shows not only how important religious matters were in the conduct of legal matters, but also, coming as it does as the final item of evidence at the end of the oration, it indicates how powerfully religious matters might be introduced into forensic argument.

Another speech for defense, *On the Murder of Herodes*, brings in divine and human law, as the calmness of a voyage made by the defendant and the consistent success of his sacrifices are offered as evidence of his unpolluted, i.e. innocent, state. Again this is the final item of evidence and witnesses are brought forward to attest the truth of the statements. This speech, like *On the Choreutes*, belongs to the last quarter of the fifth century, when Sophistic teaching had had ample time to penetrate the society, and supports the impression of another speech, made in the Assembly, not a law court, by Andocides, who had been exiled for having something to do with the desecration of the roadside statues of the god Hermes in 415. Pleading with the Athenians to allow his return in section 15 of *On his Return*, the orator asserts his innocence by attributing to the gods his preservation when he was in Athens in 411.

Although the speeches for courtroom or Assembly presentation are, like the speeches in Thucydides' text, replete with the rhetorical devices developed and taught by the Sophists from the middle of the fifth century on, they consistently refer to divine law and divine action as part of their argument. They assume that human law is in accord with divine, human law is presumed to accord with abstract principles of justice, and divine law is taken as not only knowable but congruent with the *nomoi* of human society. The gods are repeatedly introduced as supporters of the orators' positions, and they are taken to support and endorse human principles of law. The suppositions clear in the texts of jurisprudence indicate that many were prepared to accept and elaborate a morality which, though possibly limited by human knowledge and understanding, was nevertheless valid for human action. This approach to divine and human justice, obviously common as it functioned in both legal and political argument, existed in Athens alongside those perceptions that saw divine will as either antithetical to or uncognizant of human life, or saw human morality as an imperfect attempt to pattern behavior on a divine order incomprehensible to humanity. Almost diametrically opposite to some of the positions of drama, it represents a strong strain of moral thought in Athens, a strain derived from the Protagorean assertion of humanity as the measure of all things that exist.

The attitudes and assumptions we have encountered were not limited to Athenian minds. In Boeotia, the choral lyricist Pindar, who was born at the end of the sixth century and continued to write past the middle of the fifth, was one of the most, if not the most prominent of the poets who celebrated the accomplishments of the aristocrats who contended and won victories at the pan-city religious festivals like the quadrennial Olympic games and Pythian games at Delphi. Although participation in the games was open to any Hellene, it was for the most part aristocrats who could afford the time, travel and training to compete. A victor could expect to hear, when he returned to his city, a choral ode composed to honor his success. Pindar was probably the most noted of the composers of these odes, and four books of his epinician, or victory odes, survive, preserving forty-five complete odes; only fragments of the work of his rivals remain. The relationship between human and divine in Pindar's texts is very different from that of Aeschylus, his slightly older Athenian contemporary, and the genre itself seems to have been dying as Athenian drama developed.[12] Even when the Aeschylean gods act in ways complementary and understandable to humans, as in the *Oresteia*, their presentation contrasts with Pindar's presentation of the gods as suffused with radiance and glory.[13] Success in human life comes from the gods, who brighten the inferior existence of mortals and give to humans the potential of life transcending the ordinary state.[14] While some comment in the odes about moral judgment expresses reservations about human behavior,[15] comments in fragmentary poems assert that even superior human wisdom is a small thing when confronted by the impenetrable plans of divinity.[16]

So far as we can discern in the texts, human and cosmic justice[17] were related in the same way as humans to gods, and that relationship is a kind of simulacrum on the universal scale of the appropriate relationships at the different levels of human society. It is an aristocratic model. So long as people kept to the appropriate place for humans, more likely than not they would avoid the worst troubles which the gods and fates might have at their disposal.

This sense of order has resemblances to the Chinese view of the ordered universe, in which "all things are nourished together without their injuring one another. The courses *of the seasons, and of the sun and moon*, are pursued without any collison among them."[18] The Chinese assumptions, however, are much broader than the Pindaric assertion that humans can avoid the worst misfortunes by maintaining their proper place in the hierarchy in which the gods are superior. To the Chinese, the human simulacrum extends to the details of human life and the cosmic order, with parallels that can be observed and used in the ordering of human life:

> A special feature of Chinese religion was a deep-rooted belief in a mechanical, correlative, cosmic order.... much earlier than the theory of *yin-yang* and Five Phases.... The central theme of this correlative cosmology ... was that man's fate has a one-to-one correspondence with such natural systems as time and direction.... As there was no concept of divine creation, the spirits and gods were concieved as existing within, not outside, the cosmos....They were, like everything else, part of the order.[19]

The Hellenic sense, quite contrary to this, of the gods having a role in the promulgation and enforcement of some known or partly known cosmic morality clearly permeated Greek thought. The difficulties inherent in this attitude lay at the heart of a good deal of Athenian tragic writing, and the apparent contradiction between virtuous behavior and unfortunate experience has remained, since antiquity, at the core of religious and ethical thought among the descendents of the Greeks. It remained a part of that tradition even when the concept of explicit and revealed truth became a part of religious thought.

---

[1] Havelock (1957) pp. 52-64, shows Aeschylus' familiarity with sophistic "scientific anthropology" (p. 52) in his treatment of the learning of the arts, the alternative view which Conacher (1980) p. 97, chooses.

[2] If West (1971), is right that the influence of the East was strongest during the period of Persian domination of Greek areas, c. 550-480, there would have been opportunity for Persian dualism to have reached Greece. Pythagoreanism, however, was dualistic, according to Aristotle; cf. Kirk and Raven (1957) pp. 240 and 241 note 1.

[3] Quoted in Diogenes Laertius IX, 51. My translation follows the interpretation of Kerferd (1981) pp. 86-93. In much of what follows I accept Kerferd's interpretation of Protagoras' thought.

[4] I translate "ignorant," and not, as so often, "unfeeling, inhuman" (LSJ) or "callous." LSJ cite no parallel for the meaning "unfeeling" and the natural sense of "unknowing" parallels charging Zeus with "knowing" to sneak into Amphitryon's bed but not "knowing" to save his dear ones, in the preceding lines.

[5] Cf. Similar statements in Sophocles, *Philoctetes* 416 ff.

[6] Neither to me nor to W. Arrowsmith who, in his introduction to his translation of *Orestes* in Grene and Lattimore, eds. (1959) p. 190, found "stupidity"in Apollo's dispositions.

[7] Weber (1904-5).

[8] Knox (1964) shows not only that the downfall of the Sophoclean hero is unmerited, but also a characteristic of that hero in asserting character and attempting to impose his or her will on a universe uncontrollable and unfathomable, persisting in the face of all persuasion and opposition to pursue a course judged right, while divine justice remains beyond the reach of human understanding.

[9] Euben (1990) p. 105.

[10] It is worth citing Vellacot (1984) p. 45, for one idea I found useful, the argument for later (ancient) readers being able to appreciate the complexity a theater audience might miss.

[11] E.g. Antiphon I. 31, *Prosecution for Poisoning*, which concludes, "I think that those who are wronged are a concern to the gods below."

[12] As pointed out by Carne-Ross, D. S. (1965) pp. 1-2, the victory ode itself had a very short tradition, and by the time of most of the extant Athenian tragedies, was a moribund genre.

[13] E.g. *Pythian* III. 29-30.

[14] Cf. *Pythian* VIII. 95 ff. Carne-Ross (1965) pp. 58-59, points out the explicit statement of *Nemean* VI that it is through the victory that the victor somehow resembles the immortals.

[15] *Pythian* VI. 139-40; *Nemean* VI. 1 ff.

[16] Fragment 50 (Bowra).

[17] Only the occasional remark or fragment suggests that he might have treated politics (*Nemean* XI. 79-80) or mystery religions (Fragment 121 [Bowra].

[18] Legge (1960), Vol. I, *Doctrine of the Mean*, XXX, 3.

[19] Poo (1998) p. 209.

–13–
God's holy Truth[1]

In his 2004 Massey lectures in Canada,[2] Thomas King recounts and adverts frequently to a North American creation story. The woman Charm fell from a more ancient world in the sky and landed on the back of a turtle, where with the help of the animals, she built up the world as we know it. King tells of a young boy listening to the story who asked

> "If the earth was on the back of the turtle, what was below the turtle?" Another turtle, the storyteller told him. And below that turtle? Another turtle. And below that? Another turtle.
> The boy began to laugh, enjoying the game, I imagine. So how many turtles are there? he wanted to know. The storyteller shrugged. "No one knows for sure," she told him, "but it's turtles all the way down."[3]

From the sound of the laughter of the audience, the story was greeted with amusement, and there was no hesitation for belief; this was an Indian myth, and could be disregarded as just that, myth, with some acknowledgement that the native people had a sense of humor. In much the same way, for most of the centuries after Greek was no longer the dominant language or literature of educated people, Greek myth slid into allegory, naïve narrative or worse. In the early Christian centuries it was denial of the truth. It is only in the last few decades that readers and thinkers have attempted to find symbolic or psychological meaning in myth, and see in Greek – and other myth – a form of narrative truth, even in its extension to cosmogony.

The Greek mythological tradition, even when explored with sympathy, is short on cosmogony, even shorter than that of the native American. There is, of course, Hesiod's *Theogony* or *Generation of the Gods*, but this, even put together with other creation stories in Greek, does not give much of an account of the creation of the natural world, all the wondrous landscape and life about us. For an explanation of the creation of all that, we must turn to the account in the Hebrew scriptures, in Genesis. There we have the full story of creation, not only with the agent responsible, God, or Yahweh, but replete with implications for human morality and society. And it is the Genesis account of creation, with the explicit hierarchical order running down from Yahweh through men, then women, and below them the animals, that has reinforced with divine sanction many of the hierarchical and patriarchical traditions which Greek texts had already established for the future, both secular and in the later Christian tradition. As King views the contrast between the Genesis account and the North American story, "the elements in Genesis create a particular universe governed by a series of hierarchies – God, man, animals, plants – that celebrate law, order and good government, while in our Native story, the universe is governed by a series of co-operation – Charm, the Twins, animals, humans – that celebrate equality and balance." The Old Testament, not only Genesis but all its contents, was adopted and accepted as the divine word by Christian writers and theologians, and with the effective Hellenization of Christianity incorporating many Greek attitudes, the combination of traditions has had an inordinate effect in creating the attitudes, assumptions and values of two thousand years of history.

The Old Testament has generated a long and varied tradition of scholarship, criticism, interpretation and polemic, because the manner in which the text is understood establishes judgments on religion and ethics. It has been influential on thought even of those outside its religious purview, not least because the canonical works in the Old Testament show "a literary skill and imagination no less than (although different from) what we seek in great novels and poetry."[4] The history of analysis and scholarship is a long one, and has included many different kinds of analysis because of internal contradictions and statements that often challenge belief. It is now recognized that not only the text as a whole but even individual books are the work of many writers and reflect divergent opinions about history and ethical and cultic values. Over the centuries there have been many ways to approach the biblical tradition, with more recent scholarship aimed at establishing authoritative texts. By the late twentieth century, these earlier investigations merged with, or gave way to, strikingly different approaches. Writers on the Hebrew scriptures not sympathetic to its authority began applying current philosophical and literary approaches to texts and society to attempt to reveal and overthrow the manner in which the Old Testament established undesired cultural norms and even falsified history.[5] Some writers now move beyond an attempt to understand text or antiquity to a challenge of modern institutions. We can find a very different approach to the Bible in recent theological writing, and a self–conscious break with earlier studies, whereby "the Bible's function in past societies has been to socialize its people into an acceptance of the patriarchal world-view, for many ... its current function is to serve as a locus for our critique of that very system."[6]

It may well be the case that the scholarship attacking some of the traditional orientation will eventually have its effect on prevailing modern attitudes. Those attitudes are, however, still largely controlled by what many scholars call the conventional presentation of Old Testament texts and ideas, accepting the biblical endorsement of hierarchy, exercise of power and male supremacy that lead to what one feminist theologian calls the "devastating effect on women's lives [that defeats an attempt] to try to fit the notion of an authoritative sacred canon into a feminist paradigm."[7] I believe, therefore, that it is necessary first to elucidate a presentation of the Old Testament in terms that accord with this so-called "conventional" understanding. If one can show how some attitudes generally deemed desirable owe their fostering to the biblical texts which for generations were regarded as holding divine authority, the assertion that these texts also contribute to oppression and exploitation may be a little easier to accept. In this discussion I also try to take into account the "sacred" character of these texts, in an awareness of the current critical situation that David Gunn, himself convinced by many of the feminist criticisms of the texts, has referred to as making it "very hard to see where feminist criticism of the Bible can go 'constructively' without it destroying traditional notions of the Bible's authority as a sacred text," asserting that "'biblical' literature stands in its mottled complexity like any other literature that plumbs human experience, profoundly, for good or ill."[8]

For generations, the Bible was regarded as a combination of law, morality and history, and the historical aspect was always noticeable because of the traditional Jewish focus on the linear progress of events. Thus, human experience began with the event of creation, carried through the expulsion from Eden, the histories of the early patriarchs, the promise to Abraham and then the events chronicled in the historical books of the Old Testament. The traditions include the view that the Hebrews originally came from Mesopotamia and settled in Canaan, later known as Palestine (in the seventeenth century BCE according to the dating of modern historians who try to relate the biblical account to real events). Over a period of about 200 years they fought their way into the land and established a formal kingship by about 1050 BCE, under the first monarch, Saul. The next king, David, who ruled until about 975 BCE, consolidated the kingdom and captured Jerusalem, where his son, Solomon, ruled for about 40 years and made the nation prosperous in its foreign trade and diplomatic activity.

The Old Testament includes an account of Solomon's faithlessness toward Yahweh in allowing the worship of foreign gods. God then split the unified kingdom of Israel as the rebel Jereboam took control of the entire north, leaving only a small southern segment, Judah, to Solomon's legitimate heir Reheboam. Thereafter, the two kingdoms went their separate ways, often in mutual hostility. The biblical story, written from a point of view favorable to the southern kingdom of Judah, is a narrative of dwindling power and the effects of the pressure from Palestine's more powerful neighbors. The account frequently refers to the apostasy of the northern kingdom, Israel, whose kings allegedly repeatedly did what was displeasing to Yahweh.

As the centuries progressed, the people fell away from the Law, committing abominations like that of the ninth-century King Ahab, who with his wife Jezebel introduced foreign gods; the abandonment of the Law called forth the work of great prophets, Elijah and his successor Elisha. In the next century there were more such kings and prophets, and finally, in 721 BCE the northern capital Samaria fell and its inhabitants were deported by the Assyrian king, who settled foreign colonists who imported their own gods and mixed their worship with that of Yahweh.

Next it was the turn of the surviving kingdom of Judah. As its kings looked to find aid from foreign allies, the great prophet Isaiah called on the people to place their faith only in the greatness of Yahweh, and a century later, about 645 BCE, another, Jeremiah, exhorted the people with his vision of the exclusivity and magnificence of Yahweh and his Law, at the same time condemning the wickedness of the people and calling them back to obedience to the Law. By 586 BCE, after a period of vassalage to Babylon, with revolts, a siege and final conquest, Jerusalem had finally fallen to Nebuchadnezzar and large numbers of its inhabitants had been deported to Babylon. The period of exile had begun.

The destruction of the independent kingdoms and the captivity in Babylon seemed, in the Jewish view of history, to be Yahweh's retribution for apostasy. The texts of prophetic literature and the treatment of events show "in the religion of Israel from its beginning as the medium of divine action that in the crisis of the exile there was a large-scale theological revision of previous history."[9] With the Temple cult destroyed, the Jews in Palestine and those in exile depended on the scriptural texts for their understanding of the relationship between human and God. Old Scripture – the ninth and eighth century sources for Genesis, Exodus, Numbers and Leviticus, had, according to one tradition, been supplemented in 621 BCE by the discovery of another ancient book, Deuteronomy, and in the period of exile and thereafter the legal provisions of scripture were correlated and edited to provide more coherent texts so that the people could find and follow the Law. Historical books continue the narrative of the story from the time of Moses, in a narrative which explicated events in terms of a Covenant continually violated by Yahweh's chosen, called a "headstrong" people who refused to follow God's injunctions or the calls of his prophets to return to the Law. That Law was not only "cultic" in prescribing and proscribing activities connected with worship, it also formalized many ancient Near Eastern traditions into an ethical code based on the Ten Commandments and later expanded in meaning and application by the prophets. But the rules connected with the service to Yahweh, excluding from the land any pagan deities or worship of them, were frequently violated. There was pagan worship in the "high places," at altars set up even in the Temple, and pagan idols and symbols were notable from the time of Solomon's successor Jereboam; as the people stubbornly failed to take advantage of opportunities of reconciliation, the two kingdoms declined into dissolution. Only the prophetic oracles of later prophets Isaiah and Jeremiah offered hope of redemption, but this was, ultimately, a personal rather than a mass redemption, in Jeremiah's vision a new Covenant with each person individually instead of with the nation as a whole.

By the time Cyrus the Persian liberated the exiled Jews and returned them to their homeland in 538 BCE, the particular nature of the people had been formed. They had a life and ethos fundamentally different from others in the Mediterranean basin, and had virtually nothing in common with the Greeks. The difference between the two cultures goes much deeper than the Greek acceptance of pluralism in deity and rejection of that by the Jews, and was much more basic in its effect on moral, political and social attitudes. To the Jews, there was a purpose behind events, a direction that history was taking, a sense of a role for themselves in much the way the Romans saw their own role in history. To many thinkers among the Jews, however, their role was not "to rule the nations," but to live a life of purity and separateness in accord with their special relationship with Yahweh. They had been "chosen" to exemplify a life of fidelity to God and his Laws as an example to all the nations, and history moved to fulfill that destiny. They themselves were not the movers of history, but rather were its very cause. So much, I think, can be explicated from the texts without the application of archaeological, sociological or close textual analysis.

Beyond this sense of historical mission lay the effects of being the "People of the Law." Codified law had been an old tradition in the East, but it had never penetrated in its moral and ethical form to the Greeks, and especially, was never tied to the requirements of religion as it was for the Jews. The embedding of the Ten Commandments into the Mosaic code is an illustration of the manner in which ethics were validated as divine prescription, with God prohibiting such entirely human crimes as adultery, murder, theft, false witness, and covetousness of a neighbor's wife and property. These misdeeds, along with the requirement of honor to father and mother, join such religious crimes as the demand for exclusivity of the worship of Yahweh, proscription of images and misuse of the divine name, and the command to keep the Sabbath. Anthropologists can find such ethical imperatives among many early peoples, often given transcendent endorsement because of their importance to the survival of a tribe and its members. Among the Jews the commandments very early went beyond protection of the tribe and the limited requirements for communal. For example, mixed with the elaborate regulations set out for the conduct of ritual in the Book of Leviticus are demands for kindness to the poor and for honest behavior, [10] recurring often in the Book of Deuteronomy in terms of justice and protection due the poor, the weak, widows and orphans.[11] The Jewish code goes beyond the tribe to protect others: Deuteronomy 10: 19 calls on the people to befriend the strangers, "for you were strangers in the land of Egypt," and Deuteronomy 14: 29 includes the stranger amongst those who are to benefit from the triennial tithe of charity. Most striking is the phraseology of Leviticus 19: 33-4: "When a stranger resides with you in your land, you shall not wrong him. The stranger who resides with you shall be to you as one of your citizens; you shall love him as yourself, for you were strangers in the land of Egypt: I the LORD am your god."

The account here of the conceptualizations of the early books of the Old Testament, like that which follows on later pages here, is conventional and highly condensed, and it is my own version of the interpretations that seem to me to be commonly accepted or expressed. Analysis and discussion of this material over the years has been extraordinarily extensive and diverse, but to repeat for emphasis an observation I have made above, what I write here contains a reasonable summary of the ideas and attitudes I think the text has generated over the centuries. It conveys the idea of a universe controlled by a single will, that of God, in a history directed by divine purpose. All that exists does so by divine fiat, and the role of humanity in that creation is no more and no less than the duty imposed by divinity. How that still frames thinking strikes me forcefully when I think of a hymn like:

> Eternal Father strong to save,
> Whose arm doth rule the restless wave,

Who bids the mighty ocean deep
Its own eternal limit keep.
Now hear us when we cry to thee
For those in peril on the sea.

This attitude toward the cosmos and the microcosmic human experience so characteristic of European Protestantism dominated Jewish ideas from at least the end of the second millennium BCE on, and it persisted through Jewish history into Christian thought. Different from Greek ideas, which wavered between notions of the effects the gods might have on human life and the concept of an alien and uncaring cosmos, the Jewish ideas have some parallels to the Chinese concept of the "Mandate of Heaven" which authorized the imperial power. The Jewish idea is broader, however, with the divine will personal rather than abstract like the Chinese, and it spreads the relationship between the personal god and humanity through the entire people rather than creating an impersonal link between an abstract force and the occupant of the Chinese imperial throne.

The divine will, to the Jews, was for the most part exemplified by the Law, which dominated the minds of Jews from earliest times, prescribing ritual behavior and a code of "uncleanness" alongside its ethical demands. Long before the exile, religious leaders were telling the Jews that their troubles arose from their failure to keep the Covenant with Yahweh, and by the time of King David the notion of Yahweh's retribution for violation of the code had broadened to include violations of the social code as well as more narrowly ritual regulations.[12] In the eighth century the words of Isaiah[13] place ethical requirements at the core: the prophet deplores the fact that no justice is provided widows and orphans, that unrighteous laws refuse justice to the unfortunate and cheat the poor. Isaiah's text claims that kings should rule by integrity, which will bring peace, and use justice to produce lasting security. Yahweh brings the true justice, frees the captive from prison, opens the eyes of the blind,[14] and Isaiah opens with words that have rung down through the ages to express an interpretation of God's attitude toward humanity:

> I am sated with burnt offering of rams....
> Your new moons and fixed seasons
> Fill Me with loathing,
> They are become a burden to Me
> I cannot endure them....
> Put your evil doings
> Away from My sight.
> Cease to do evil;
> Learn to do good.
> Devote yourselves to justice.
> Aid the wronged.
> Uphold the rights of the orphan;
> Defend the cause of the widow.[15]

Utterly unlike the Greek tradition, words like these are the carriers into western religious thought of the sense of sin, transgression and rejection of God that marks the conscience and removes all possibility of a pervading Confucian sense of the natural goodness of humanity. The prophets return again and again to themes like these, with not only ritual at stake, but fundamental morality and ethics.[16] The prophetic tradition also understands the Law and its violation as the explanation of evil in the world, for evil and trouble arise from human failure to keep the Law, and the people are responsible:

> Surely this instruction which I enjoin on you today is not too baffling for you, nor is it beyond reach. It is not in the heavens, that you should say, "Who among us can go to the heavens and get it for us and impart it to us, that we may observe it?" Neither is it beyond the sea, that you should say, "Who among us can cross to the other side of the sea and get it for us and impart it to us, that we may observe it?" No, the thing is very close to you, in your mouth and in your heart, to observe it.[17]

There is no suggestion in this concept of divine order of any difficulty on the part of humanity in understanding the will of God; the concept is quite different from the sense of doubt, uncertainty and ambiguity that pervades Greek thought and even begins to appear in later Jewish wisdom literature's insistence on the obscurity of wisdom.

The early idea that transgression and punishment is a collective matter affecting the entire people of Israel began to erode by the time of the Babylonian captivity. At the end of the seventh century BCE the expression of personal religion by Jeremiah rejects the old notion of collective responsibility, the concept of the punishment of the sons for the sins of their fathers: "In those days they shall no longer say, Parents have eaten sour grapes and children's teeth are blunted. But everyone shall die for his own sins."[18] Jeremiah is certain about the nature of divine law, and of the punishment brought by its transgression. In his words and those that express similar views, the Jewish tradition offered a very different attitude from the Hellenic doubts about the nature of divine law or whether divinity was friendly or hostile, involved with humanity or detached and remote.

By the fifth century BCE, according to the biblical account, some of the Jews had returned from exile and lived a peaceful existence as part of the Persian empire, although the numbers of Jews in different parts of the Mediterranean world suggests that the numbers outside Palestine always remained larger than those in the promised land. After the conquest of the Persian east by Alexander, the Jews of the East began to experience the impact of the Hellenism of their rulers, and became acquainted with a culture from which they had been hitherto remote. In these same centuries they accelerated their spread beyond the territorial limits of Palestine. These are the centuries that began the tradition of the so-called wisdom literature, the books of Job, Psalms, Proverbs, Wisdom and others like these. Apart from the Psalms, some of which go back to early times and may even have been composed by David himself, the wisdom books were all created in the post-exilic period with little input from earlier sources. Job is probably a work of the early fifth century BCE, possibly with some later intrusions, and Proverbs also was probably put together in that century. Other books, Ecclesiastes and Wisdom for example, came later, in the period after Alexander the Great.

While the wisdom books contain some concepts apparently new, for the most part they continue earlier attitudes: Yahweh is the founder of the earth;[19] the emphasis on the Law continues,[20] with the concept of God the judge coming more to the fore,[21] the deity Himself caring for the orphan, the widow and the poor.[22] There may be some aspects of change, possibly post exilic in origin, in the more frequent references to the compassion of Yahweh, as in Psalm 103, or His everlasting love, as in Psalms 136 and 138, but there is little or nothing in these books that cannot find strong and legitimate basis in the earlier texts of scripture.

One wisdom book, Job, has been thought to introduce new and specifically Greek ideas, but even here, occasional similarities of thought and expression are overwhelmed by the fundamental differences in world view. The questioning of divine justice that permeates the book as Job's friends advise and try to comfort the wretched sufferer may evoke some aspects of the questions in Athenian tragedy. Job's assertion that God is unjust or his enemy has reminded some readers of the maleficent Zeus in Aeschylus' *Prometheus Bound,* and Job's conviction that he is right has often been noted as similar to the attitudes of Sophoclean heroes. Sophoclean theodicy seems to appear as well as the work comes to its climax, with Yahweh thundering his awesome poetry out of the tempest:

> I will ask and you will inform Me.
> Where were you when I laid the earth's foundations?
> Speak, if you have understanding....
> Have you ever commanded the day to break,
> Assigned the dawn its place,
> So that it seizes the corners of the earth
> And shakes the wicked out of it?[23]

To this sequence of questions Job has no answer, but the words of Yahweh do bring him understanding:

> I know that you can do everything,
> That nothing you propose is impossible for You.
> Who is this who obscures counsel without knowledge?
> Indeed I spoke without understanding
> Of things beyond me, which I did not know.[24]

Job has learned the lesson of the supremacy of Yahweh, and although the story bears some resemblance to Sophoclean tragedy, the basic attitudes are different. Unlike Sophoclean heroes, Job continually protests his lot, until at the end God restores him to good fortune. For Job and the other Jews, the rules are known in detail as laid out in the Law, and Job is insistent that he has obeyed not only ritual requirements but also the obligations of social justice. What Job learns is the overwhelming supremacy of God, and the negligible quality of created humanity in comparison to the majesty and power of the creator. It is an acceptance of the insignificance of humanity utterly different from the centrality of the human condition in Greek thought, and it also differs from the Chinese in its stress on the role of a creator and the absence of the sense of a natural bond between human beings and the rest of the universe. In the view of the cosmos found in the Book of Job, only Yahweh and His will directs life and proposes meaning to it. Thus, the work ends with Job gaining an even greater prosperity than he had before, an outcome never achieved by the Sophoclean tragic hero. The text carries forward into wisdom literature the strong theocratic character of Jewish life, a sense of the relationship between human and God undiminished from the perceptions of earlier scriptural writings, and a powerful influence on religious thought in times to come.

In my sense of the impact of biblical writings on readers throughout the centuries, the assertion of divine command validated the ethical stance of the canonical texts, and this divine authority has made these ethical positions central in western culture for two millennia. While I and others no longer have as much confidence in divine prescription to validate these ethical values, in that idea, I still find myself seeking support for my ethical judgments from texts of the past. It is also true, though, that the opening of texts to critical analysis has provided the opportunity to see negative effects of those texts, and to show the manner in which their ethical and social stances can be challenged. It seems to me that any dispassionate reading of the biblical text will recognize that however varied and numerous the individual contributions to the text may be, most are based on the acceptance of male supremacy, patriarchal power in a hierarchical structure, the application of force, slavery and perhaps even some forms of racism, and in aggregate reinforce those assumptions. The widespread recognition of biblical support for the first two or three of these attitudes is demonstrated by the repeated assertion of biblical authority by those who advocate those practices. It is hardly surprising, then, that the Hebrew canon has been subjected to repeated analysis of its stance on these issues by feminist writers and those advocating changes in the power ethic of contemporary society. The Bible has been argued as "a human product of elite males," providing "seeming authorization of the exploitation of any who are not in-group, elite males."[25]

It seems to me that the problem is even greater than that cited by those attacking the oppression justified by the Hebrew scriptures. A very strong current in the western tradition has washed society along a path of increasing, perhaps even accelerating, liberation. Thus the authoritarian tendencies of the Old Testament run counter to the direction of other attitudes and texts which, I believe, emerge out of some Hellenic attitudes. Put differently, in a number of areas attitudes are ambivalent because tradition is ambivalent. This ambivalence was not immediately apparent in antiquity, certainly not in the medieval period, but has come more to the fore in recent times when the thrust toward liberation and expanded participation in society has been advocated more and more forcefully.

The religion of the Hebrew Bible and its successor Christian books, while complementing some of the Hellenic attitudes of hierarchy and male supremacy, supplanted completely the paganism of the Greeks and the Romans. The early Christians saw clearly how their tradition contradicted the religious attitudes and practices of the Greeks, and made every effort to eradicate Greek (and Roman) religious practice and belief, once they had the power to do so. The acceptance of the monotheism of these texts has so dominated the world view of Jews, Christians and Moslems that many treatments of their religion regard those three so-called "prophetic," or "religions of the book" as a higher, more advanced form of religious thought. It seems to me that even some who do not profess themselves believers in the truth of the texts make this assessment. It is a valuation that favors the three book religions even though they are quite exceptional among human cultures.

Jews reacted to Hellenic ideas at first with hostility, and Jews and Christians saw themselves at war with the Greeks, regarding Greek ideas as anathema – worse than heresy. The Greek universe was inhabited not only by humans, animals, plants and the objects of the earth and sky, but by *theoi* – a word we translate as gods. The *theoi* were, for the most part, immortal, and they did – or did not, according to some Greek writers – have effects on human life and activities. There were other spirits as well, of trees, rivers, natural places, and these might or might not have individual identities or names, just as creatures called *daimones* and even ghosts might exist and act, unnamed but nevertheless with some power, to be respected and propitiated by sacrifice. All of this made for a cosmos that was multi-faceted, with contradictions and conflict at the non-human as well as at the human level, all to contribute to the seemingly inconsistent and illogical nature of Greek religious comment and practice.

The acceptance of the notion of a supreme individual with intelligence, will and purpose swept all this away in the populations that inherited Greek traditions and occupied the parts of the world in which Judaism, Christianity and Islam prevail today. For me, for most of my life, it was easy to accept the idea that shamanistic or polytheistic or animistic ideas characteristic of so many peoples of the world attested a less rationalistic and less reasonable approach to the cosmos. Buddhism, Daoism, of which I knew only the philosophical strains, I could fit into the more accepting attitude, and it is only as I have become more aware of the real nature of other religious forms that I can appreciate how much they accord with what now I see as a more general human religious mood. As a part of so ancient, thoughtful and learned a culture as the Chinese, for example, Chinese religion may not ratify the attitudes of such diverse communities as North American Indian, Polynesian, and Hindu, but it certainly sides with them against the unusual biblical traditions.

It seems clear now, after the excavation of early sites in China, that the Chinese from earliest times included in their religious practice a multiplicity of approaches to entities beyond ordinary human perception. The early oracles on shoulder-bone and turtle-shells show divination, a practice that persisted in one form or another for centuries, The ritual of sacrifice became more formalized with the Son of Heaven – the emperor – as the agent with authority to make sacrifice for the entire people. Although with the advent of Confucianism, in the troubled times of the so-called "Spring and Autumn" period, a thrust to what many call "humanism" penetrated Chinese practice, the ecstatic trances and service of shamans carried on. The patterns of worship and sacrifice to Heaven and Earth continued, regularized and performed for state purposes by the emperor, but even as time passed and Chinese ideas became influenced by Daoism and Buddhism, basic aspects of Chinese attitudes never disappeared. Life continued to be "dominated by the belief in ancestral spirits. The bond between the human and the divine was especially assured by communication between the ancestral spirits and their living descendants, or communication between the human and the divine through the mediumship of diviners or shamans."[26]

While there is is some similarity to the Greek and Roman oracular priests and their interpreters, the Chinese pattern goes much farther in recruiting the supreme temporal power into the structure of contact with the non-human powers. And it certainly differs violently from Hebrew law, which directs that "You shall not practice divination or soothsaying.... Do not turn to ghosts and do not inquire of familiar spirits, to be defiled by them. I am the Lord your God."[27] While it was permissible for Hebrew priests and prophets to assert their own elucidation of God's will, that will in itself was exclusive and allowed for no other affect on human life but that of God. Even in the rare instance of a spirit revealing truth to a living human, as Samuel did for Saul, the ghost reveals the will of God in his role as prophet.[28] And, finally, in the many levels on which Chinese religion differs from Greek, Roman or Hebrew-Christian, it even carries a strain in which the human is thought to be able to control one's future:

> Unlike the religions of the Greeks and Romans, therefore, one hardly finds a sense of mystery in the everyday religion of personal welfare in ancient China. Neither was there divine revelation concerning the fate of man such as that found in Judeo-Christian traditions.... a person could change his fate either by choosing to follow systems favorable to his particular needs, or by propitiating the spirits and employing mantic tools ... fundamentally based on a belief in magic....

The act of "changing one's fate" one might add, is still a popular subject in the fortune-telling business in contemporary China.[29]

Confucian thought, with its emphasis on the essential good nature of humans, represents a profound difference from the underlying attitudes of biblical concepts. Whether carried to its extreme by a subsequent thinker, Mo-tzu, continued by Mencius or denied by others, the Confucian attitude had a permanent impact on Chinese attitudes. There is nothing like the idea of the Fall of humanity exemplified by Genesis nor the sense of driving purpose assumed of God by Jewish and Christian thinkers alike. Its particular characteristics imbue Chinese religion with differences perhaps even greater than those allowing for diversity, multiplicity of extra-human entities, varied methods of approaching the divine through sacrifice and ritual. And despite the existence of written doctrines in the translations of Buddhist texts, the Sutras never achieved the status of authority accorded the biblical scriptures by Jews and Christians. Sects developed and coexisted, and with rare exception, the diversity of belief and practice was tolerated both by state and by the multifarious religious groups. As a result, one speaks of Chinese religions, a pluralism, and a pluralism in which the most ancient shamanistic and oracular practices continued alongside, and even permeate, humanistic Confucianism and the most mystical aspects of Daoism and Buddhism.

I do not propose here to consider how Chinese traditions affect contemporary Chinese thought and behavior, beyond asking in passing whether the diversity of religious experience might lead to diversity in modern Chinese thought. My interest is in tracing how the biblical tradition influences my own way of looking at the world. Here, I am struck most forcibly by my own pursuit of certainty; I am impelled, I think, by a tradition that encourages a strong sense of truth and falsity. A society framed to accord to the rules of a single entity that created the universe is a society that divides action into compliance and disobedience, and true belief is necessary to determine right action. My own pursuit of accurate understanding and explanation is a mild form of the attitudes which, in their extremes, produce the violent fundamentalisms of the three biblical religions. The very existence of "The Book" provides a basic contrast to the variability and flexibility of the Chinese tradition. There, over centuries, indeed millennia, commentary and discussion, debate and disagreement about interpretation of a wide varied of "classics" and Buddhist sutras do not support the citation of chapter and verse to reinforce argument and action of an exclusive nature. Rather, they create commentary and discussion to explore the significance of respected writings. Among the peoples of the biblical religions, there is always the book to cite, a sacred text that is taken to record the will of the single divinity that rules the universe. Out of this atmosphere has come both good and bad, the insistence on the importance of the individual with a soul, the concern of the divine ruler even for a sparrow, the moral law of affirmative doing "to others what we would have done to us," rather than the Confucian abstaining from that which we would not have done to us.

It was in the centuries after Alexander, when the Macedonian successors ruled Palestine and established Greek settlers in the land, that Hellenic influences began to be felt in Jewish thought and writing. Those influences are notable, in fact, in the historical writing that recounts the great Maccabaean revolt against Antiochus IV. The revolt began after a series of internal conflicts among the Jews, reported in the non-canonical works, Maccabees 1 and Maccabees 2 and in the Book of Daniel and in Josephus' *Jewish Antiquities*. Trouble began when Jason, the brother of the high priest, obtained the endorsement of the new king, Antiochus IV, to become high priest himself. With the king's support, he had Jerusalem established as a Greek city, Antioch-in-Jerusalem, an act that included the establishment of Greek polis institutions, some of which were controversial among the Jews. When Jason was ousted in favor of one Menelaus, civil war broke out, the turmoil occurring during Antiochus' expeditions against Egypt, the second of which ended as a result of Roman demands in 168 BCE. In the course of all this, there was a sack of the Temple by Antiochus and revolutionary activity against him. When the king finally returned to Palestine in 167 BCE he instituted the famous persecution of the Jewish religion and installed pagan cults in the Temple, and decreed, among other things, that observation of the Law was to be banned, along with keeping the Sabbath and the circumcision of boys. Resistance and martyrdoms followed; one Mattathias, a respected man in the town of Modein, killed a Jew who was about to obey the king's officers, then killed the officer as well, and fled with his associates. Among the group were the sons of Mattathias, who, beginning with Judah, known as Judah Maccabaeus, led the revolts against Antiochus and eventually gained control of Palestine as an independent state.

The writers of the Jewish accounts, as I read them, represent these events as related almost entirely to religious affairs, with the revolt generated by Antiochus' religious persecution. The accounts present Hellenization as a corrupting influence, a point of view that persists in Josephus' account that portrays the revolt as a brave fight for religious freedom. Whatever the realities of the affair were, complicated in fact by divisions among the Jews themselves on the very issue of Hellenization, it is what people think about it that counts in the long run, and the battle for independence under the leadership of the Maccabees remains even today a symbol of liberty and religious freedom.

Independence did not curtail Hellenization among the Jews of Palestine, and Hellenization may be traced even in the accounts of the revolt. Maccabees 2 was actually composed in Greek, and shows all the characteristics of Greek historical writing, at the same time preserving the traditional attitudes of the earlier prophets by portraying the troubles of the age as brought on by the people falling away from the Law. The compiler of the work shows an easy familiarity with Greek culture as well as language, and his references to the king's activities, the correspondence with the Jews of Egypt opening the work, and the reference to the Romans in 11: 34-8 shows a mind acquainted with the world of the wider Mediterranean. Maccabees 1 has the same world outlook, even if in this case the Greek text is based on a translation of a Hebrew original. The author knows the main lines of recent Roman history and shows the influence of the Hellenistic historians' use of documents, comfortably quoting the record of diplomatic relations between Jews and Spartans.

The political life of the new kingdom was even more strikingly influenced by Greek models. To all appearances, the court of the Hasmoneans – as the Maccabee brothers and their successors are called – exhibited many of the characteristics of the other Greek and Macedonian courts of the time, and Simon's court and court protocol followed the patterns of the royal behavior of many minor dynasts of the period. Later rulers even added Greek inscriptions to the Hebrew of their coinage, and it was only with the plundering of the Temple by John Hyrcanus,

Simon's son who became high priest in 135 BCE, that the Hasmoneans encountered any opposition.

The impact of Hellenic ideas on the Jews of Palestine is apparent in the later books of the Old Testament. A great deal has been made of the external influences on the Book of Ecclesiastes, showing pessimism evocative of the Egyptian work, *Dialogue with his Soul of the Man Tired of Life*, and its insistence on the value of pleasure in this life as influenced by Greek Epicureanism. Similarities of expression and the third century BCE date of Ecclesiastes allows for influences from the west, not only an Epicurean flavor in passages like "Thus I realized that the only worthwhile thing there is for them is to enjoy themselves and do what is good in their lifetime,"[30] while there is a Stoic ring to the expression of the idea that "There is nothing worthwhile for a man but to eat and drink and afford himself enjoyment with his means."[31] Even so, while these passages may share the outlook we can find in the works of Zeno and Epicurus, they may not demonstrate any direct influence, and may be no more than commonplaces of current wisdom like the observation that "A lover of money never has his fill of money."[32]

It is interesting to compare Ecclesiastes' assessment of death with the Homeric:

> For the same fate is in store for all: for the righteous, and for the wicked; for the good and pure, and for the impure; for him who sacrifices, and for him who does not; for him who is pleasing and for him who is displeasing; and for him who swears, and for him who shuns oaths. That is the sad thing about all that goes on under the sun: that the same fate is in store for all.[33]

The language evokes Achilles' words in *Iliad* IX. 318-20:

> Fate is equal for a man standing back, the same if he fights vigorously. In one honor are we all, the despicable and the noble. The man who accomplished nothing dies equally with him who has done a lot.

The differences in thought, however, are a great deal more significant than the similarities in words. In the Homeric concept enunciated by Achilles, the alternatives of conduct are bravery and cowardice, the life of nobility and that of meanness, while in Ecclesiastes the choices are ethical and moral, between virtue and wickedness, purity and impurity, observance or neglect of religious obligations. But there is no escaping death, whether one follows the Law or violates it, and in Ecclesiastes, interestingly enough in view of the emergence of the idea of bodily resurrection in Jewish writing of the next century, death is unalterable, irrevocable:

> For in respect of the fate of man and the fate of beast, they have one and the same fate: as the one dies so dies the other, and both have the same lifebreath.... Who knows if a man's lifebreath does rise upward and if a beast's does sink down into the earth?[34]

We are in a tradition very different from that which incorporated the Socratic and Platonic speculations about the psyche.

Greek ideas have been found in other scriptural works,[35] but such Hellenization as did occur in the religious, moral and social attitudes of the Jews never offset their sense of submission and devotion to God and God's Law. While later writers like

Philo, the completely Hellenized Jew of Alexandria, might struggle to rationalize through allegory some apparently conflicting ideas in scripture, neither he nor any other believing Jew ever doubted the fundamental message of the Pentateuch, the five books of Moses that set out the basic relationship between divine and human and prescribed the obligations of the latter to the former. Essentially, Jewish thought would contribute to western attitudes a confidence in the absolute validity of certain ethical and moral norms. While the Hellenic tradition might see in human centrality a basis by which humans might make moral decisions, those decisions would always have the ambiguity and uncertainty inherent in human ideas. Although Greeks had the confidence in the possibility of human knowledge, they lived with the awareness that such knowledge, being human, must always remain limited. To the Jews, for whom God was always at the center, the very insignificance of humanity provided the possibility for genuine, final and complete knowledge. What God might reveal, humanity could know, and since God had made a revelation, human beings had knowledge that went beyond human to the divine.

Later mediated through Christianity, many of the ideas and values found in the texts I have cited persist to present days. But the Jewish texts, as they carried on into Christian thought with its Hellenic characteristics, brought with them one attitude that was fundamentally different from anything Greek. While thinkers from the sixth-century Xenophanes to third-century Stoics and Epicureans might debate the role, nature and even existence of the divine, Jews and Christians shared a concept and a confidence in their knowledge of the divine nature. Xenophanes might quip that if oxen and horses had hands and could produce works of art, they would produce images of gods like themselves; Stoics might conceive of the cosmos as the interaction of an abstract *Logos* working on matter; Epicurus might assert that if the gods existed, they cared nothing for humans and took no role in human affairs, responding to a strain in Greek thought that denied the very existence of the gods. Jews and Christians never doubted the existence of a personal Yahweh who had created the universe, had a plan for it, was conscious of what happened in it and acted on it, even on its most particular parts: "His eye is on the sparrow." This attitude, particularly as it interacted in Christianity with Greek ideas about the nature of the human being and its place in the universe, had an enormous effect on later thought and action.

---

[1] These words describe the Bible in the dedication to King James by the translators. I was tempted to use the King James translation for my quotations of Hebrew text below, since that translation was so influential on the English-speaking world, but, since that translation came relatively late in the history of thought, I have instead chosen to use the translation published as *Tanakh, A New Translation of The Holy Scriptures According to the Traditional Hebrew Text*, 1985, Philadelphia, The Jewish Publication Society.

[2] King (2003).

[3] King (2003) pp. 31-32.

[4] Jobling, D., "Methods of Modern Literary Criticism," in Perdue, ed. (2001) p. 23.

[5] Surveys of the most recent literature are well presented in the relevant sections of Perdue, ed. (2001); see also McKay, H. A., "On the Future of Feminist Biblical Criticism," in Brenner and Fontaine (1997) pp. 61-83.

[6] Fontaine, C. R. "The Abusive Bible: On the Use of Feminist Method in Pastoral Contexts," in Brenner and Fontaine (1997) p. 111.

[7] Milne "No Promised Land: Rejecting the Authority of the Bible," in (1995) *Feminist Aproaches to the Bible*, Washington, D.C., Biblical Archaeology Society, pp. 69-70.

[8] Gunn, D. M., "Reflections on David," in Brenner and Fontaine (1997) p. 565.

[9] Albertz (1994) p. 387.

[10] Leviticus 5: 21-6; 25: 35 ff.

[11] Deuteronomy 10: 18; 14: 28; 24: 10-21; 26: 12-14 ff., etc.

[12] Cf. 1 Samuel 22: 21.

[13] Isaiah, like other prophetic books, such as Jeremiah, treated below, is not a simple report of a single prophetic voice. It is a complex editorial creation drawing on a number of sources (see Schmidt (1984).

[14] Isaiah 1: 23; 10: 1, 2; 32: 1, 17; 42: 3-4, 7.

[15] Isaiah 1: 11, 14-17. Cf. also, 59: 12-14, by one of the followers of Isaiah.
[16] E.g. Amos 2: 6-7; 5: 21-4.
[17] Deuteronomy 30: 11-14.
[18] Jeremiah 31: 29-30.
[19] Psalms 24.
[20] E.g. Psalms 7, 119.
[21] As in Psalms 7; 58; 94, etc.
[22] Psalms 9-10; 113; 146.
[23] Job 38: 3-4; 12-13.
[24] Job 42: 2-3.
[25] Fontaine (1977) "The Abusive Bible: On the Use of Feminist Method in Pastoral Contexts," in Brenner and Fontaine (1977) p. 93.
[26] Ching (1993) p. 48.
[27] Leviticus 19: 26; 31. Similarly, Deuteronomy 18:10.
[28] The story of Saul's consultation of the witch of Endor, who raised the ghost of Samuel for consultation, is clearly a story of violation, not only of divine law, but of Saul's own human legislation against such activity.
[29] Poo (1998) p. 210.
[30] Ecclesiastes 3: 12, repeated in 8: 15
[31] Ecclesiastes 2: 24; cf. the same idea in 5: 17.
[32] Ecclesiastes 5: 9.
[33] Ecclesiastes 9: 2-3
[34] Ecclesiastes 3: 19-23.
[35] For examples, the sense of the universality of humans appears in Sirach (Ecclesiasticus) 10: 19, written about 200 BCE and later translated into Greek. There is a representation of God as mindful even of non-Jews living in Nineveh, in Jonah 4: 11, and the additions to Daniel in Chapter 14 of the stories of Bel and the Dragon resemble the wonder tales told in Greek of Alexander the Great.

–14–
To Live In Christian Times

There might be some parallel to the Chinese experience in the religious patterns of the Mediterranean basin in the final century or two of the last millennium BCE or the first centuries of the new era. A person seeking connection with the non-human, the superhuman, the divine, or knowledge about life and the cosmos might have recourse to Greek oracles, sacrifice to Greek or Roman or other gods, commune with divinities associated with new or modified national worship practices like that of the recently hellenised Egyptian cult of Isis. One might be a Jew, and there is evidence of the spreading of the Jewish religion in the establishment of synagogues in many cities of the now-Roman world. There were atheists. There were followers of the philosophy of Epicurus, who acknowledged the possibility of the existence of gods but denied their significance for human affairs. There were followers of the religious philosophy of Stoicism, who believed, in the words of one of their writers, that the cosmos, organized according to reason and providence, was "a living being, rational, alive and intelligent,"[1] and they might accept divination and call on Zeus as the unique ruler of all existence, himself the reason, or *logos*, that informed all creation, including the lesser gods.

Into this mix came Jesus and his followers. Most writers I have read accept the "real" historical existence of a "Jesus" whose life and ministry provided the basis for the texts we know as the Christian testament. Again, there are great divergencies in contemporary interpretation of these Christian texts, with major disagreeements as to what information is "historical" or which sayings and ideas of Jesus belonged to the actual figure of history. The challenge can even extend to denying the objective reality of Jesus, seeing the texts as deliberately fashioned in forgery and fraud to create out of myth what was then alleged to be a true narrative, so that "the Christian story itself, which most likely began as a kind of spiritual drama, together with a 'sayings' source based upon the Egyptian material, was turned into a form of history in which the Christ of the myth became a flesh-and-blood person identified with Jesus (Yeshua or Joshua) of Nazareth."[2] Many, including myself, will regard this interpretation of the texts as extreme, but it illustrates the possibilities, particularly when an attempt is made either to validate or deny validation to the texts on the basis of their historical veracity. In any case, through the centuries, it seems to me, interpretation has been based on the meaning of the texts for an understanding of the nature of Jesus and God, with an assumption of a historical core to the story of Jesus. The doctrinal arguments have focused on differing views of the real nature of divinity and also on what the historical truth of Jesus' ministry might have been. As in the case of Hebrew Scripture, Christian texts have come down from ancient through mediaeval time to modern to influence society and public culture as well as personal actions. My own orientation as a non-Christian leaves me more open to non-religious interpretations: personal, scholarly, anthropological reading rather than statements of received truth by religious leaders. It is with that point of view I tell the history as I see it, and narrate a Christian story that I believe to have been at the heart of a great deal of Christian interpretation and narrative

In the first century of the common era, Palestine, known to the Roman administration as Judaea, was the scene of disturbances of a religious nature that prompted reaction on the part of Roman emperors and their administrators. In Jesus' time, the Roman emperor was the authority accepted by the Romans and the provincials. At the start of Roman administration, Augustus, the first Roman ruler we designate as emperor, controlled Judaea through a local Jewish king, Herod the Great. Herod built lavishly and worked largely within a Hellenic mold, celebrating quadrennial games of the Greek type in his new city of Caesarea and in Jerusalem as well. He maintained peace in the kingdom, despite conflict with Jewish religious leaders, and received for his efforts additional territories along the borders of Judaea. In Jerusalem he built a new temple to provide focus for Jewish worship, and part of that building, which was destroyed in the Jewish War of 70 CE, still remains as the venerated Wailing Wall in Jerusalem.

Herod's reign came to an end amidst quarrels and bitterness between him and his wives and sons, so grievous that Augustus once remarked that he would "rather be one of Herod's pigs than one of his sons."[3] On his death in 4 BCE, the realm was split among three remaining sons, once again leaving the Jewish territories under divided administration. In the shifts of administration that came after, Roman procurators administered

Judea for the thirty-five years that saw the life and crucifixion of Jesus under the fifth procurator, Pontius Pilate, who during his term of office used miltary forces to confront many disruptions in Judaea. Just about the time of Pilate's appointment in 26 CE, there was a general strike in Jerusalem protesting the appearance in Jerusalem of Roman standards with the image of the Emperor Tiberius on them. Pilate removed them, choosing the more conciliatory route rather than killing the offending Jews, an action that might have provoked a more serious rebellion in the province. Other incidents came, ultimately producing Pilate's recall, and the next procurator, appointed by the Emperor Gaius, had to deal with more trouble, and the emperor himself almost provoked a serious incident when he ordered a huge statue of himself set up in the temple of Jerusalem.

There were religious factions among the Jews of the time, according to the later writer Josephus, who wrote a number of works in Greek dealing with the society and history of the Jews in this period. There were the ascetic Essenes, about four thousand of them, as well as Pharisees, Sadducees and proponents of the so-called "Fourth Philosophy." According to Josephus, he investigated the matter and began "following the system of the Pharisees, which was nearest to that called the Stoic by the Greeks."[4] Josephus presents the Pharisees as the dominant faction, and his comments, probably tendentious, have been pressed to yield what scholars seek to know about any opponents of Jesus, so his claim that the Jews followed the system of the Pharisees is usually accepted in the interpretation of New Testament statements. As a result, the Jews of Jesus' time are often seen as they appear in Josephus' description: the Pharisees, not literalists, accepted and expanded upon an oral tradition of interpretation of scriptural texts, while the Sadducees accepted the Law as made explicit in scripture.

The "Fourth Philosophy" was a sentiment that led the Jews into their disastrous revolt in the last third of the first century, and Josephus does not discuss it very much from his safe position among the Romans. The leadership of that group centered in Galilee, a district in which Josephus was appointed to a military command in the later war, and in which Jesus spent most of his three and a half years of ministry. The tenacity of this attitude among some of the Jews of Judaea illustrates the manner in which scriptural authority influenced political behavior, so that the revolutionaries expected success in their assault on a ruler of overwhelming material superiority. Jewish literature and tradition asserted that the Covenant with Abraham assured the Jews that ultimately they would prevail over their enemies and rule in their land. Defeats, destructions, deportations and the like arose not from an imbalance in the power relationship between Jews and others but from the Jews' own failure to follow the Lord's rules.

The different philosophies reported by Josephus were probably not known or debated much in the countless little hamlets and villages throughout the countryside, maintaining their Jewish life far from the temple cult in Jersualem. Life in the villages, with their squat, almost windowless houses, was the same agricultural life of herdsmen and farmers that had served the Jews of the time of the writing down of the laws in the books of Leviticus and Deuteronomy. The Jews of Galilee to whom Jesus brought his message were much like the Israelites of the time of Abraham, Isaac and Jacob, of David, Solomon, and Isaiah. The cities were different however. Not only in Jerusalem but in the thriving and prosperous centers of Caesaria in Samaria and Tiberias in Galilee, many city Jews followed Hellenic patterns to a significant extent. Greek civic gymnasia, temples and public buildings co-existed with synagogues, many Jews conducted their lives in Greek, and Josephus mentions Jewish contemporaries with abilities like his own. The court of Herod and the capital cities of his sons used the Greek language, and the port of Caesarea did the same. And of course, alongside the Hellenized and non-Hellenized Jews were the Greek-speaking non-Jewish inhabitants whose religious life followed the many diverse patterns of the different religions of the times.

The diversity of Jewish life and the progress of Hellenization made for variety and conflict among the Jews of Jesus' time. Rural Jews kept to the old ways, for the most part; prophets repeatedly appeared. One came from Egypt and led crowds into the desert until repression came from the Roman government. Another, Herod Antipas killed: John the Baptist, whom the Christians made a precursor of Jesus.

Jesus himself had a following of more permanence than John the Baptist. Josephus does not tell us much about Jesus or his followers, but the crucifixion itself was noted enough to prompt a mention in Tacitus' account of the times,[5] if the passage in the *Annals* is genuine.[6] There is little apart from the Gospel accounts themselves to cast light on the lives of the Jews, of Jesus, and of the Jews who followed him in his own lifeime or in the years immediately following the crucifixion. These Gospels, however, were written as documents of proselytization, to justify and explain the faith. They were not contemporary accounts of what happened by dispassionate observers, and they were written some decades after the crucifixion. To some readers, they were taken as things done and said; for others, they guided the steps along the road Jesus had taken. In the lifetime of Jesus himself and in the years immediately after his death, the followers saw the events and the accounts of them as extensions in time of the prophetic words and actions Jews had experienced from the time of Jeremiah. As I read the Gospels, they primarily set out and clarify Jesus' warning of the coming last days – the same warning as Jeremiah had given – repeated now because the end was imminent. This prediction about the coming of the Kingdom of God had long stood in Judaism, and there was nothing heretical in believing it, so that the Jews who followed Jesus were those who were convinced that God's promise for Israel was about to come true. Even the writings in Greek for those who might never have encountered this Jewish belief carry Jesus' proclamation of the last days as a fundamental part of the message.

Jesus preached his message for only a short time, probably only in the years 28 and 29 in Galilee, then in Jerusalem in 30. The Galileans who received his message were mostly country people from the north, and none of his immediate followers seem to have been the Hellenized Jews of the urban areas. The Gospels, in fact, try to stress the point that they were ordinary working people. This following of Jesus seems to have been a group different from any of those noted by Josephus, not aligned to any of the defined groups. They were Jews following a charismatic leader, and they conducted in Jewish terms any debates among themselves as they settled into life as their martyred leader's disciples. Conflict between them and other groups – Sadducees, Pharisees or priests – focused on their acceptance of Jesus' message of the coming kingdom of God and the life and preparations needed to enter therein. They were actively carrying their message to other Jews.

Within a decade they carried their message beyond Jersualem and then even outside Palestine to Jews who had settled among the Greeks and Romans. In the Egyptian port city of Alexandria there were many Jews, and had been for a long time. The community in Rome was large enough in Jesus' time to have built a large synagogue, the ruins of which still stand near the airport at Fumicino. From the numerous Jewish inhabitants of the eastern city of Tarsus came Saul, a thoroughly Hellenized Pharisee born with Roman citizenship, who later experienced conversion and under the name Paul became a leading exponent of the message of Jesus. Paul's words were not, for the most part, accepted by many Jews, even though the proclamation of the kingdom of God had been part of Jewish tradition. His letters were now addressed to members of particular assemblies of followers in Greek cities, as well as to non-Christian Jews. On their part, Christians rejected much of the familiar approaches to religion practiced by first-century Jews, apart from continuing the assertion of the coming kingdom of God. The Christians never considered the literalism of the Sadducees, and the Gospel accounts made the Pharisees into Jesus' enemies. Then, they early abandoned any connection between the coming kingdom and a revival of the political kingdom of David, so they had nothing in common with the "Fourth Philosophy" and took no apparent part in the great revolt of 66-70.

Even the ascetic movements attracted only some of the Christians. The elaborate structure of rules formulated for Jews by texts like the Mishnah after the destruction of the Temple in 70, whereby the Jews could serve God through self-regulation, had no impact on Christian behavior, which approached the Father God through the intermediation of the Son. Finally, after the subsequent renewal and defeat of revolt by Bar Kochba, the Jews came to tems with the changed situation, while the new Christians went their separate way. But even before the revolt of 66, things had been changing, and the destruction of the Temple served as a kind of seal separating the groups, Jews from Christians, Jews from Greeks. By this time, there were congregations of followers of Jesus in a number of Greek cities outside Palestine, and we can find in the letters of Paul the evidence of an attempt to regularize the concepts that were being disseminated among them. St. Paul's letters are, in fact, the earliest statements of what Jesus' followers thought of Jesus' life and the events that followed the crucifixion, and they must be taken with the Gospels to understand the ideas of the early Christians. The complexity of understanding the texts of the Christian testament is illustrated by the relationship between Paul's letters and the story in Acts of the Apostles, since certain "historical" events mentioned in Acts as coming before Paul's activity must in fact have followed that.

    The documents of the Christian Scriptures became legitimized and regarded as sacred by a process that began with the writing of a record of what some Christians believed had happened, some two generations after Jesus died on the cross. There is a fairly general modern consensus that the Gospels presented as written by those who knew Jesus come, in fact from writing of the last third of the first century. Three of them, Matthew, Mark and Luke, the "synoptic" Gospels, so-called because of their potential of being viewed together, are interrelated in some ways, while the fourth, John, represents not only a different tradition but emerged somewhat later than the other three. Many modern students of the texts also believe that a number of the letters attributed to Paul were written by others, and some also argue that the letters of John are not all the work of the same hand that wrote the Gospel. Added to the difficulty of penetrating through the texts to some kind of "historical reality" is the controversy and difficulty of assessing the nature of the sources used by the Gospel writers, the compiler of the Acts of the Apostles (actually a continuation of the Gospel of Luke), and such works as the genuine letters of St. Paul, agreed by most commentators to predate the composition of any of the Gospels.

Not only the composition of the texts is strung through a half century or more of developing Christian life; there was also debate among the early Christians about the validity of texts – not only those of the Christian testament we know today, but a great variety of texts regarded by Christians as non-canonical, without the authority of the accepted texts. Works like *The Shepherd of Hermas* and the *Gospel of Thomas* were composed in this period, but were rejected in favor of the accounts of Jesus in the now-canonical texts. There continued to be dispute about this, and there was even a movement at one point to reject most of the Gospel testimony to create a consistent account from a single Gospel. On top of this is the awareness, certainly today and probably even in early times, that the Gospels were all composed in Greek,[7] something that might be seen to bear on their nature as testimony. The resolution of the debates about the authenticity of texts resulted in a canon of accounts of the life of Jesus that contains interpretations often mutually inconsistent factually and ideologically and make it difficult, if not impossible, to reconstruct not only the "facts" of Jesus life and ministry, but of the beliefs and conceptions of it by his immediate followers of the early church. In order to resolve the questions we may have about the "primitive" church, we would have to resolve satisfactorily the question of what is early and what is late in the Gospels, the story in Acts and in the various apostolic letters. On decisions about these matters depends judgement on what was said and done by Jesus and the early apostles.

I have little doubt that much of what is said today on some of these matters is correct, at least in general terms. It seems to be right to interpret the texts to conceive of a division of the early Christians between the "Judaizers" who believed they should adhere to the Mosaic laws and those who believed the message of Jesus allowed most of the Law's details to be abandoned. The genuine letters of Paul explicate not only his own theology but shed a great deal of light on emerging Christian concepts. But I do not believe that we can devise a valid account, at least in detail, of what Jesus said and did and thought during the two or three years of his ministry, and I view with caution the contemporary studies that claim to have sifted through the material identifying the "genuine" sayings. Nor do I have much confidence in the reconstructions in detail of the development of the early church or the views and actions of the apostles during the two decades after the crucifixion, the period of the so-called "primitive" Christianity. Too much happened in those vibrant years, there was too much debate, too many historical, theological and doctrinal issues resolved or left moot before the time when the first writings we have – the letters of St. Paul and the earliest Gospel – to allow for much firm assertion about the ideas of the time. Thus, while I am sympathetic with the reformist goals of feminist writers like Elisabeth Schüssler Fiorenza, I am not convinced that the evidence permits a reconstruction of the relationship between Jesus and the disciples to confirm that "from their very beginning early Christian community and life did not conform to the patriarchal ethos and structures of their own society and religion ... reform movements within Judaism that stressed the gracious goodness of the Sophia-Creator God who wants the wholeness of everyone in Israel without exception."[8]

So I believe that there is not much we really know about Jesus, the apostles and the Christian movement until about the last quarter of the first century. But then the Gospels emerge, at the earliest in the decade before the destruction of the Temple in

70, and more probably, after that. From then on we have the body of texts that, once the canon was established, became the fixed statements that Christians referred to in understanding their faith, and struggled with to resolve perceived contradictions and understand and infuse meaning into the story of Jesus. These are the texts that influenced the development of the Christian world. Together with the Hellenic texts I have already discussed, and in fact itself influenced by them, the Christian testament made its impact on the world and still largely frames the relation to the religious world of many modern writers and thinkers, moralists, and as we have learned, politicians.

---

[1] Diogenes Laertius VII, 142-3; cf. 138.

[2] Harpur (2004) p. 12.

[3] A pun on the close similarity of the Greek words for "son" and "pig."

[4] Josephus, *The Life* 12.

[5] *Annals* XCV, 44 (see next note) mentions that the Christians, blamed by Nero for the fire at Rome, took their name from the Christ executed by Pontius Pilate during the reign of Tiberius.

[6] Tacitus' mention of the crucifixion, and the references in Josephus, have been challenged as later interpolations by some modern scholars, but the texts have existed for a long time to establish for believers the historicity of the Jesus story.

[7] Greek is conceded as the language of composition of the Gospels by almost all students, and the argument that Mark was a translation from Aramaic is, I believe, a minority view today.

[8] Fiorenza (1993) pp. 219-20.

"YOU ARE NOT ALONE"

–15–
Saving Humanity

As I approached the writing of this chapter, I felt a deficiency, a lack of empathy for the religious and theological approach to trying to solve human problems. As I expressed my sense of bafflement in a letter to a friend and colleague, "I think my inability to empathize with the approaches the West has taken to these texts has to do with my upbringing. God was a non-issue in my family. God did not play a large role in my thought or my life. I called myself agnostic, if anyone asked, not because I had a religious view, but because I was not interested enough to think about it." Now, I am interested. One way I tried to make up for this perceived lack was to read a lot of the work of contemporary feminist theologians, whose perceptions of the needs and goals of society seemed much like my own, but who seemed to want to preserve a relation to both Jewish and Christian Scripture that so often militates against fulfilling those needs and reaching those goals. There were two major different approaches to the Bible that seemed to me relevant to the manner in which I am trying to treat texts; one is the effort to reinterpret the texts to make them useful and meaningful in a world with values very different from those that appear in the Bible; the other is a forthright rejection of the biblical texts as authoritative.[1]

Many of the texts feminists struggle with, notably the story of the creation of humanity in Genesis, come from the Hebrew Scriptures, but there are many issues among the Christian documents as well. The prescriptions of Paul against the participation of women in church activity are cases in point. The concerns are as valid as those directed to the Hebrew texts, and I will refer to some of the issues below. However, one of the strongest and most consistent of the ideas running through the texts of the Christian Testament, the concept of the impending arrival of the Kingdom of God, seems to me to affect the patriarchal and androcentric weight of the writing less than many of the texts.

The Gospels repeatedly recount Jesus' warning that life as it was being lived was about to end. His warnings, exhortations and explanation of the life to be lived in the face of the change remained current for at least a generation, as the First Letter of Peter sets the time of writing as "the end of the ages."[2] That letter, attributed by different scholars to different writers, and datd variously from the middle of the first century to the beginning of the second, shows that whatever date in the period one chooses, for some time after Jesus' death some Christians were still expecting the kingdom to arrive. The Revelation of John shows that the idea persisted at least to the end of the first century.

This apocalyptic vision, that the world as it had so far existed was about to come to an end with the arrival of the Kingdom of God, had found room in Jewish thought for at least two centuries. Works contemporary with the composition of the

Christian books, Baruch 2 and Ezra 4, show it in Jewish terms, and the doctrine was preached by John the Baptist before Jesus. For Christians, however, the concept was strikingly different. In the first place, it was not a political message, in the sense that the end would bring about the fulfilment of the promise to Abraham of a political kingdom. Then too, it was a belief fundamental to Christian thought, because it was connected with Christ's role in its proclamation, organization and salvation of the living and the dead. For Christians, Jesus' message gave them hope for the present, in that they could remake their lives to make them eligible for inclusion in the coming kingdom. To the writer of Revelation, the "beast" – Rome, Nero or whatever – was the agent of the Evil One, in slaughtering some of the virtuous and seducing others. Those who stood fast, however, would be rewarded, as the thundering destruction of the existing world would mark God's victory over the forces of evil to bring about a new heaven and a new earth in which would stand the new Jerusalem.

While the events in Revelation are similar to those described in Baruch, Ezra and Daniel, the writer gives the faithful hope by making Christ their ally, with the possibility of personal victory coming with the universal victory of God. The writer makes the "beast" and Satan not God's agents but the enemies of God and the faithful in Christ. This distinction is implicit in the Gospels as well, with Jesus' exhortations and the basic concept of God's plan in the Sermon on the Mount, as Jesus urges his followers to abandon their concern with the things of this world and emulate the lilies of the field:

> Not everyone saying to me "Lord, Lord," will enter the kingdom of the heavens, but the one doing the wish of my father in the heavens. Many will say to me on that day,

"Lord, Lord, did we not make prophecies in your name, and in your name did we not cast out demons, and in your name did we not do many miracles?" And then I shall say plainly to them, "I never knew you; go off from me, workers of wickedness."

Everyone then, who hears these words of mine and does what they say will be like the thoughtful man who built his house on rock. And the rain fell and the rivers rose and the winds blew and fell upon that house, and it did not fall, because it was established on rock. And everyone hearing these words of mine and does not do what they say will be like the foolish man who built his house on sand. And the rain fell and the rivers rose and the winds blew and struck that house, and it fell, and its fall was great.[3]

The words to which Jesus refers are the moral and ethical exhortations of the Sermon on the Mount, words to be taken not as a call to make this world better but for the believers to reform themselves so that they will be able to enter the new Jerusalem.

Jesus asserted that the end would come before all those to whom he was speaking had "fallen asleep," that is, before they all died. But all the hearers died and still the end did not arrive, and it became necessary to interpret the words. There were answers like that in the Second Letter to Peter, explaining "that one day for the Lord is just as a thousand years, and a thousand years are just as one day."[4] But this justification of the text, asserting that the delay allowed time for repentance, was later than the other texts of the Christian Testament – it probably was penned at the end of the second century – and its presence in the official canon shows that the issue of the impending Kingdom of God remained an important part of mainline Christianity.

The apocalyptic vision made Christ essential to the salvation of the faithful; other themes in the early Christian books developed particular roles for Jesus in Christian concepts. Beyond specific items of dogma like the virgin birth or miracles, which are easier to believe as an act of will or faith than it is to follow the prescriptions for behavior in the sermons, there are peculiarly Christian aspects of Jesus that appear as early as Paul's letters. Christ exhibits an ambiguity permitting a whole range of conceptualizations of him: as human; as God; as intermediary between God and humans; as spirit; as God's logos; as resurrected flesh; as savior. Whether or not all these were known to the early apostles, all emerge from the earliest writings, and all had their impact on later thought and belief. There was a continued debate and an exploration and interpreting of the texts to establish for Christians the meaning of Jesus' life on earth. The desire to understand – and then to require conformity to an understanding of – Christ's nature created a great deal of Christological speculation and focused attention on the Christ-figure. Ultimately a doctrinal resolution emerged in the formulation of the Trinity, with consubstantiation of God and Christ and the Holy Spirit, and the determination to define this nature in Trinity came from the problem of understanding the Jesus of the Gospels and apostles.

It has been argued that the early church evinced a non-hierarchical structure at the outset. However likely or unlikely may have been the "equality of discipleship,"[5] at least for women, in the early church, the need for resolution of disagreements was quickly felt, and the first of whom we know to take the lead in asserting authority was St. Paul. Modern sympathizers with the ethical pronouncement of Jesus but hostile to the power and theology of the church as it later emerged often lay on Paul the responsibility for aspects of Christian theology they do not like. The complaint has only to recommend it that it obviates the need to wrestle with Paul's difficult and often ambiguous Greek. Paul's authority was accepted later, for he wrote as an organizer, concerned to assert authority as an aid to the salvation of the faithful, and he did no more than countless theologians who followed him. The very act of interpreting texts can be an act of authority, and as, over the centuries, interpretations of the texts multiply, so too multiplied the efforts to restrain belief in assertions about God and Christ that the leaders of the churches believed wrong.

The wider, Greek-speaking world to which Paul's letters penetrated had much in common with this Hellenized Jew from Tarsus. His choice of language, along with the language choice of the Gospel writers – Greek – meant that however Jewish the ideas of Paul and the others might have been, expressing their ideas in Greek rather than Hebrew or Aramaic inevitably bent it to Hellenic meanings, an illustration of McLuhan's dictum, "the medium is the message," but at a deeper level. Paul took concepts of Judaism that would have been understood by the Jewish followers of Jesus and used words in Greek to convey them. Greeks familiar with mystery religions as well as Jews would understand what was meant by *soter*, "savior"; so too would they comprehend *pneuma* which we translate "spirit" but which in Greek was close also to our meaning of the word "breath. The concept of conversion was known, while other of Paul's concepts, that the redeemer Christ still lived and appeared to people by the action of the *pneuma*, that the *pneuma* was in some way both part of and independent of God, that Christ passed to individual humans the grace that freed from sin – these ideas were difficult for Jews and Gentiles alike.

The difficulty of these concepts explains why Paul wrote of them again and again, but they were not the only ideas in the letters. He called members of the churches to the moral behavior often called the "Christian virtues" and rallied them to the Law which was to be summarized by the command "Love thy neighbor as thyself,"[6] and called on them to clothe themselves "in feelings of pity, kindness, humility, gentleness, patience and over all these, love, which is the unifying bond of completeness,"[7] and to "love one another and the whole human race."[8] Many modern readers draw attention to the failure of many Christian individuals and many Christian institutions and churches to follow these injunctions, and insist that they were observed more in their breach than followed. This may be true, but Paul cannot be faulted for that, any more than he can be blamed for the notorious command that wives be subservient to husbands[9] in a text almost surely not written by him. Nor is it Paul insisting on the final and New Covenant making Christ's death a sacrifice to cancel the sins of the times before his coming, replacing the old covenant, concepts enunciated in Hebrews, a text probably written at the beginning of the second century.

These texts, and the ideas in them, were given authority as they were incorporated in the canon of authoritative texts that included the Gospels. Those accounts of Jesus' ministry began to appear in the four decades after Paul's last letter was composed. In three of them, the so-called synoptic or "viewable-together" Gospels, there is a common base of incidents and events, and even sometimes identical language, as they organize their stories along the same lines. The three are closely related, although not all modern interpreters agree on the nature of that relation. They all present themselves as first-hand narratives, histories of Jesus' life, teaching and death, and they provide the basis of the Christ story that has lasted to modern times as their legacy. But each has a different objective from the others, each has a different emphasis, and each is written in a different style. Mark is vivid and dramatic, in an abrupt and unclassical Greek that has led some modern readers to claim it is a work of translation. Matthew is carefully structured and has a style closer to classical Greek. Almost every incident in Mark can be found in Matthew, but with rearrangements, notably the pulling together of statements of Jesus into a single, coherent "Sermon on the Mount." Matthew also adds to Mark the long genealogy tracing Jesus' ancestry to David, tacitly making him a legitimate successor to the kings of Israel, and the text gives the story of Jesus' birth, the visit of the Magi, the unparalleled (in other Gospels) account of the flight into Egypt to save the child from the wicked designs of Herod. All this aids the Gospel writer in presenting Jesus as a lawgiver parallel to Moses; of course superior: Jesus the emissary of God brought a replacement of the Law in a manner even more miraculous than the story of Moses.

Quite apart from this focus, Matthew's account established belief in the virgin birth, in Jesus' descent from David, the stories of the Magi sent by Herod when he heard of the birth of the king of the Jews, and even the flight into Egypt, perhaps puzzling to early readers since it is a story missing from the fuller account of Jesus' infancy in Luke. Some of Matthew's variations are minor, but some, even short passages, are of great theological importance, as in the addition to the words in Mark, "For this is my blood of the covenant, which is poured out for many," Matthew adds the vital concept "for release of sins." And the grand scale of the composition of the Sermon on the Mount combines the ethical heart of Christianity with the fundamental assertion of the impending Last Days. Here are injunctions based on the Mosaic code, combined with an emphasis on gentleness, mercy and forgiveness. Here Jesus' words command the choice between God and money, the injunction to store up treasures not on earth but in heaven, with the psychological insight "for where your treasure is, there will your heart be also."[10] All the moral prescribing is interwoven with instructions for prayer, to create a single, all-inclusive statement of Jesus' preaching, a great outpouring of human self-idealization that still stands to tantalize Christians who believe they represent valid standards for human conduct.

The third of the synoptic Gospels, Luke, while corresponding in broad terms to the other two, is very different in approach. In excellent Greek with a proper classical introduction, it is made up of the earlier sections of a longer work on the history of the church completed as a separate history entitled Acts of the Apostles. The two works, Luke and Acts, cohere to present an account of Jesus' life and teaching and the subsequent reception of teaching and preaching authority of the apostles. For example, in Luke, the story of Jesus' apearance after the crucifixion is very different from that in Matthew: after two disciples see Jesus and go off to Jerusalem to tell the others, Jesus appears and frightens them, as he insists on his corporeality. "A ghost has not flesh and bones," Jesus says, presenting his hands and feet to their touch. "Do you have anything here to eat?" he asks, and eats a grilled fish as proof of his corporeality. The Gospel leaves no doubt that the resurrection was in the flesh, and the appearance to the apostles is a sign of their authority. They go off to Bethany, and the story is picked up in Acts when Jesus promises them they will receive the power from the Holy Spirit. The promise is fulfilled when the Holy Spirit comes to validate the apostles' preaching and dissemination of God's message, coming to them as they are gathered in one room:

There was suddenly from the heaven a sound like the force of a driving wind, and it filled the whole house where they were sitting, and separating tongues as if of fire appeared to them, and settled down on each one of them. And they all were filled with the Holy Spirit [*pneuma*] and they began to speak in other tongues, just as the spirit [*pneuma*] gave them the ability to speak.

The text presented by Luke and Acts weaves theology into the account with the effect that the narrative justifies doctrine. The apostles in Acts call people to the same repentence and mercy as Jesus did, and with the story of the Jews resisting in stubbornness, Paul in sadness more than anger is forced to turn from the synagogue to the pagans. The story as told justifies the authority – and force – later exercised by the church, and contains more than just the kernels of attitudes that in succeeding centuries and millennia would generate dispute and unrest among Christians and in Christian dispute with others.

The last of the four Gospels preserved in the canon is John, so different from the other three that it is always classed and considered separately from them. It is not a matter of the synoptic Gospels giving a more "historical" account, even if they seem to do so by the more narrative nature of their account, but that the fourth Gospel, John, presents an essentially different picture. The locale is diffferent – Judaea for most of the story instead of Galilee – and the time implied by the number of passovers is longer, perhaps as much as four years. Jesus, rather than being the gentle shepherd of Luke or Matthew or the moral preacher of the synoptic Gospels, is more remote, a god-like figure, Word made flesh but not quite human flesh. For example, at the end, Jesus' last words on the cross are not the agonized "My God, my God, why have you deserted me?" of Mark and

Matthew, mentioned in Luke as a cry coming immediately before the final words "Father, into your hands I place my spirit. [*pneuma*]." Even those words are too human for the portrait of John. Jesus says, "I am thirsty," in order to fulfil scriptural prophecy, and his last words are the detached observation, "It is finished."

John is also much more Hellenic than the other Gospels, sharing many of the Greek philosophical notions of the first century, and affected by abstractions like the *logos*. The "holy infant so tender and mild," on which much of the Christmas story rests, becomes an abstract logos without human birth, from a virgin or anything else, but is simply "made flesh." And from Prologue on, John portrays a Jesus deliberately, unflinchingly and fully knowing, proceeding toward the denoument on the cross. John the Baptist knows in advance of "the lamb of God that takes away the sins of the world,"[11] and Jesus tells Nicodemus that "Thus God so loved the cosmos so that he gave his only begotten son, so that every person believing in him might not perish but might have eternal life,"[12] and repeats in parable and metaphor: "I am the bread of life"; "I am the resurrection"; "I am the Way, the Truth and the Life."[13] And the words John gives to Christ have a fully developed doctrine of the Eucharist, as Jesus more than once speaks of himself as spiritual food, and provides meat and drink for the future transubstantiation debate. The Jesus passing human understanding, who can say "Truly indeed, I say to you, before Abraham existed, I am," is a metaphysical view of reality beyond human experience, more comprehensible to Greeks with a Platonic background than Jews firmly rooted in Hebrew Scripture.

John's Christology gave the world not so much a messenger of God announcing the imminent end of the world and arrival of God's kingdom, but the eternal existent *logos*-Son of God. Often viewed by Christian believers as an account on a deeper level of meaning than the other Gospels, as a result its sometimes conflict of narrative could be dismissed. John contributed a mystical, symbolic and metaphorical interpretation of Christ to stand alongside the literal interpretation, an approach which might sometimes be considered heretical when stated openly, but could always be the basis of private faith. So too, matching the First Letter of John, the Gospel of John makes the same references to the logos existing from the beginning, the same exhortations to the Christian community to guard agains sin, and in the same way as the Letter, focuses on love: love of God for Jesus, Jesus for his people, the people for God, Jesus and one another, a perception that has survived the concentrations of other canonical texts on salvation and the apocalypse, and even the actions of churches and preachings of clerics, to provide an alternative vision of Christ for those alienated by churches and dogma.

    The body of Christian texts, once accepted as the approved literature for the early church, progressively took on authority until it was regarded as revealed truth. That the texts were in Greek meant inevitably that Christian discussions should be framed in the context of Greek thought to present ideas in the philosophical and religious language of Hellenism. As time passed, and the kingdom of God did not arrive on an earth not yet ended, essentially non-Hellenic aspects of Christian thought took on a Greek, even Platonic cast as salvation was more and more seen as an elevation to God's higher existence. The influence of Hellenic modes of thought shows in the appearance of many Greek philosophical ideas in early Christian texts, and perhaps most striking, we can see the influence of Plato more vivid and influential in Christian philosophy as Christian writers discounted the importance of this world in confronting preparations for the next. Slaves remain slaves, masters their rulers, and the authority of temporal powers stays in place. For entirely different reasons than the search for harmony characteristic of Confucian texts, the Christian social order allowed for the same hierarchal, stable and authoritarian regime supported by the Chinese texts.

Within this core of the ideas of the Christian canon were the seeds of many beliefs and attitudes, which grew along many different lines. Christian gnosticism was rooted here, and so too the loving treatment and feeding of the poor for which Christians became known in late antiquity. Salvation in and through Christ, understandable to so many familiar with Hellenic mysteries that promised merging with the god, gradually developed into a complex doctrine of life after death that neither Greeks nor Jews would have recognized in Jesus' time. One idea that had begun to emerge in late Greek ethics, and which might have been seen to be validated by Christian doctrines of the soul, has left only traces in the texts of the Christian testament. The principle of the basic equality of all humans to which the Roman philosopher-statesman Cicero alluded and supported to some extent, and was also endorsed by some of the later Stoics, has little emphasis in the early Christian writers. Even though Christians might conclude that all souls were equal in God's love, the concept was not developed in theology and certainly not carried into social philosophy. Apart from the assertion in the Letter of James that the members of Christian churches should not despise the lower and poorer members of their synagogues, social equality was not a behest found in the texts that became canonical.

There may have been, however, equality among the early Christians that was suppressed by the patriarchal orientation of the leaders. Elisabeth Schüssler Fiorenza's feminist exploration of the texts insists that in the suppression of reports of the work of women, most of the evidence of the equality of discipleship has been lost.[14] She argues for interpretation of the texts to correct this invisibility and for finding in the Christian writings support for a "church of women" that is not only a historical characteristic of Christianity but a force for overthrowing all kinds of oppression in the present and for the future: "The 'discipleship of equals,' then, should not be understood as a founding, finished event but a constant call and an ongoing process which has yet to bear its fullest fruit."[15] The discipleship of equals, however, as a possible force in the early church and a theme looking forward to a world in which the oppressed might have hope for this life, was not an influence on the dominant leaders – perhaps in the first instance because it did not seem a very important matter in view of the impending end of this world. Then, as time passed and the leadership became more and more concerned with regulation of Christian life in this world, the definition of ethical behavior responded more to the words of Jesus and the apostles than to a theoretical and not very prominent construct of Greek philosophy – or the yielding of wealth, power and authority to the women, slaves and poor.

For the most part, the texts remain even today as support for the dominators of society, usually not read as feminists propose them to be reinterpreted to radically change the world of their readers. I think that most who give authority to the Christian texts today regard them as guides to salvation and a life with God after death. In that interpetation, I believe, they are not so far from the comprehension of Jesus' ministry by his contemporaries and immediate followers. Many others, however, prefer to place greater emphasis on Jesus' moral and ethical preachments, rejecting the emphasis on faith over good works, but that position fails to acknowledge the force of the texts that insist upon the doctrine of sin and its redemption through Christ, the apocalyptic pronouncements, the assumption of an eternal reality on a different plane from that of existence, the denigration of flesh and the senses, the assertion of authority.

All these stand in the texts, even though they may not have been in the genuine messages of Jesus. As early as we know it, Christianity absorbed the long-standing hostility to the everyday world, that world accessible to the senses and significant to the body, that had been one of the threads that made up the fabric of Hellenism. That aspect of thought which was so much a part of the philosophy of Plato, and had survived the onslaughts of the science of Aristotle and the materialism of Epicurus to lodge even in Stoicism, had an even more vital role to play in Christianity. The early Christian texts may have received this orientation through Hellenized Judaism or may have got it direct in the creation of the first Christian texts, but they were molded by it. For almost a thousand years thereafter, the central concerns of writers – thinkers, politicians, theologians whose words have been preserved in later texts – would not be the things of this world and what could be understood and done about them, but the nature of the next world and how a person could fare well in it.

It is obvious to me, as I consider what I have written here, not only how different these concepts are from my own attitudes toward the world, but how strikingly they differ from my understanding of the Hebrew tradition. Even more, they seem to me to bespeak almost a different universe from that inhabited by the Chinese. In that eastern tradition, there are no texts that represent absolute truth in the manner of the Gospels and the Christian scriptures; there is no figure like that of Jesus, nor any prescriptions for a means of living in order to provide a happy life in another world. There are no other worlds, in Confucian thought, and even Buddhist or Daoist mystery does not provide for the denigration of the body, the exaltation of "soul" that Christian doctrine accepts. There is not even a "God" of the nature of the Hebrew and Christian traditions, nor a supreme entity of the sort proposed by later Hellenic mysticism.[16]

What many writers see in Confucianism as "humanism" makes the Confucian attitudes attractive to me and many others in my own society who have no commitment to the truth of the Scriptures. But it is also true that the absence of authoritative texts that require belief materially affects the whole notion of objective truth and its comprehension, an attitude that has driven so much of thought and philosophy and science in the cultures derived from the Greek-Hebrew-Christian tradition.[17] The texts with the Hellenic-Hebrew-Christian modes of thought not only allow for the existence of a truth, however learned; they demand its pursuit. They encourage the dogged determination to eliminate what is perceived as error, encouraging what many see as a deleterious aspect of that tradition. That determination to pursue truth also, however, has had the benefit of encouraging a scientific exploration of reality.

---

[1] These may be contrasted in two essays in (1995) *Feminist Approaches to the Bible*, the first by Phyllis Trimble, "Eve and Miriam," the second by Pamela Milne, "No Promised Land: Rejecting the Authority of the Bible."
[2] Peter 1: 20.
[3] Matthew 7:21-7.
[4] 2 Peter 3:8-9.
[5] Asserted by Elizabeth Schüssler Fiorenza in e.g. (1984) p. 183 n. 21; (1998) pp. 112-14; 119-120. Her argument for equality of women in the early church, set out in "You Are Not to be Called Father: Early Christian History in a Feminist Perspective," in (1993) pp. 151-179, leads me to the assumption that the equality proposed would extend to men as well.
[6] Galatians 5:14.
[7] Colossians 3: 12-14.
[8] 1 Thessalonians 3: 12.

[9] in Ephesians 5: 22-4.
[10] Matthew 7: 21.
[11] John 1: 20.
[12] John 3: 16-17.
[13] John 6: 35; 11: 25; 14: 6.
[14] Fiorenza, *inter alia* in (1983); (1984); (1992); (1996).
[15] Jobling (2002) p. 59.
[16] Jullien (2000) pp. 303-4, comparing neoplatonism with Taoism, : "At the outset the problem appeared the same. Apropos of the ineffable from which everyting proceeds, Plotinus and Wang Bi, the Neoplatonist and the neo-Taoist, logically resort to the same paradox.... [but] on a subject so apparently universal as mysticism, thought remains attached to its cultural horizon. Among the Greeks, contemplation of the One passes obligatorily through predication (katagorein: even if it is to refuse any predication to the One), and this predication is developed on the basis of categories (which correspond in principle to the various cases of Indo-European languages), which can be found in the hypothesis in *Parmenides* and at the center of Aristotle's *organon*....To emerge from the impasse to which it is led by the impossibility of predication in relation to the One, Greek thought proceeds to a doubling of planes.... It is precisely this doubling of planes, through successive abstractions, that Chinese thought lacks....Thus the great image does not refer to a reality other than its own individual and concrete reality; but in detaching us from a particular character, it allows us to see the limitations and exclusivity of the individual and the concrete. It does not give us access to a hypostasis higher than it, but it liberates us from being bogged down. It gives us access to things that unfold spontaneously, as sources of immanence, in nature."
[17] Chan, ed. (2002) p. 75; Roger Ames, following Angus Graham, draws a distinction between Chinese thought and the styles of argumentation familiar in the West: "Dialectical dispute is driven by the possibility of certainty and is characteristic of people who would ask, What is the Truth? The 'art of accommodation' (*jianshu*) on the other hand is driven by a sense of melioration and is characteristic of people who, recognizing the performative and perlocutionary force of communication, would ask, How do we, harmoniously and productively, make our way together?"

–16–
The Great Chain of Being

As I proceed with this project, reading, thinking, talking about what I have been reading and thinking, and writing, I am often struck by how much I am learning about myself and how I became the collection of ideas and attitudes and values that I recognize as me. When I began reading translations of Chinese philosophy and discussions of Chinese philosophy, I encountered comments by western philosophers that there was no real philosophy among the Chinese, and observations that the great difference between the Chinese and western thought was a western preoccupation with the questions of being and essence, not given much attention by the Chinese. I missed the significance of all this until I began addressing the question of the fundamental relationship between Hellenic thought and religion and the cosmology behind Jewish and Christian thought, compared to the Chinese texts, which show the Chinese were "less concerned with cosmogony, or the origins of the cosmos, than with the comportment of human life within a universe that was not created just once but was continually generating and regenerating itself."[1]

The consensus of those who read and think about Greek philosophy makes the period from about 700 BCE to about 450 BCE (more or less Karl Jaspers' "axial period") one in which the basic thrust of Greek ideas first appears. As Jaspers did, most modern readers see these years for Greece as the great period in the formation of the western world; in Werner Jaeger's words, "Our history still begins with the Greeks."[2] The affirmative judgment on the accomplishment of the thinkers of this period are expressed unequivally by the Canadian Louis Dudek: "... the shift [from primitive to modern rational consciousness] happened only in Greece in this comprehensive way, and only there with the clarity and with the decisive effect on all future history that we know the west has had."[3] The shift, many students of Hellenism state, was a shift from mythological thinking to rational. The favorable assesment of "rational," of course, is a modern view and a modern value judgment.

However, shift or no, the focus of the attention of the earlier philosophers known as Presocratics seems to have been cosmological, and perhaps even more important, trained on the issue of identifying "what is real," in the belief that what is real can be discovered by humans and described in human terms. This, as my understanding develops the idea, is the major distinction between Greek and Hebrew cosmologies. And here lies, in Karl Popper's view of the world and science and knowledge, the major characteristic of the world-view of the tradition descended from Hellenism, an assumption of a "what is" as real. Even with human inability to do more than conjecture and hypthesize about it, the conjectures and hypotheses can be, as time goes on, better and better. Popper argues for the use of what he asserts as established by the Presocratics as "conjectural explanation. This, even if guided by intuition, always remains tentative, and contrasts with essentialist or ultimate explanation."[4] Popper asserts that "that only the first method, conjectural explanation, is valid, and feasible, while the second is just a will-o'-the'wisp."[5] In my view, Popper is a brilliant example of the tradition of knowledge and investigation which, from as early as we know western culture, focused on discovery of "what is," and I, as heir to that tradition, find my thoughts resonating with his insistence that there is something real, and objective, "out there," even if we shall never know it.

Students of Chinese philosophy claim that the Chinese did not and do not focus on such issues, and, in my judgment, neither do the texts of the Hebrew scriptures. And so, as I review the preceding chapters in pursuit of what History is "for," I ask myself how this confidence in and inquiry about what is "real" unites the unquestioned acceptance of the ineffable so strong in Hebrew thought with the assumption of the comprehensibility and accuracy of revelation that marks the centuries of the Christian texts. Does this union influence the attitudes and values of the modern world? The answers that come to me have to do with assertion, construction, and perhaps less desirable, hierarchy, and they call for some discussion of the earlier Greek philosophers dealing with "scientific" matters. As I proceeded to set out these ideas, I found that in an earlier attempt at an exposition of the development of my concepts after the publication of *The Promise of the West,* I had actually begun an exposition of the exiguous remains of what the presocratic scientists had taught. Although what I write below orients itself for a different view of that material, it is interesting (to me, at least) that I earlier had some inkling of the importance of this material to my project.

Among the Greeks, parallel to the concern with justice and the moral order and its implication for the human sphere treated in earlier chapters above, thinkers inquired into the natural, or physical world. First attested at Miletus on the west coast of Anatolia, a tradition of investigation of the cosmos and the phenomena of the world developed a whole series of explanations of reality, almost all of them based on speculation, or, what Popper calls more approvingly, "conjecture." Many moderns call the members of this group the "doxographers," the writers of opinion, as their conclusions seem also to be based on speculation and mere opinion. I use the word "seem" in this regard because our information about their views is fragmentary and incomplete, based on quotes and references in a wide variety of ancient and even medieval writers, and, as Gadamer insists, "in general all the passages on which the tradition is based should not be viewed as documents and testimonies that inform us in a historically valuable way about the Presocratics.... the citations collected under the title 'Fragments of the Presocratics' ... are quotations that at least reflect the interests and points of view of the later authors who quoted them."[6]

We have no complete or even nearly complete statements of what they believed, but it seems clear that among the issues they treated was the question of the origin and nature of the universe. They approached the question not in the manner of Homer's assertion that Oceanus and Tethys were the parents of the gods, or Hesiod's *Theogony*, tracing the generations of the gods. The Ionian philosophers thought about questions like that of the material from which creation emerged, or how it did so. They also examined the nature of reality, and the substances from which the world, or the cosmos, was made. Thales of Miletus claimed that water was the first cause of things; Anaximenes and Diogenes chose air instead; Heraclitus of

Ephesus designated fire as the first principle, while Empedocles asserted four principles, water, air and fire, adding a fourth, earth.[7]

We have little argumentation presented by these sixth-century writers, and some of the fragments appear quite bizarre to a modern reader, as, for example, an opinion attributed to Anaximander of Miletus: "the stars are a circle of fire divided from the fire in the cosmos, surrounded by air. Furthermore, there are breathing-holes, a kind of passages, flute-like, through which the stars are seen."[8] The physical speculation characteristic of the Ionian coast continued from the sixth century BCE on into the fifth, and eventually produced the atomic theory of Leucippus and Democritus. The idea that the physical universe was composed of minute entities, atoms, floating through the void and linking up to create the compound bodies we know is, on the face of it, more attractive to moderns with our evolved atomic theory, but it is no better verified than the other early Greek notions. And, when we consider the idea of variously shaped atoms, hooked, concave, convex and the like, that link up by chance swerving, the theory is really no better than any other that has not been subjected to experiment or verified in some way. Later Greeks, like Aristotle, would put all this speculation in a single category of thought, along with unitary, non-material theories, like that of the eternal, perfect, unchanging One posited by Parmenides of Elea in Greece, or the mystical claim of the Sicilian Pythagoras that reality at its basis was number — that things were numbers.

For the moment it is enough to show that thought evolving from the eighth to the fifth centuries BCE was not limited to moral speculation about justice, but probed external matter as well. The physical speculation was a material counterpart of the moral, in that both based themselves on the supposition that human beings can know something beyond self, either of the moral or of the physical makeup of the universe. Both are, in a way, an intellectual attempt to impose human understanding on an apparently chaotic and obscure universe. Even more than this, the theories about the material universe illustrate something even more basic about the Greek attitude toward self and the world, the objectification of the external world, which also becomes an objectification of the self. It is an attitude toward cosmology quite different from, for example, a Chinese stance, which sees humans united to the rest of the universe in a seamless continuum.

This Hellenic characteristic of separation of the thinker from the objects considered is a fundamental characteristic of western thought, and shaped everything that happened in western religion, philosophy and science. Its origin is obscure, lost in time like the origin of language itself, but it is a characteristic that persists and affects the development of scientific investigation in cultures influenced by the Greek tradition, and we see it first obviously affecting scientific thought in the sixth century BCE. It controls not only the development of cosmologies like those we have just mentioned, but the later development of science, and it affects human self-understanding and consideration of values and moralities as well. This tendency to separate the observer from the observed allows for analysis of the human as a combination of separate mind and body, or soul and body, and permits even so basic a notion of human nature as the existence of the human soul, immortal or not. When we look further at Greek thought, we see it developing along lines that would have been impossible were it not for this basic bifurcation, and is this characteristic of Greek thought, more than the development of logic or the establishment of the techniques of proof, that opened up the possibility of the transforming change in western culture that many still call the scientific revolution.

That I introduce science, so important in the formation of western life for the past four centuries, is justified at this juncture, indeed required, because the early stage of Hellenic development produced some forms of scientific thought that demonstrate particular attitudes toward the cosmos. These attitudes are of fundamental importance to the development of Jewish and Christian thought once those traditions felt the influence of Hellenism. Science itself can be attested early among the Greeks with advances in astronomy, leading Otto Neugerbauer to push back the beginnings of science to the turn of the sixth to fifth centuries BCE, with the remark that he considered "astronomy as the most important force in the development of science since its origin sometime around 500 B.C. to the days of Laplace, Lagrange, and Gauss."[9] By the end of the sixth century BCE a number of vital astronomical conclusions had been reached: the earth is round; the moon shines by the sun's reflected light; the sun is not smaller than the earth; there had been the discovery of the gnomon (a stick, marked in measurements and placed vertically in a horizontal plane to throw a shadow all day long); the obliquity of the ecliptic was known; solstices were known, and the intervals between them could be determined.[10]

By the end of the fifth century BCE the understanding of the motions of the astronomical bodies had advanced to the creation of the geometrical model, with a number of theories, as, for example, the idea of the planets, sun and moon traveling along separate orbits around a central earth, while other theories displaced the earth from the center. By 432 BCE some Greek astronomers had proposed the 19-year cycle for controlling lunar months, at least a half century before the common usage in

Babylonia that generated the myth that the Greeks learned the cycle from that source.[11]

There is a great deal of disagreement among scholars about the nature and quality of Greek science, and even more about the meaning of the fragments of the sayings or writings of the doxographers. There is, however, broad agreement that their thinking was in some way rational, and even Jonathan Barnes, always so scrupulous to inform his readers of any scholarly disagreement with his views, sees no reason to defend his statement of early Greek rationality: "in holding that the Presocratics were the fathers of rational thought, I hold only that they were the first men self-consciously to subordinate assertion to argument and dogma to logic."[12]

The identification of what they said is not germane to what I want to examine here. Rather, it is their general concern that is of significance to my discussion, that they tried to deal with the nature of being, the essence of reality: "what is." Classical scholars have always stressed this aspect of their work, and its importance as a differentiation of culture has long been recognized by the historians of Chinese thought, at least western commentators on Chinese thought, who trained as they are in the tradition of philosophy that was molded by such cosmological questions, quickly noted the general lack of interest in them on the part of the Chinese.

The rationality, the conjectures evinced by the Presocratics, focused on the effort to identify the reality of "what is," a reality that they thought lay behind the appearances of phenomena in the world of the senses. It seems to me that the entire history of western philosophy and science has been based on this early assumption that by investigation one might penetrate the illusions of sensed phenomena to ascertain the true nature of things – physical nature and moral reality alike. This characteristic world view is more clearly seen, and shown to be particular to western culture, by comparison with Chinese approaches to reality, religious and philosophical. Rather than investigate "what is" (and commentators have often noted that the absence of a word for "being" in Chinese may account for the absence of the pursuit of "being"), Chinese thought assumed a correlation between human life and conditions and that of the cosmos:

> Correlative cosmology asserted a fundamental homology between human affairs and cosmic order, both of which were governed by certain cycles, rhythms, and patterns of change and transformation. The relationship between the human and natural worlds was seen as organic but asymmetric; although changes in one produced corresponding changes in the other, ultimately the human realm was subordinate to the inexorable logic of the underlying principles of self-generating metamorphosis imbedded in the cosmos.[13]

Greek cosmology assumes a separation between the human sphere and the cosmos, a separation that may be crossed by the exercise of human reason, science, or in philosophy what we call metaphysics. The separation is different from that presumed by Hebraic thought, which supposes an unbridgeable gap dividing the divine from humanity. The Jewish gap is one of understanding: the God of Job acts and rules in a manner incomprehensible to Job. The ultimate explanation of creation in Genesis is simply the will of the divine, and issues that are, to Christian thinking, important matters of comprehending the arbitrary acts of a supposed good and merciful God, seem in Jewish scripture not even to be approached. What humans can know about the cosmos, its nature, or the will of the divine, is limited to information transmitted by God, and any human relationship to the cosmic order that can be achieved is gained only through prophetic explication of the rules and prophetic denunciation of disobedience. There is nothing like the Greek effort to achieve knowledge through reason, or to create what we call science.

As a result of their incorporation of Hellenic attitudes and cosmological thinking, Christian texts and Christian thought diverged greatly from their Hebraic roots. Early Christian texts were soon subjected to scrutiny and evaluated in terms of their supposed accuracy in delineating the nature of God, and those not deemed valid by authorities were excluded from what became the canon of Christian scripture. Even the accepted texts were subjected to interpretation to force conformity to the views of those in authority in the church, and, as David Rutledge has observed, the process of interpretation was "simply that Christianity has inherited, to a large extent, the Greek metaphysical position concerning matters of language, truth and interpretation."[14] The violent doctrinal disputes and persecutions of heresies in the early (as well as later) Christian times owes a great deal to this inheritance of Hellenism. The conception that humans can, by reason – for that was the technique the Christian authorities claimed to use in their interpretation of their texts – establish the nature of the divine, represented the same effort as that of the presocratic philosophers attempting to establish the nature of "what is." The dualism and opposition between "right" and "wrong" that modern feminists assert as the characteristic of authoritarian patriarchy played a major role in the establishment of authority in the church.

[1] Sommer (1995) p. 3, a textbook anthology presenting, with concise introductions, a selection of translations of texts relating to Chinese religion from antiquity to the present, and illustrating the dramatic differences between Chinese religious attitudes and those of Greek or Jewish and Christian writers.
[2] Jaeger (1965) Vol. 1, p. xv.
[3] Dudek (1994) p. 65.
[4] Popper (1998) p. 244.
[5] Popper (1998) p. 245, and see also p. 7: "The questions which the Presocratics tried to answer were primarily cosmological questions...."
[6] Gadamer (1998) p.72.
[7] This is a condensed version of Aristotle, *Metaphysics* 984 a 1-10; there are many different evaluations of Aristotle's rendition of the thought of the doxographers, *inter alia*, Guthrie (1962, 1965, 1969) and works cited below. The important fragments and testimonia of these and other doxographers or Presocratics are conveniently presented, with discussion, in Kirk, Raven, Schofield (1983).
[8] Hippolytus, *Refutatio* 1, 6, 4.
[9] Neugebauer (1962) p. 2.
[10] For the evidence, see Samuel (1972) pp. 22-23.
[11] Neugebauer (1962) p. 140. For the date of the cycle's introduction in Greece, see Samuel (1972) note above, pp. 42-49.
[12] Barnes (1982) p. 5.
[13] Von Glahn (2004) p. 35.
[14] Rutledge (1996) p. 59.

–Part Five–
The Individual and the Cosmos

–17–
Epic Times

In a kind of reversal of the normal order of things, we come in the last part of this treatment of the attitudes that influence us deeply to those that I see as fundamental, basic in both time and significance. The literary work that most influenced the Greeks contains and promulgates attitudes and assumptions about the human being and the cosmos that dominate Greek thought and persist to fashion basic attitudes toward life that affect our own concepts and actions. From time to time in preceding pages I have referred to the *Iliad* and to attitudes I call "Achillean" from its hero, and it is now time to focus on that text and that personality as the most basic to all that has gone before. Because this text and its protagonist had so fundamental an influence on three millennia of history, it seems to me to be worth examining the work in more detail than anything else I have discussed hitherto. What is it? What did it mean to the Greeks who read it once it was established as a text? What does it still mean to us?

I first encountered the *Iliad* as poetry as an undergraduate in the early nineteen fifties. Standing in an alcove of the Hamilton College library, I pulled a new issue of *Poetry* magazine from the rack, and leafing through it came across a translation of some of Homer's hexameters by Richmond Lattimore. I can still recall the awe with which I read those lines, soon to be published as the translation of the *Iliad* that would become so familiar to readers in the last half of the last century. I had read some Homer in Greek, although I no longer remember the classroom experience with the vividness with which I still recall my discovery that this, to me, difficult and unfamiliar dialect, could be real poetry.

My next encounter with the epic was not a matter of literature but an aspect of scholarship aimed at understanding the nature of the hexameters that made up the twenty-four books of mayhem, death, human perversity and self-assertion. This was at Yale, and I was a graduate student, recently returned from three years of active duty as a junior officer in the navy. Settling into what I planned as an intellectual life, I met, in rapid succession, the Minoans with their graceful painting and ambitious architecture, and the Mycenaeans recently revealed to have been Greeks and thus the exemplars for the heroes of epic. I also met the ideas of Milman Parry, whose explanation of the nature of the oral poetry[1] was by then accepted by all students of Greek and ancient literature. I learned of the oral tradition of early twentieth-century Serbo-Croatia, still vital in Parry's own time. The oral poet did not present a song as a memorized work, but rather took a known narrative and fashioned each performance out of a repertoire of established formulas carrying the concepts, information and description needed for the occasion. This was "formulaic diction," with identical words, phrases and verses repeated to describe specific people or similar events; the pattern appears in the *Iliad* and *Odyssey*, where over one third of the verses or lines are used more than once. Parry and his followers stressed the limits imposed by this technique, where the poet is constrained by the content of the repertoire and the scope of his formulas and his own ingenuity in using them. Creativity is possible, nevertheless, as an occasional singer may invent to enlarge the body and leave greater range to his successors. The system is still conservative, for the casting of the formulaic verses in meter preserves old ideas, words, or information to the extent that the meter is rigid and discourages the abandonment of anything that works, and ideas recur again and again in the recitation of epics that may be short or long at one time or another depending on the extent to which the specific formulas are compounded or omitted.

At the time, and for decades after, this explanation of the epics made sense to me, and it is only in recent years, as I struggled to comprehend the nature of the *Iliad* as a foundation for Greek thought, that I felt it necessary to come to terms with the questions that literary critics posed as they considered the art and thought of the *Iliad*. I have not been alone in this. For a long time, this so-called Parry-Lord thesis of the nature of Homeric epic has been the foundation of modern discussion of the *Iliad* and the *Odyssey*, sweeping away the old disputes between so-called "unitarians" and those who insisted on a multiplicity of authorship. Scholars have accepted the notion of formulaic composition, but have debated issues arising from the nature of composition. How can formulaic diction create a poem that has a coherent attitude toward the world and the human condition? That the poem did so seemed as obvious to me and modern readers as it did to the Greeks, for whom the *Iliad* and *Odyssey* provided the intellectual, ideological, poetic and artistic platforms for everything that followed in Hellenism. Of the two, the *Iliad* can safely be said to have exercised more direction over Greek literature than any other work; its psychological depth, its inclusion of so many religious, moral and philosophical concepts established many parameters of thought in later times. It has often been said that "the *Iliad* was the Bible of the Greeks," but this seriously understates the importance of the *Iliad* for Greek thought and mentality. Few educated modern people in the western world, even the religious, have a familiarity with biblical texts that remotely approaches the knowledge of the *Iliad* that was common among literate Greeks.[2] Homer was quoted with great frequency, not only for literary purposes but for evidence about the past, as, for example, the historian Thucydides used Homeric texts to justify his claim that no wars before his time were as great as the monumental conflict between Athens and Sparta in the fifth century. It is this dominance of the epics that led to the dismay of the philosopher most concerned with the impact of poetry on ideas, that is, Plato, who regarded Homer as the most influential, and accordingly asserted that his work should be banned as expressing views of men and gods that were not only wrong in themselves, but had a harmful influence on thought and behavior.[3]

Beyond challenging the possibilities of oral composition lies the question of timing, the period when the oral poetry was vital, creative and capable of producing works of the extraordinary quality and length of the Homeric epics. I did, as a student, consider issues like this, for as I developed more interest in historical issues and bypassed literary problems, I explored what was known at the time about Mycenaean society and speculated that the *Iliad* (whose archetypal role in the framing of the attitudes of the European world was not yet at issue for me) might actually go back to the Bronze Age. These seemed to me to be issues of paramount importance. Later, however, I had a different attitude toward the scholarly debates. The questions of date and composition were still matters that impinged upon my desire to read the epic as coherent thought, but I framed the major question differently: Before the *Iliad* was reduced to writing, could the Homeric oral way of thinking develop a coherent view of human experience, and communicate that perception in a way suitable to oral presentation, a genre not obviously amenable to the argumentation and complex narrative writing characteristic of later philosophy and history?[4]

I had a number of considerations to fit into any picture I might construct. It is possible to argue that the poetic and intellectual stance (but not the historical picture) of the *Iliad* fits into a picture of the Greek world as it was in the midst of the turmoil of the Late Bronze Age, when Mediterranean societies were disrupted by a general upheaval caused at least in part by invasions, pillage and destruction. It is also possible for historians to insist on a correlation between epic society and that of the so called "dark ages," when the only society "Homer" could know was a rude life of war and plunder in a world in which prosperity and social and economic structure had declined from the level that had been overturned.[5]

The choice between these alternatives would determine my view on how far back the attitudes exemplified by the *Iliad* might go. This was a problem for me, however, and not for the ancients, and I gradually came to think that it was not at all relevant to an understanding of the impact of the epic on the Greeks. They themselves had no knowledge of the alternative interpretations, either of the nature of oral poetry or its place in time. No one in antiquity had any comprehension of Bronze Age civilization, and some Greek writers saw its few physical remains, like the monumental fortress of Mycenae that glowered down from its citadel at passersby, as the work of giants who inhabited the earth before the advent of humankind. The enormous blocks of stone making up the walls certainly justified the assumption that the builders were far beyond the size of mere humans. The Greeks who later read the *Iliad* also misunderstood the performances of the rhapsodes who passed down the epics in earlier times, not realizing that long narrative poems like the *Iliad* were refashioned, even "recomposed" over the generations so that their forms and conception emerge out of the interaction between audience and creating singers. And they were not constrained by an idea of oral poetry that challenged the possibility of subtle and reflective thought, because they attributed the creation of the poems to a single mind, "Homer," a single and real poet, responsible for creating the entire poems from inspiration, not tradition.

I decided then that I was not concerned with the origin of the text, nor even the manner in which it might have been composed, but rather the effects on the Greeks (and us) of this text once it was established. This happened, according to Greek tradition, at the behest of the sixth-century BCE Athenian tyrant Peisistratus, but the conversion of the oral story to written text might have been much earlier, at the start of Greek alphabetic writing, as Barry Powell argues.[6] Whatever may be the resolution of the debate over the date of origination, if ever it is resolved,[7] the timing does not matter to an understanding of the effect the text of the *Iliad* had on later Greeks, for they had the text, and that text was more or less agreed once it had been reduced to writing. What had been important to me when I was writing about this epic two decades ago, and still more so as I come back to treat it again, is the effect the *Iliad* has had on the manner in which the Greeks, and we as their heirs, view ourselves as human beings.

As I write this latest attempt to present a notion of what the *Iliad* text might have meant to Greeks encountering it after the period of oral development, I have become very aware of the extent to which modern readers, scholars and critics have worked to show how such an oral poem might exemplify an extraordinarily high level of literary art. Among the earliest of these explorations came Gregory Nagy's work in 1979,[8] and this was followed by a raft of works arguing for a gamut of literary techniques by which the epic could portray various aspects of poetic narrative.[9] All of this tends to support my own desire to treat the *Iliad* as coherent thought, but the debate about orality is quite beside the point for me, since my interest is in the text as a written artifact, tracing the manner in which the ideas found in it might have formed attitudes and ideas in latter times.

At quite a late stage in the development of my ideas, it occurred to me how much the scholarship and analysis of the epics was part of a kind of feedback loop in which the nature of discussion was affected by the attitudes established in thought by the epics themselves. By that I mean that the notions about human activity and purpose established in our tradition by the epics come to affect the manner in which the analysis is made. My ideas about the impact of Achilles' story on our thinking will emerge later; for now I want to say that I think the attempts to establish understanding about composition, origin, date and the like are probably not accessible to satisfactory objective demonstration of fact, but they are a kind of Achillean attempt to assert control over intractable material. My own presentation of individual understanding as a parallel to accretion and advance in knowledge is a demonstration of confidence in the possibility of human knowledge. The whole enterprise is quite remarkable when it is compared to the approach the Chinese, for example, take to the understanding of their own classics, which though originally oral like that of the Greek epics, are based on a tradition of writing earlier and different from the Greek.

I think the consensus among western and Chinese scholars accepts a time well back in the second millenium BCE for the Chinese to have begun using their form of rendering words into visual form. In the case of the Chinese, the manner of writing was a system that, while much modified over time, never changed its approach to the manner in which visual presentation rendered ideas and sound. Some of the earliest Chinese graphs remain poorly understood, it is true, but those that we do understand yield to analysis on the basis of the resemblance to later forms. This is quite different from the experience of rendering Greek. The manner of writing the language in the script called Linear B, a syllabary in which the signs represented consonant-vowel combinations, such as ba, ka, ta, bo, ko, to and the like, was abandoned after the end of the second millenium BCE. It was completely forgotten by the Greeks, who subsequently adapted the "Phoenician" alphabet to write their sounds and words in letters, with individual signs for vowels and consonants that correspond to sound and create strings of meaning.

When the Chinese came to look back on their classics, their approach was much like that of the early Greeks: they regarded the collections that made up the early books of *Songs*, of the *Spring and Autumn Annals* reporting the events of the early first millenium, the *I Ching* of comprehensible prognostication, and the *Book of Documents* dealing with the interaction among the particular states at a time when the area thought of as China was not a unified empire, as compiled, edited or actually composed by single minds. In the case of the Chinese, however, those minds belonged to identifiable people, not like the temporally vague Greek Homer whose very origin and location was disputed among a number of Greek cities that claim him for their own. No one disputes the Chinese location of Confucius, or even his travels among the warring Chinese principalities and his relation to such rulers as the king of the state of Lu. We know his dates. The Chinese have long placed his birth in the year 551 BCE and his death in 479; no western revisionist disputes this.

The western and Chinese traditions differ in the treatment of the classics mentioned above and that of the Confucian texts, the *Analects* attributed to Confucius himself, the so-called *Great Learning*, the *Doctrine of the Mean*, and the so-called *Mencius*, a book of philosophical discussions believed by the Chinese to have been written by the philosopher Mencius, or Meng-zi, who was supposedly taught by Confucius' grandson. The treatment of all this material by the Chinese is stunningly different from the manner in which western writers approached the Homeric tradition.

First of all, the Chinese never departed from their focus on the contents of their early classics. It is true that Buddhist writings and ideas penetrated China, and other streams of thought like that of the vaguer personality Lao-tze joined the mainstream of Confucian discussion, and literature broadened to include what we would call "history" and fictional writing as well. However, for the most part, Chinese philosophy, scholarship and commentary focused on the early writings and created a massive literature that accreted over the centuries. It is only recently, and then under the influence of analytical western scholarship working with Homer and the Old and New Testaments, that Chinese scholars have joined westerners in the assumption that the early books are "layered," and show accretion due at least in part to an oral tradition that may go back to earlier times. There is now an archaeology of analysis, parallel to the archaeology of discovery that has in recent years brought forth very early writing on so-called Oracle Bones – inscriptions on the heated bones and the carapaces of turtles reporting the meanings of the splits and cracks on the material thought to contain value for prognostication. There also have been brought forth from tombs some very early texts that introduce enough variety into the presentation of early ideas to confirm – for westerners and some Chinese at least – the notion that early Confucian thought was not unitary.

Even so, the western way of dismantling and analyzing our basic texts has by no means won out over two thousand years of tradition in China. To read the discussion of the four basic books of Confucianism by Chen Li-fu, a member of Chiang Kai Shek's Guomindang government on mainland China and later one of the modern Confucian scholars and philosophers, who died at the age of 100 as the twenty-first century began, is to read a commentary and an explication that for the most part could have been written in the first centuries after Confucius himself.[10] On the other hand, modern analysis of the basic texts of the western tradition bears little resemblance to the tradition of earlier centuries.

As I considered our treatment of our basic texts in light of what I was learning about Chinese attitudes, I wondered whether the power of these texts over our attitudes is not demonstrated by the very manner in which we study and analyze them. The strength of the influence of the *Iliad* on our tradition, not only literary but conceptual, is illustrated by the approach to discussion of the poem in the decades after the Parry-Lord thesis became generally accepted among classical scholars. Readers and thinkers were uncomfortable with the notion that the kind of formulaic diction and composition evinced by the bards discussed by Parry and Lord could have been responsible for poetry so long and so comprehensive of both art and human experience. The epics have been approached with all the conceptual literary analyses applied to modern, written works, at the same time maintaining that as oral composition they can in one way or another maintain the "literary" stance the critic perceives in them.

In all this, there has been a pervasive drift back to the hypothesis of a single author, somehow in the oral tradition or at the end of it fashioning the traditional poetry into the work that exists today, and that tendency has now met a challenge in a "full circle," so to speak, and a demand that we admit "incoherence" in the text to the extent that we should envision a communal effort, in which "The guild or community of bards produced the *Iliad*, or something very like it, in order to achieve permanence and authoritative status for the epic, and, characteristically, assigned it to a single figure, 'Homer.'"[11] A completely different explanation of the literary and intellectual unity of the epics stresses the coherence of the tradition itself, with the monumental epics representing "the culmination of perhaps over a thousand years of performer-audience interaction."[12]

As I reviewed what I wrote about the *Iliad* in 1980, I knew that my observations were dependent on my assumptions about what was possible in the kind of composition I envisaged, and with the caution of the traditional academic, I decided to examine recent scholarly writing to ensure that I had not missed some discovery that would alter my approach. As I read, I was struck again by the manner in which the enormous outpouring of scholarly writing on the question of the composition of the epic is itself illustrative of the importance the *Iliad* has for my tradition. It is true that many of the approaches to the contents of the text deal with concepts, ideas and values for the most part explicitly stated either in narrative voice or in the voice of one of the protagonists rather than the underlying assumptions that I will be discussing. However, even those issues are sufficiently fundamental to modes of thinking in the modern world to make the epic a challenge to interpreters. The treatment of the text by modern writers reminds me that the issues dealt with by the *Iliad* established many themes in the body of ideas about the human condition, so that the importance of the *Iliad* to western culture long after the end of Greek civilization meant that the *Iliad* continued to permeate culture more deeply than other epics known to western literature and read by educated minds or put before students in "western lit" courses. Literary constructions like Vergil's *Aeneid* or Milton's *Paradise Lost* are from time to time taken down from bookshelves, and national epics like the *Nibelungelied*, the Irish *Táin* or *The Song of Roland* are important to certain traditions. It is safe to say that none of these are as widely known or so often read as the *Iliad*, with the result that the *Iliad*'s rendition of the human condition continues to affect our view of ourselves, while the slowly emerging of respect for female power and rights in modern times has little to do with the presentation of the dominating women in the German and Irish epics.

Scholars who attempt to interpret the *Iliad* remind me that other characteristics of oral or traditional poetry are important to us, and many of the studies I refer to here connect the experience of creating such an epic with other human enterprises of composition, performance and ritual. Because the performance of such works implies the presence of audiences rather than single deliberating readers, we can trace in such poetry fundamental, even if tacit, assumptions about humanity and the cosmos that are common to large elements in the population. Furthermore, when such poems are relayed through the ages, those assumptions are preserved for later generations and become part of a collective mentality that makes it possible for readers thousands of years later to understand the poetry and derive meaning from it. This is the "resonance" pointed out by Barbara Graziozi and Johannes Haubold, who with me, see the Homeric poems as part of a tradition in which early listeners did not entertain questions of authorship and composition of works that described a past they knew from an entire body of oral poetry.[13] However important the funerary texts or other writings of Egypt may have been to the literate among the Egyptians, they are relegated to specialist scholars in the western world because they have never assumed centrality to our culture, and the assumptions those texts made about human life may or may not be meaningful to many of us. And this is not a matter of translation, as it may be in the bewildering differences between translations of, let us say, the Chinese of Lao-Tse. In the case of Greek literary works like the *Iliad*, implicit concepts remain understandable and influential, whether they appear in antiquated versions like Chapman's Homer that aroused poetic comment in itself, or ponderous renditions like Bryant's, or brilliant accurate and poetic translations like Richmond Lattimore's mid-twentieth century *Iliad*.

I also thought, as I compared the experience with my classic to the Chinese with theirs, that the effect of mine is, so to speak, double-barreled. The *Iliad* affects us not only as we read it today and have done so over centuries, it affects us in the ways that it formed Hellenic ideas and the civilization of the Greeks, which then affected us in ways that diverge from the influence of the story of Achilles. For the Greeks, the Homeric epics offered specific guidance and information that reinforced the effect of the poetry to frame and preserve fundamental ideas about the human condition. The epics comprehended many ideas essential to Greek culture and religion, and far more than they might serve as mere entertainment or even purely intellectual literature, or as a model for later poetry – although they did all that – they expressed specific religious and philosophical truths and they provided the Greeks with the only record of the part of their past that preceded the arrangement of Greece at it was in the historical period. In this way the epics, along with other poetic and oral narratives that came down through the dark ages into the historical period, provided the Greeks with a sense of their origins and their past. When Thucydides asserts that at the time of the return to the Peloponnesus of the sons of Heracles, all the peoples of southern Greece were displaced and only Athens held out against the invaders, he bases his historical writing on information which, even if it had been reduced to writing in his own time, owes its existence to an earlier oral tradition. The *Iliad* preserves an important part of that tradition, and Herodotus used it to portray the Trojan War as part of a sequence of reciprocal grievances exchanged between Europe and Asia, leading ultimately to the Persian Wars. As we have seen, Thucydides could employ the text to provide a measure against which to stress the size of the armaments and the importance of the Peloponnesian War of his own time. The actions of particular heroes of the *Iliad*, and the chain of events they began during or after the war, became ramifications for their descendants and the cities of Greece long after the war was over. Finally, the portrayal of a common effort by Hellenes acting in concert against a barbarian enemy helped established a concept of an essential unity that co-existed with the particularism so characteristic of the world of individual Greek cities, and the events of that war, the reactions and responses of the heroes to those events, offered later Greeks some historical perspective on their own conflicts, and yielded a set of examples for later appropriate Hellenic behavior in military and even political disputes, even while molding opinion in its own time.[14]

At least equally important as the historical implications of the tradition were its religious, ethical and moral effects. There were representations of the gods that showed their interactions with one another and with human beings and interpretations of their impact on human success or failure. The epics contain attitudes toward mutual obligations, usually of nobles, and the appropriate behavior of inferiors to their superiors and vice versa. They present a reasonably consistent code of conduct for members of the warrior class, with the expected courtesies of combat and the values a warrior class seemed to live by. "To help one's friends and harm one's enemies" is a comprehensible code, and one that could adapt to the deceitfulness of an Odysseus as well as the blunt stubbornness of Achilles. These may have been values of a class, but more than other literature, the values of the *Iliad* were the values of a whole class, not only the product of the reflections of individuals but also of the reactions and acceptance of the audiences that heard them. The attitudes expressed by the heroes of the *Iliad* were meaningful and instructive to a whole social group, perhaps a whole society, and the poem, along with other epics, maintained some common values until our texts were committed to writing.[15] This is what Graziozi and Haubold forcefully argue, that "archaic audiences were not interested in towering, isolated texts, but in texts that could resonate with what they already knew about the cosmos."[16] These texts, however, and the *Iliad* particularly, did become towering isolated texts for later Greeks, and even more so to us, who have lost virtually all the rest of that early archaic tradition.

In the presentation by the Homeric epics of the virtues of kings, princes, soldiers, wives, children, and servants, the list of aspects of human relations and what makes up *arete* or nobleness is almost endless, astonishingly broad for two poems apparently limited in their subject matter. There are filial and wifely responsibilities and feelings, the duties of hosts and expectations of guests, honors owed to friends and comrades, limits of maltreatment of enemies, ranging from practices and courtesies to the appropriate treatment of the dead. However divergent the ways of life of different cities or hostile their populations, the epics provided a touchstone common to all Greeks, something we can see in a concrete manifestation as Alexander the Great patterned the honor paid to his deceased comrade Hephaestion on the funeral ceremonies Achilles accorded to his fallen friend Patroclus. While many of these individual rules of behavior, pertaining as they do to a particular time, society and class, are hardly applicable to modern life, they are understandable, partly, at least, due to the fact that modern society remains committed to the underlying values of epic society and the tacit assumptions about humanity that support those particular values. And some of the particular values seem to have persisted, or at least have molded similar values. To help one's friends and hurt one's enemies is only a step removed from Jesus' words, "He that is not with me is against me,"[17] and the harshness of the Homeric dictum is understandable to and perhaps even in part responsible for a society prepared to overwhelm a weak opponent, acting on George W. Bush's Homeric intention to destroy as enemies any who not help him.

---

[1] Enunciated in the papers collected by Parry, ed. (1971), and restated in Lord, (1960. In addition to other works cited in the notes here, the issue has been discussed by Kullmann (1984) pp. 307-23, Thornton (1984), and more recently, the intellectual potential of the *Iliad*, despite its oral nature, has been treated by Mueller (1996).

[2] The intellectual impact of the epics shows not only in the continual reference to them by later writers, but by physical remains, which show that in the period for which we have good evidence, from the third century BCE down to

the fifth of our era, Homer dominated libraries, at least the libraries held by the Greek-reading residents of Egypt. There, of the literary texts discovered among the preserved papyri, Homer accounts for almost 800 pieces, while the next most common authors, Demosthenes and Euripides, can boast only about 100 each, and the pattern is consistent from the earliest time of Greek occupation of Egypt down to the Arab conquest.

[3] Plato, *Republic* 606e, refers to the "praisers of Homer, saying that this poet had educated Greece," an idea found as early as Xenophanes (fr. 10). The reason for Homer's importance is argued by Havelock (1963), as being the fundamentally oral nature of Greek society, for which Homer served as a kind of "tribal encyclopaedia," formidable opposition in Plato's time; cf. also the implications of a wider interpretation and potential of "oral."

[4] See my discussion, Samuel (1992) pp. 6-11.

[55] The material, and the earlier discussions, are reviewed by Luce (1975.

[6] Powell (2004) pp. 22–34.

[7] The composition of the Homeric poems is generally placed after the beginning of the first millennium BCE, after the collapse of the great Bronze Age palace centers, usually in the two centuries 900 to 700 BCE. Some scholars have argued that the formulas were developed in the Bronze Age itself, or even earlier, even though they do not reflect much of the articulated and proto-literate society we think we see in the physical remains and bureaucratic texts of the period.

[8] Nagy (1979, 2nd ed. 1999).

[9] For examples, the manner in which "Homer" uses different modes of speech and speech words, by Martin (1989); gesture and body signals and the like, by Lateiner (1995) citing, usefully, esp. p. 25, important studies of the artistic aspects of oral poetry; there is a whole series of special studies published by Rowan and Littlefield that I do not cite here, as not relevant to my investigation, but which illustrate the current tendency to treat the epics as amenable to the same kinds of investigations we might expect for purely written texts.

[10] Chen (1986) The vast majority of the text reads as though it could have been written in 300 BC. There are perhaps a dozen modern references: to Sun Yat Sen, rare references to Chiang Kai Shek, the Communists, nuclear destruction and physics (p. 193), Christianity (pp. 195 ff, esp. 199-200), the modern physical notion of four dimensions (p. 196), Chinese open-mindedness (p. 200), sine curve (p. 225), automobile (p. 278), western industrial society (pp. 397, 408), western missionaries and Pope Pius XII and his Dec. 9, 1939 permission to Chinese Christians to perform post-mortem sacrifices (p. 404); "Iron curtain countries", p. 566.

[11] Wilson (2000) p. 72.

[12] Nagy (1999) p. 15. Nagy stresses this a number times, as, e.g., p. 47: "The structural unity of such epics results, I think, not from the creative genius of

whoever achieved a fixed composition but from the lengthy evolution of myriad previous compositions, era to era, into a final composition."

[13] Graziozi and Haubold (2005).

[14] As argued by Hammer (2002) p. 13.

[15] Just what the nature of this oral tradition was, and its potential for freedom, need not be limited by the categories of the Parry-Lord thesis. The subject should not be considered without reference to Finnegan (1977) which sets forth the evidence for the diversity of types of oral composition and emphasizes the importance of the interaction between poet and audience.

[16] Graziozi and Haubold (2005) pp. 33-34.

[17] Matthew 12.30; Luke 11.23.

–18–
The Optimism of Pessimism

I remember as a graduate student talking about the parlous state of the world in the early 1950s, with my teacher, C. Bradford Welles, who had served in the army during World War II and had seen much more of life than I had. Listening to my catalogue of troubles, Welles answered, "despite my better judgment, I am an optimist," a remark that I think of, a half-century later, as Achillean. Welles' unjustified optimism, after two world wars, a great depression, a holocaust that consumed millions, in a world threatened with nuclear annihilation by the United States, the Soviet Union, or the cooperative enterprise of both, would have been understood by the hero of the *Iliad*. Achilles would probably even have endorsed that optimism. Welles, like Achilles, thought that despite all the evidence of ruin to the contrary, resolute humans might manage to avert the worst disasters. The whole mindset may be summed up in the proverb, "If at first you don't succeed, try, try again."

This is not a necessary human attitude, and alternative views are expressed in a satirical way by the various Murphy's laws, like "If things can go wrong, they will," or "You can't fall off the floor," which if taken seriously would surely discourage human action. Such remarks are perhaps like the Chinese *wu wei* – "don't act" – known from some Chinese writings. There are certainly societies not nearly so proactive as ours, although with the advent of the global village most of them have yielded, at least in part, to appreciation of western activism in pursuit of the material advantages they see enjoyed by members of western society.[1] That in itself is in part responsible for the antagonism towards the West and its outstanding exemplars by those who do not accept some of the basic principles of life I see in the history of my culture.

This, of course, is a personal view. Like any self-reflection, it has the potential of one-sidedness and self-deception. It also risks self-satisfaction, and for a long time, I was inclined to see this attitude as generating many of the beneficial characteristics of western society without considering how it might also be responsible for some of the patterns of behavior I deplore. It is only with the reading and thinking I have been pursuing in recent years that I have come to regard this basic orientation of western society as a major contributor to the problems we create for ourselves, and to be aware of alternatives that, though they may not lead to our successes, also avoid our failures.

This change in view on my part suggests why it is so difficult for me and others to modify the negative characteristics of our way of life; I think that this basic attitude is deeply ingrained. It goes back, I believe, all the way to the *Iliad* and the story of Achilles as the epic tells it. Even the first word in this monumental poem, *menis*, wrath, is a signal of the problems impending. It is a word that has been argued to mean more than the emotion of anger as it is commonly translated, but a concept of deeper cosmic meaning,[2] and the impact on our society is not the concept of *menis* or wrath itself, but the epic's treatment of that wrath by the central character, Achilles. In its narrative of over 15,000 lines, the epic traces Achilles' actions in response to that wrath, how he justified it, maintained it, renewed it, redirected it and finally laid it to rest. Achilles' wrath is more than theme, for it and his response to it are the fundamental causes of all the events that fill book after book of fighting, in a presentation of the human condition with a coherent intellectual and philosophical stance.[3]

After ten years of besieging the city of Troy, Achilles withdrew from combat, enraged when Agamemnon took his prize, the girl Briseis, in reaction to Achilles' advice to return her to her father, the Trojan seer Calchas, in order to lift the plague that Apollo had inflicted on the Greeks. Agamemnon's exercise of authority was a direct attack on Achilles in terms of a system that recognized achievement, provided reward and constituted the basis for assessment of self-worth in the warrior culture that heard the songs of the rhapsodes. In this value system, worth was measured and repute gained from excelling – in combat, in games, in counsel, even in craftiness – and the competitors to be outstripped were others of one's own class. This ethos of an aristocracy, this competitiveness, called *agonistic* from the Greek word *agon*, for contest, remained characteristic of Greek culture, wherein "the aim of the talented Greek, since Homer, was 'always to be the first and outshine the rest.'"[4] Successful competitors received prizes, and men exchanged gifts to demonstrate esteem, and the culture was not one in which self-esteem, internalized, arose in supreme self-confidence without the assurance of worth by the material demonstration of the opinions of others. The opinions of others generated feelings of self-worth, and even then, only when those external opinions were demonstrated by visible evidence. When Agamemnon removed Achilles' reward for excellence, he did more than insult Achilles by implying that Achilles might deserve less than he thought he had earned, he actually *diminished* Achilles' real worth. It is not a concept promoted by modern psychology, but it was a motive force in the Homeric system known as a "shame culture" by anthropologists, and in the context of that culture Achilles could hardly do other than attack Agamemnon in response. When he failed to do so his inaction could be explicable in terms of divine action – in this case, the intervention of the goddess Athena who held him back by his hair, an intervention the epic portrays as Achilles experiencing as a reality, not an allegory or metaphor or psychological phenomenon.[5] When the goddess pulled him back from combat, Achilles sought an alternative to his justified lunge at Agamemnon: withdrawal from the war, a second-best alternative, perhaps, because it showed Achilles' excellence only by default, rather than excelling immediately and directly by defeating Agamemnon. All of this would have been understood by the earliest listeners to the epics, and it remained clear to Greeks for centuries.

    The demonstration of Achilles' worth came with Zeus' interference, as Achilles' divine mother Thetis prevailed upon the ruler of the gods to turn the tide of battle in favor of the Trojans as a demonstration of the value of Achilles to the Greeks. In thousands of lines to the end of book viii success went to the Trojans as they forced the Greeks back to the ships lined up along the shore. Their backs to the sea, with Agamemnon himself suggesting that they forsake the siege of Troy, the Achaeans – another name for Greeks – confer and prevail upon Agamemnon to conciliate Achilles. Agamemnon announces that he will grant the sulking warrior egregious gifts to bring him back into the fighting ranks. Agamemnon claims his earlier act to have been one of madness, due, he asserts, to Ate, the divine force lying in wait to strike men down. Again, the explanation is not psychological but external reality: Agamemnon's loss of reason under the impact of a force outside himself. Agamemnon's return to reason brought the dispatch of emissaries to Achilles.

Many modern commentators regard the entire embassy episode as a later accretion to the *Iliad*. Certainly the disjunction between the mention of three envoys, Phoenix, Ajax and Odysseus, and the words immediately following, "so these two walked along the strand," to tell of their progression to Achilles tent, make Phoenix's inclusion suspicious, and this aspect of the narrative becomes more noticeable in view of other factors: grammatical forms confirming the intention to denote two and the fact that although Phoenix had been appointed leader, in speaking Odysseus began the parlay and reported Agamemnon's offer to Achilles. Phoenix's words to Achilles may, therefore, not have been included in the poem. Achilles' response, on the other hand, is completely consistent with the story, and provides no justification for regarding the embassy episode as incompatible with the rest of the *Iliad*, for his reply is almost essential to the narrative of his wrath. The hero's anger stands, its cause unaltered, although expressed by an Achilles who has changed his view of glory.[6]

Achilles rejects Agamemnon's attempt at reconciliation for more reason than his hate for the king. The hero disavows the basic premise of his decision to participate in the Trojan War to achieve the glory that would live on after the short natural life allowed to him. Although it was the issue of that glory that had impelled him to his fury in the first place, now Agamemnon would fail to assuage the damage he had done though offering greater honor, because Achilles now challenged the validity of the principle itself. At the beginning of his reply he points to death as a determining fact: death comes to the brave man who fights just as it does to the coward. However much or little a man does, he comes to that same death. Although Achilles presents other ideas in his speech, such as the impossibility of compensating him for the "heart's affliction" he has already suffered, there is nothing so important or outstanding as his derogation of the worth of glory gauged against the magnitude of death. It is a thunderingly deviant position, and no one else in epic, in the *Iliad* or the *Odyssey*, ever says anything like it. If his words leave any doubt about his meaning that glory is not worth dying for, he repeats the idea a few lines later after a stream of insult directed at Agamemnon. The rewards of cattle, sheep, horses, can be had for the taking, but a man's life cannot be brought back, neither stolen nor regained by force, "once it has crossed the barrier of his teeth." It is a "far more radical line of criticism,"[7] not only of Agamemnon's offer but of the human condition. Achilles refers to his alternative fates, to stay at Troy to die young after gaining everlasting glory, or return home to live a long but undistinguished life. A long life or a glorious one; Achilles chooses the former, and advises others to do the same.

Although Achilles decides not to leave Troy, as he initially threatened to do, his refusal to fight is disappointing news to the army. But in six more books of battle, wounds and deaths of heroes and loss of men, they fight on. Then in book xvi, as the Achaeans are on the verge of destruction, Achilles' comrade Patroclus begs his friend to allow some help to the Greeks. If Achilles himself will not throw his weight into the balance, he might at least allow Patroclus to borrow his armor and battle in his place. If the Trojans think that Achilles has rejoined his fellows, they might mitigate their assault and give some relief to the Greeks. Achilles answers, reminding Patroclus how Agamemnon had taken his prize Briseis from him as if he were "some wanderer without rights," but the answer also concedes another change in Achilles' attitude, allowing that he will let the anger be a thing of the past, as it was not in his heart to maintain it forever. Achilles lends Patroclus his armor, but warns him to do no more than drive the Trojans away from the Greek ships and not to pursue them in attack, for he does not want to risk the possibility of either losing his own prestige in light of Patroclus' possible success, nor does he want Patroclus' life to be endangered.

The passage is notable for apparent inconsistency, for when Achilles restrains Patroclus from possible detraction from Achilles own glory, so that ultimately the Greeks will give him back his woman with gifts in addition, his words contradict the fact that the offer had already been made and he had refused it, a discrepancy presented as evidence that the embassy episode is a later insertion that did not really belong to the narrative. What seems inconsistency, however, may merely be a reference to a concern on Achilles' part that Patroclus not lose him the honor already promised, or may merely be unimportant in the speech, the drift that may be a holdover from oral composition. In any case, both passages are in the *Iliad* as it came down into writing, and both must be considered in terms of the impact of the developing portrayal of Achilles. Important in book xvi is the implication that Achilles' anger has passed, and he seems to be moving back to his earlier self, another stage in "the examination of Achilles' motives, his possible disillusionment with the honor code on which his life has been based, now seen in light of the possibility of death."[8] Now, less satisfied than before with the prospect of a long life and enjoyment of his possessions at home, he has gone from white-hot anger through bitterness to a certain calm, some balance, and a willingness to help his comrades in their great need, accepting again the traditional goal of helping one's friends, with hate for Agamemnon impelling him less.

Yet another change soon comes. Soon after Achilles arms his men and sends them to throw the Trojans into retreat with many of their best men dead, Patroclus himself lies among the fallen, killed and stripped of Achilles' armor by the Trojan leader Hector. He had disobeyed Achilles' injunction and pursued the Trojans to the very walls of the city, where he fell to Hector after being stunned by a blow from the god Apollo and a spear wound in his back. Achilles now fell into almost limitless grief for his beloved comrade, and lamented his loss to his goddess-mother Thetis, whom he told of his new resolution, to avenge Patroclus' death by killing Hector, even though this means that his own death would soon follow. Now his dominant emotion is sorrow, expressed again in the anger against Patroclus' killer.

During a meeting of the Achaeans at which Achilles calls for immediate attack, the hero's mother goes off to arrange for new armor to be made for him by the god Hephaestus, allowing for the colloquy in the camp that shows Achilles motivated by a new principle of action and a new purpose that will make his life meaningful: revenge. Originally dedicating his life to the traditional pursuit of glory that justifies a warrior's existence and rewards his struggle with reputation that lasts beyond his death, he moved through anger to a mellowing that allows him to feel concern for his friends. Then, with the death of his dearest companion Patroclus, a new goal and a new principle dominates his life, a new anger prompting a relentless search for revenge by killing Hector. Back in battle, retribution is again a matter of anger. "The man is near who has particularly touched my anger," Achilles says as he pursues his quarry, four times charging futilely into the mist in which Apollo has secreted Hector.

Leaving off the pursuit in frustration, he turns against the other Trojans, slaughtering ruthlessly as the gods intervene as well and dispute with one another, until at last, in book xvii, Achilles confronts Hector and kills him.

We see the wrath again in all its immensity, as Achilles answers Hector's last request to yield his body to the Trojans for a decent burial: Achilles will accept no ransom for the body, but he will leave it to be picked at by dogs and birds, and he wishes that he had enough rage in him to chop away Hector's meat and eat it raw. Calling on the other Greeks to return to the ships to prepare a funeral for Patroclus, he continues himself on his rampage against the corpse of his enemy. He makes holes in Hector's lifeless feet, draws leather thongs through them to tie the body to his chariot, and then, under the walls of Troy from which the mourning Trojans watch, he drags the corpse through the dust.

Achilles has not yet reached the end of the changes the epic will recount. The story moves through the account of the funeral of Patroclus, recalling the mixture of sorrow and anger as Achilles calls on his dead companion, kills some Trojan captives and places them on Patroclus' pyre to be burnt with his dear friend's body. Even now, Apollo protects Hector's body from putrefaction, while at the funeral there is more divine activity as Achilles remembers to offer prayers to the winds, North and West, so that they kindle the flames into a great blaze. Now, finally, Achilles can rest, but even then he rises from sleep to bury the ashes of his friend Patroclus and arrange for funeral games in his honor. Now, more than 600 lines present the contests of the games, with accounts of the leaders of the Achaeans and an example of the competition and reward that lie at the heart of the events that began with Achilles' first eruption into wrath. That anger is still not satisfied or at its end; it is there at the beginning of the final book of the *Iliad*, as Achilles, sorrowing and unable to sleep, at dawn wreaks further outrage on Hector's body by dragging around Patroclus' tomb three times that body still fresh, protected by Apollo, twelve days after Achilles took away its life.

We are now unrolling the last in the bundle of papyrus rolls that hold the text of the *Iliad*. The gods intervene again, not striking or aiding warriors in combat, but telling Achilles explicitly what they want him to do. There is no ambiguity here, no riddling oracle, but an example of the possibility of accurate human knowledge of divine will and order. Achilles' mother Thetis announces that Zeus wishes Achilles to allow Hector's father Priam to ransom the body, and Achilles complies without hesitation. When Priam, advised by the gods, appears at Achilles' tent, the hero receives him courteously, and apart from a brief caution that Priam not stir him up to anger, treats him with the respect due a king and yields the body for burial. Only the slightest trace of anger remains to Achilles, who is even willing to share his sorrow – sorrow for Patroclus and his own father, who like the king of Troy will survive to mourn his magnificent son. Achilles even goes so far as to grant Priam a truce so that the Trojans can provide an appropriate funeral, and accepts the full eleven days Priam proposes for the ceremonies. Here, Achilles goes beyond the respect for the body commanded by Zeus, apparently, as one reader puts it, "motivated instead principally by a feeling of common humanity in the face of common mortality,"[9] his own idea of mercy demonstrating the generosity now possible for him. We have come to the end of the wrath, and Achilles has come to a new spiritual point, so that after the short description of the funeral games for Hector and his burial, the epic comes to an end.

The readers of modern novels, following the twists and turns of protagonists in the face of unfolding events, will not find the development of Achilles' character difficult to follow. Achilles progresses in an almost Hegelian dialectic through thesis, antithesis and synthesis searching for a reliable rule of conduct in an imperfectly understood world that produces the hero's "disillusionment."[10] There is, for Achilles, no prescribed moral rule, no validated ethic, no "ten commandments" on which to base action, and modern human beings who do not have faith in received divine decrees can grasp this difficulty. No more to Achilles than to us are the rules of the gods clear. These so-called "Olympian" deities of Homer, who were revered along with unnamed spirits, family gods, ghosts and so many other obscure forces and daemons common to many religions, were neither personifications of the forces of nature nor merely people writ large with the extra quality of immortality. They are beings of superhuman power, pass over the earth and influence it, affecting human lives and acts. They can be pleased by human worship, by sacrifices and festivals, and people can expect to receive return for religious investment, although the gods may not always grant what is asked, or grant it quite in the manner hoped. Nor, save in the rare instance provided by the encounter between Achilles and Priam, does there seem to be ethical or moral content in the relationship among the gods or with humans, and there is no clear corollary between what might seem to be just or ethical conduct in the human sphere and approval by the gods. There are certainly no rules established in advance for the guidance of generations to come. It is this sort of universe that Achilles must face in working out his destiny, with no rationale on which he can base his decisions; it is a condition that might be described as moral chaos. Although people are expected to worship the gods, they do so in a service of ritual and sacrifice rather than conformity to a moral code, without established principles of human social interaction commanded or in any way endorsed by religion, in a world of "paradoxical quality ... one in which human action exists within the context of a divine universe...."[11] Thus Achilles had no external standard to follow as a guide in his quest for some form of happiness, unless he were to base his life on the entirely human principle of competition and striving to excel, the very principle that failed him at the beginning of the epic.

I am not proposing here that the *Iliad* is a text with a philosophical theme created by a bard who proceeded to present his answer to these problems in epic form, or that the story of Achilles is told as unconscious mythic thought that surfaces from human psychology.[12] It is rather the case that philosophical and religious issues underlie and fashion the language and myth making up the poem, with the bards singing their lines and recounting the acts of their characters according to norms they and their audiences know and understand, based on "a highly developed self-consciousness about moral and political values."[13] The events of any man's life, and so, Achilles,' must conform to phenomena understandable and believable to an audience familiar, at least in part, with the experiences portrayed, placing the account not only "within a wider history of the cosmos,"[14] but in the context of the listener's understanding of the nature of the cosmos. Whatever the interpretation we put on Achilles, as modern readers seeking comprehension of the significance of the figure, we are dealing with "an artistically unified *Iliad*"[15] that accords with the Iliadic society's assumptions about the human condition, produced by a tradition of oral performance that presents a complex character to be interpreted by listeners and later, readers. Just as we can understand a modern writer's assertion that "it is part of the greatness of Achilles that he is able to contemplate and accept his own death more fully and more passionately than any other hero,"[16] in terms of modern uncertainty about the nature of any future life or even the possibility that it exists at all, so Greek audiences empathized fully with the sequence of reactions Achilles presents: to the choice he must make between long or glorious life; to Agamemnon's dismantling of his reward; to the proposal for reconciliation; to a relaxation of anger in the face of the army's need and Patroclus' plea; to Patroclus' death; to his defeat of Hector; to the orders of Zeus; and finally, to commiseration with Priam in his tent.

Achilles is a hero; he was a hero, with all the qualities the word implies and the paradeigmatic function that is part of the meaning of the word hero to the Greeks, and so we accept him as this kind of figure and search for the qualities that made him so. The quality that makes Achilles outstanding above all others is not just the choices he makes but "the heroic sort [of ethics that] exists – the ethics of crisis ... and the great heroes it produces exist as a reminder of the ultimate cost of human consciousness."[17] A vital part of his significance is above all his persistence in making choices at all, and his story establishes in our tradition a model of human indomitability in the face of repeated failure. Achilles again and again reorders his principles of behavior on the basis of events, without, except in the two instances that begin and end the tale, any divine prescriptions or advice. He continually asserts his own judgment and his own will to delineate the nature of the life he will choose as best for himself. At the beginning of the epic he has chosen the life of active valor to assure eternal fame, but when this does not work out and his glory is diminished, he tries something else, withdrawal, as a demonstration of his quality by the effect of his absence. That leads him to a new principle, enunciated in book ix, *carpe diem*, as the Latin has it, "seize the day," or "eat, drink and be merry" in a long life that will allow him the enjoyment of the good things of life he already possesses. Still he encounters failure, for the result of his next choice is the death of his friend Patroclus, and however one may interpret ambivalence in his last conversation with his comrade, Patroclus' death destroys any satisfaction he has in the course he is pursuing and impels him to a new choice of revenge as a principle of behavior. But even that choice fails in satisfaction, and we leave him choosing a generosity and human sympathy that moves him in a new direction, different from what we might expect in the society in which he lived. And also, because the story of Achilles emerges from a shared understanding of human life and its difficulties, the "heroism" of Achilles is not a deliberately fashioned statement but rather a tacit reflection of assumptions and shared attitudes about the human condition. In this it is even more potent for its archaic hearers and later readers throughout the centuries, and more influential in establishing attitudes in centuries to come.

This was my interpretation of the Achilles-figure when I wrote about it 20 years ago, and I still believe that the impact of this kind of Achilles has been fundamentally influential in framing a set of attitudes that dominate the way I and others look at life in our culture. The epic tells of a man for whom nothing worked, and yet does not present him as a failure. To me, and I believe also to the Greeks, his nobility, not his failure, distinguishes him; his larger-than-life emotions and actions, his refusal to quit in the face of repeated dissatisfaction with the outcome of his choices, his persistence in the face of adversity, misfortune or even divine opposition. He maintains his determination to impose his will on his surroundings. At every setback he chooses anew to follow a different program to find happiness and satisfaction in human life, and despite the absence of universal rules that may make failure inevitable, he continues to pursue that goal. He is a figure to be reckoned with by the ages, and he has been admired from earliest Hellenic times on.

As I looked at this view of Achilles years ago, my natural optimism and my desire to validate values in which I believe led me to see only the benefits deriving from this kind of exemplary figure. In a life based on the possibility of some human comprehension of the cosmos and humanity's place in it, but informed by the awareness of the incompleteness of that knowledge, Achilles seemed to me to be a paradigm of the western human being. His assumptions lie behind every effort over the centuries to test human ideas against the seemingly disordered cosmos, with its moral incomprehensibility, its chaos and its uncertainty. My affirmation of the Achilles-figure led me to think – and I still believe – that neither Darwin nor Einstein would have been possible without the example of Achilles, and it is only in a culture derived from admiration of his indomitability that these thinkers or most others in western history could have developed. The extent to which the "Achilles attitude" forms and informs western attitudes shines forth even in defiance of prevailing ideas. For example, a feminist work challenging long-standing theological and metaphysical ideas as the basis of our culture asserts "the reason for hope is not to be found in the knowledge or rational calculation that our efforts will succeed in saving life on earth but rather in the conviction or inner knowledge that it is right to try.... Even if we knew for certain that in two hundred years there would be absolutely no more life on earth ... it makes no sense to say that our efforts to preserve and enhance life come to nothing."[18] The words could have been uttered by Achilles.

Our history is replete with "magnificent failures." For all of Faust's faults, we admire and empathize with him for his insistence on asserting his will and accepting a dubious bargain to do so. There are real figures in history, who, if looked at dispassionately, are hardly to be admired for their moral qualities, or for that matter, their unalloyed success, but they are "heroes" to our history: Napoleon, who ended his life defeated, and in exile; Caesar, assassinated; Alexander the Great, dead at 33 amid plans for yet more conquest, Martin Luther King, advancing his goal by his very death. The Achilles attitude, if I may call it that, also lies behind what I believe to be a generally western disdain for authority, the "unwillingness to accept the word of another" that Paul Veyne, examining Greek attitudes towards myths and legends, designates as "a character trait."[19] Thinkers and scientists not only rejected the ideas of their predecessors or at least challenged them, but refused to bow to the authority of political or religious leaders who insisted on adherence to the "truth." Copernicus is an example, publishing his theory of a heliocentric system in the face of the religiously endorsed view that the earth was stationary. Galileo's contest with the Church provides another example of the struggle of ideas against authority.

    I am not suggesting that Achilles' refusal to abandon the attempt to assert his will over the cosmos in which he lived was an example deliberately chosen by Greeks. Nothing so blatant. Rather, I tell the Achilles story to show how, in a text fundamental to Greek, and then western thought, the assertion of human will and human ideas over the unknown forces with which we must contend established an attitude that promotes that sort of independence, and along with it the derogation of tradition and authority, conformity and yielding. Homer's Achilles established for the Greeks the concept of the hero who is, as Bernard Knox writes, "a reminder that a human being may at times magnificently defy the limits imposed on our will by the fear of public opinion, of community action, even of death, may refuse to accept humiliation and indifference and impose his will no matter what the consequences to others and himself."[20]

It is important to realize that this attitude, seemingly so normal because we have grown up with it, nurtured by approval of what we call "independence of thought," is a particular cultural inheritance, not a necessary attribute of human nature. I now believe that we must probe deeper into this dominating work, the *Iliad*, to learn whether there are aspects of the inheritance we might not wish to accept. When I formulated these ideas 20 years ago I saw only good in the legacy of Achilles and the *Iliad*. To make the point, I entitled the book in which I offered the idea *The Promise of the West*. But I have done a great deal of reading and thinking in those 20 years, and more than that, of living and observing the culture I wrote to celebrate.

I will take up first, not the attitudes toward the cosmos I believe evinced by the story of Achilles, but some more obvious aspects of the epic that have gone unchallenged as "normal human behavior" in our tradition. The epic has been seen as a glorification of war itself, although this may be denied by one or another interpretation that sees Achilles challenging the so-called "Heroic Code." There is certainly an endorsement of competition that seems to lie at the heart of the contests, not only those between the protagonists for each side in the war, but among one another by fighters on each side. This is the "agonistic" or competitive nature of Greeks asserted by Burkhardt, and accepted as characteristic by most analysts since. However much Achilles may ultimately display "magnanimity"[21] or retreat from anger, the poem itself celebrates and endorses the effort to be "best." With regard to the epic's stance toward war, modern interpreters of Achilles, perhaps more disillusioned about the exercise of war and force than critics of earlier generations, have tended to find in him a similarity to another hero, Sarpedon, the paradigm of rejection of the code of the warrior. However, even if among these varied interpretations there is some truth, the tradition, ancient to modern, has been consistent in treating Achilles in terms of his quality as warrior. Even if a minority of readers in antiquity and mediaeval times used the Achilles figure as a vehicle to attack war, for the most part his story exalted military valor, and with the return of classicism in the Renaissance, Achilles would "again function as an inspiration for those who would win immortal glory in deadly war ... through our own times, continuing to imbue war death with transcendent value," as Katherine King sees the reception of the hero. She suggests, however, that

> The charismatic Iliadic paradigm is again the enemy: A modern East German novelist who seems to question whether the warrior function can continue to hold any place, any rank, in the nuclear age and who has woven her own paradigm of the war hero from the most negative strands of all the various traditions expresses both the goal and the apparent impossibility of fulfillment in the words of her first-person narrator, Kassandra: "If only I could wipe out the name, not merely from my memory, but from the memory of all men living. If I could burn it out of our heads – I would not have lived in vain. Achilles."[22]

There are contemporary efforts to deny a Homeric endorsement of military valor and the glorification of death in battle. Just as feminist biblical scholars have been engaged, for a decade or more, in challenging the ratification of patriarchy in the Bible (OT & NT both!) either by denying the validity of the texts or offering radical reinterpretations, we can begin to see a dramatic turn in views of the *Iliad*. Suzanne Wofford, for example, argues that the epic

> tells two stories at one and the same time: it tells the story of the making of a formal, patterned meaning of mortal experience, and it tells the story of the warriors, a story of violence and death, unmitigated by the possibility of future honor or fame.... Two stories are told, then, but one seems to me finally the more powerful. In concentrating the war story more and more on the fact of death, the epic shows that death for the individual is the final of the forces that drive the cosmos' reality, whatever immortality may be claimed in the larger order of art or in the continuity of family or society.... The society represented here depends, the epic suggests, on seeing force as alien to itself at the same time it is informed by it.[23]

Maybe so. Teachers will have to ensure that future generations break thus with the past, however, if the *Iliad* is to stop influencing the admiration for martial prowess and glory.

I do not, however, with "Kassandra" advocate the erasure of the name of Achilles, nor am I a Platonist who would eliminate the *Iliad* from our schools or libraries. But, with those who strip bare the deleterious aspects of our religious texts, I believe critics and readers who confront the epic must recognize how much the tradition of war and the warrior mentality has promoted militarism in our culture – note, for example, how modern American leaders choose to refer to their troops not as "soldiers" but as "warriors."

In much the same way as it endorses the warrior mentality, the epic assumes and endorses hierarchic patriarchy as the correct organization of society. However much the female Hera may attempt to deceive and outwit her husband Zeus, the divine ruler of Olympus, the *Iliad* both subordinates her to him and portrays her as fearful of his power. For all that modern critics try to salvage some meaning and value for the women portrayed in the epic – Achilles' concubine Briseis, the Helen who caused the war in the first place, Hector's wife, Achilles' divine mother Thetis, females play a role distinctly subordinated to men. In a presentation of the nature of gods and men, women virtually do not count: "conceptually [Zeus] is envisaged as the head of a huge family tree which includes gods and men but, leaving aside very few and explicable exceptions, does not include women."[24] This is not just because the epic is about war; it is implicit in everything the epic says about the relationship between male and female, and of course this implicit presentation influences countless subsequent generations who openly or perhaps tacitly used the Homeric epics in the formulation of later works.[25]

All this is fairly obvious, however, and the encouragement of violence and endorsement of military valour is a reasonably clear characteristic of the *Iliad* that teachers, critics and readers can challenge when the epic is made part of a presentation of our cultural heritage, as it so often is. What, however, about the tacit, more subtle and more pervasive aspects of the Achilles figure as I have delineated them – the insistence on standing in opposition to cosmic forces, if necessary, in an attempt to impose the individual human will and the derogation of yielding to authority or conformity to arbitrary patterns of behavior?

This message, as I already have pointed out, permeates Greek society and carries forward to the present to influence our own attitudes heavily. So long as I could see only the affirmative effects of this attitude I could celebrate the Achilles figure, but as I see some deleterious effects, I face a dichotomy, a conflict that is doubly difficult in that some of the negative aspects of these attitudes promoted by secular literature are reinforced by religious texts, as we have already seen. And there are several negative effects.

The insistence on imposing the individual will, while encouraging a view of life and society that puts the human at the center, also promotes the domination by humans of all other aspects of the cosmos. As the advances of science can be seen to flow from the ideology promoted by the Achilles-figure, so too can the attitudes of domination that develop and lead to the human–centered exploitation of the fauna and flora of the earth, and of the earth itself. The attitudes that lead to this sort of behavior are not universally human, nor are they produced by some natural human relationship to the environment. They derive from assumptions about the relationship of the human with the cosmic background established in significant measure by the influential Achilles-figure. They all the more influential by being tacit, secular, literary, dramatic, and, of course, reinforced in their molding of other influential writings and ideas. These are negative effects of the "heroic" expression of the will established in the western tradition by the *Iliad* and its leading figure Achilles. It is important, I think, to recognize both how rooted our culture is in these assumptions, and how they generate both good and bad attitudes and behavior. If we fail to see both, we will be like the emperor on the one side of a Roman coin who never knows of the eagle on the other.

---

[1] See Smart (1985)..

[2] Mueller (1996) p. 129, formulates the position that mênis is "... nothing less than the *nomen sacrum* for the ultimate sanction that enforces the world-

defining prohibitions, the tabus that are basic to the establishment and perpetuation of the world of Zeus and the society of mortals he presides over."
[3] Without assuming that the scope of potential in the oral tradition is so restricted as to force the conclusion that the epic was created in writing while the skill was very limited in its application, as Mueller (1984) pp. 163-5, hypothesizes a "master poet" whose lengthy acitivity accounts for repetitions and inconsistencies. The evidence against extensive use of writing in composition of the *Iliad* has been reviewed by Kirk (1985) pp. 11-14, in an introduction that summarizes the generally held theory of lengthy development of the epic tradition and maintains Kirk's view of an eighth-century date for the creation of the *Iliad*. Virtually all the subsequent works cited here in the notes assume this coherency.

[4] Burkhardt (1998) p. 71.

[5] I want to stress the perception of this act of the goddess on the part of Homeric bards and later Greeks as reality, not hallucination or some psychological phenomenon like the means of reconciling the two sides of the brain, as in Jaynes (1976, 1990) esp. pp. 72-83.

[6] Mueller (1984) pp. 173-4 summarizes and maintains the argument that "Book 9 represents a late stage in the growth of the Iliad," while accepting it, of course, as the work of the final poet. Most recent work accepts the embassy episode as an integral part of the *Iliad*, with little or no argumentation. Vivante, for example, makes no distinctions in his treatment of the epithets in that scene, just as MacCary (see note 352 below) makes the episode integral to his discussion, while Schein, S. (1984) passes over it in note 35, p. 125, distinguishing the approach of analytical scholars from those who "recognize merely a narrative inconsistency arising from Homer's reworking of a traditional story"; briefly also, against the idea of the late reworking, Lloyd-Jones (1971, 1983). Nagy (1999) pp. 52-55 sees the duals as a progression in the narrative whereby they refer to only two of the three sent on the embassy. Wilson (2000), p. 11, accepts the view that the duals derive from an earlier version in which they were appropriate, but insists that the reader or hearer would in the first instance "find it confusing and inconsistent."

[7] Graziozi and Haubold (2005) p. 130.

[8] Zanker (1994).

[9] Zanker (1994) p. 129.

[10] Described by Rabel (1997) p. 117, as a "pattern of disillusionment and error that characterizes his behavior through the poem." Rabel has a view similar to my understanding of the basic attitudes of the poem.

[11] Hammer (2002) p. 56.

[12] The proposal of "an 'Achilles complex' as the thematic core of the *Iliad*, and a formative stage in the development of every male child," in MacCary (1985) p. 95, has at least the merit of explicating carefully the tradition out of which

such interpretations emerge, as well as reviewing the structuralist and "humanistic" approaches to the Achilles story.

[13] Osborne (1996) p. 157.

[14] Graziozi and Haubold (2005) p. 40.

[15] Nagy (1999) p. 78. The urge to posit "artistic unity" is illlustrated by a recent argument seeing the epic as unified by the actual selection of formulae and diction and choice of words to present a cohesive account of Achilles' pitilessness resolving into pity in three successive stages: Kim (2000).

[16] Griffin (1980) p. 15.

[17] Saul (2001) p. 66.

[18] Christ (2003) pp. 176-177.

[19] Veyne (1988) p. 31.

[20] Knox (1964) p. 57.

[21] Zanker (1994).

[22] King (1987) p. 234.

[23] Wofford (1992) pp. 94, 95, 96.

[24] Graziozi and Haubold (2005) p. 99.

[25] As, to cite an extreme and controversial case, the alleged imitation of Homer by the writer of the Gospel of Mark: MacDonald (2000).

Criticizing the Tradition

Where does all this leave us? Or rather, where does it leave me? I have pursued these issues as much to clarify to myself what their significance might be in guiding future behavior, and I think, after a great deal of reading and pondering, I can assert some conclusions for myself. But before I attempt to explain what this discussion with myself has meant to me, I want to lay out what I believe is the dominant problem of my time. After that, I can discuss what I believe to be the influence all these texts have had on the creation – and possible solution – of this problem, and the manner in which I intend to approach it.

The problem is easily set out: it is the challenge of climate change and the threats it brings to society – and human life itself. All other issues with which I and others have been concerned – poverty, injustice, oppression, violence, disease – all human problems pale in the face of the potential of the collapse of everything that supports us. I am confident that I do not overstate this; many of my contemporaries say the same thing. I need not go into the details or practical causes of this impending disaster; that has been done well and frequently enough to convince me. It is enough for the purposes of this book for me to state that I believe that we are at serious risk of creating enough change in the earth's climate to overwhelm civilization with a series of disasters that will end it. And by civilization I mean all civilizations: Chinese, Japanese, Islamic, East Indian, African, that of aboriginal peoples – all those as well as the civilization I call mine: that of western Europe and its inheritors in the Americas, Australia, New Zealand and so on. That is the civilization about which I have written in this book, the civilization created by Greek texts and biblical texts, and that is the civilization so many accuse of causing the threat to all.

At the end of the preceding chapter I suggested that the "Achilles attitude" contributes to the human attempt at domination of the cosmos, an attempt that many believe is pushing the ability of the earth to support, even to tolerate, human activity. That belief has led some people to seek alternative attitudes, so that some find attractive the Chinese, or at least Confucian Chinese, sense of the unity of everything in creation, with the goal of humans not domination, control, self-assertion and autonomy, but harmony. I responded to this attraction, and as I read the eastern texts I frequently felt drawn to their conclusions, although I was aware that I often did not share their suppositions. As I read and thought, however, something from my own tradition repeatedly tugged at me. Recently, rereading a collection of essays by Karl Popper, the source of the tug came clear. Popper wrote:

> In spite of our great and serious troubles, and in spite of the fact that ours is surely not the best possible society, I assert that our own free world is by far the best society which has come into existence during the course of human history.

Thus I do not say, with Leibnitz, that our world is the best of all possible worlds. My thesis is merely that our own social world is the best that has ever been – the best, at least, of which we have any historical knowledge.... I have in mind the standards and values which have come down to us through Christianity, from Greece and the Holy Land; from Socrates, and from the Old and New Testaments

At no other time, and nowhere else, have men been more respected, as men, than in our society. Never before have their human rights, and their human dignity, been so respected, and never before have so many been ready to bring great sacrifices for others, especially for those less fortunate than themselves.

I believe that these are facts.[1]

There it is. I reread that and it expresses, for the most part, what I feel about my current position.[2] Popper wrote it in 1956, in the age that, with all the threat of nuclear obliteration, was for me the years of optimism. That optimism persisted. Ten years later Alvin Toffler suggested that the world was about to change dramatically in ways that few people might expect.[3] Then came the first warnings of the Club of Rome: there was a "Limit to Growth." The warning undercut for some the confidence that whatever problems the present (then) might face, growth and technology would ameliorate them. The oil crisis of the mid seventies seemed to support the view that there were natural limits on what humans could do. Next followed computers, the PC revolution that people predicted would dramatically alter the nature of life on this globe. The last fifteen years or so have been a period of "globalization" that has changed the way people work and communicate, generating, according to one view, enormous opportunity for individual growth if the dangers created by globalization do not result in violence that will overturn all that the new technology can gain.

I want to take up that one view for a little while, because it exemplifies what those who object to my civilization cite as the world's main problem, and yet offers the promise of what I find so enticing about my tradition. Thomas Friedman[4] argues that in the recent decade, the expansion of access to computers, the web and the connectivity it provides, the ability of software to offer dramatic new ways of carrying on business activities, and other apects of technological change all have created a world in which nations, countries, companies, institutions are so interconnected and interdependent as to have created a world qualititatively different from the past. And it is a world that unites people of all different traditions, the Chinese with that based on Hellenism, for example, a uniting that Friedman argues can be both practically and intellectually rewarding while still preserving the unique features of different cultures.

To Friedman, this new world thus offers great promise, and he embraces it with all the enthusiasm of a twenty-first century Achilles. He is not naïve, however, for he recognizes that the characteristics of the new world bring new threats: insecurity can win out over imagination. And some of what he writes relates to the problem that is for me the primary issue. He sees energy consumption as an issue, and the current state of oil exploitation with oil's high price as a major factor in creating current political problems: "Give me $10-a-barrel oil, and I will give you political and economic reform from Moscow to Riyadh to Iran."[5] He warns that "all sorts of natural habitats are threatened. If these trends go on unchecked, with the natural habitats being converted to farmland and urban areas, and the globe getting warmer, many of the currently threatened species will be condemned to extinction."[6]

Including us, as I see it. Bringing China, India, the remotest parts of the world, into the plenitude that residents of New York, London and Canberra experience will have more than the "geopolitical impact" Friedman worries about in a preceding paragraph. Even if the energy consumption is drastically cut by these developing societies to reduce the political impact of their arrival on the scene of what Friedman calls the "Flat World," I don't see how all the manufacturing, production and transportation can be carried out without accelerating the rush toward disaster. Yet, the arrival of these societies at levels of social, political and legal comfort as well as material, are to Friedman, and to me as well, desirable goals. They are desirable precisely because they fit with the right direction for the free society in which Popper and I believe, and they are achievable (unless we die first) because of all the attitudes and aspects of the tradition I have been expounding in earlier chapters of this book.

They will not necessarily be achieved, however. Success will only come if we are able to make some major changes in the ways we treat ourselves, one another, our societies and our world. Human civilization can only go forward into a better future if we find ways to make political arrangements, economic structures, social institutions and the provision of everyday human needs in a world of billions of people congruent with the available resources of the world in which we exist. This is not an easy matter and hardly possible in an atmosphere of "business as usual" or in pursuit of simple solutions. We – or I, still imbued with the Hellenic conviction that human beings matter and human welfare is worth pursuing, must find ways of maintaining the achievements so far won while we alter the activities that threaten our very existence. Change will not come easily, and it will be particularly difficult to make changes in human practices that do not destroy the benefits that past practices have brought us. The Achillean tradition still holds promise; Confucian values have a place beside it. Neither can replace the other holus–bolus in a rejection of its past.

I offer no specific solutions or proposals here, and I did not write this book with the thought that I could map out a course for the future. I wrote, rather, in the hope that understanding ourselves, our past, our traditions and assumptions will make it possible to embark upon changes that will be creative and realistic, and that this appreciation of ourselves will inspire us to make those changes. Most of our tradition impels us to personal aggrandizement, as I see it. We have built a civilization that maximizes the benefits and salutes the accomplishments of domination. If the aggrandizement that spills over into ruinous exploitation of others and of the planet is to be restrained without the loss of the benefits it has brought, the change will occur on the individual level before it sweeps politics and economics on the macro level, or so I believe.

In simple terms, it seems to me that if the world is safely to achieve an increase in the material well-being of billions of us, then at least a billion of us must aim at reducing our own individual material consumption. I think we are more likely to do that if we want to do it, changing our goals with a revision of our understanding of what makes us "heroes" like Achilles. When the meaning of achievement is recast, actions change, and with that change our demands of our political and economic institutions. That is an abstract objective, but I think it is reachable and can be couched in self-questioning on the everyday level. When we buy a new car, and make our choice, shall we in future ask ourselves, on the deepest level possible, "why do I make this choice?" When we go to a public meeting and judge what we are told, do we ask ourselves, "why do I believe this?" When we consider purchases at the store, paying wages, disposing of obsolete but usable equipment, can we ask "why do I do this?" When we make decisions about our relations with ourselves, with others near and far, with the land and water itself, do we ask whether we can feel part of the system we are effecting and break away from millennia of feeling superior and separate from it? All this is necessary, I believe, and will come to pass when we have a fuller understanding of ourselves and how we have come to be what we are.

Furthermore, in the formulation of responses to the changes called for by the increasingly close connection among the different parts of the world discussed by Friedman, comprehension of historical experience and the attitudes it engenders is vital. The reactions to the Chinese treatment of Tibet, both in China and the rest of the world, is a case in point. Outside the Chinese tradition, the debate operates with attitudes and assumptions very different from those held by the Chinese. The perspective of the Achilles-attitude gives "human rights" the priority in evaluating events and the concomitant Chinese actions: oppression; reaction to the exploitation of China in recent centuries; improvement of economic and political conditions in China. Chinese responses, on the other hand, are strongly affected by long-standing attitudes promoted by the Confucian tradition, a tradition still influential among people who were born outside of China but share the Chinese background and culture. The Chinese in China regard their expatriates as *huaqiao* – overseas Chinese – and the *huaqiao* not only accept that definition for themselves, they share many of the attitudes and assumptions of the Chinese who remain in China.

Those attitudes include the comprehension of governors – emperors, presidents or commissars – as parents of the people, and in that context influence the evaluation of the contemporary government as a benign parent aiming to improve the economic condition of Tibetans and give them the standards of China in areas like women's rights and the demotion of the importance of religion. Actions are assessed as much or more in terms of the Confucian goal of harmony rather than a priority of human rights: "Let the ruler *be* a ruler, the minister *be* a minister, the father *be* a father, and the son *be* a son." The ideas of Confucian writers mold the tacit assuptions of young Chinese students in Europe and North America who in fury write letters to the western newspapers. If we – and the Chinese – are not aware of our assumptions, issues like that of Tibet will generate conflict rather than change, when change is needed. This goes far beyond issues like that affecting Tibet, and carries on to the desperate need for all societies to create attitudes that will protect the planet for the future.

I believe that an awareness of our long-standing attitudes is essential to understanding ourselves. Without an awareness of our tacit assumptions about human beings, about society and the world in which we live, we risk making unsuitable changes, or we will fail to make necessary changes because we do not understand our motives or the attitudes that frame our decisions. In a way, then, this book is an attempt to aid in one ancient pursuit, a dictum of Hellenism, of Socrates, and a motto at Apollo's shrine of Delphi: "Know thyself."

---

[1] Popper (1956) pp. 496-97.

[2] I would like to note here that Popper's words are themselves an expression of the Achilles attitude toward the world, and written in 1956, still preserve the tradition in which people are called "men." That we have changed in this somewhat, and are willing to call females by a more appropriate term, is to me an illustration of the development of the virtues Popper claims for his society.

[3] Toffler (1965) *Future Shock*.

[4] Friedman (2006).

[5] Friedman (2006) p. 564.

[6] Friedman (2006) p. 501.

Appendix: Mentality

The term mentality has been much used in recent years, particularly by historians writing in French, and it is offered as an explanation, at least in part, for the actions taken by members of a society. Its explanatory value is assumed, based on the idea that a given society's mentality leads to decisions different from those that might come from a society with a different mentality. The mentality alleged, to be a useful concept, must be specific enough to generate discrimination, and it must be supposed to be general enough in the society to affect all or almost all the society's members. The concept has been used without much questioning of its validity, until a recent challenge by Geoffrey Lloyd argued that the concept will not stand up to examination when tested with some of the historical characteristics deemed most affected by "mentality," using, for his argument, evidence from Greek antiquity.

In the matter of science, for example, evaluating the assertion that a change in mentality led to the Hellenic developments, Lloyd argues that science must "be understood against the political background of ancient Greek society, especially the very extensive experience that many Greek citizens had of debates in the assemblies, and the law courts, of evaluating evidence and arguments there in matters both of private legal disputes and of strategic public concerns."[1] This is generally the line taken in his discussion, asserting that the political context rather than "mentality" can explain changes and events. For example, in setting out the Greek approach to proof, that is, how ideas can be tested and positions proven, Lloyd claims that proof was sought as much for polemic, or more so, than demonstration, in the arguments of the scientists, and concludes again, "the political and legal background plays a role at least at the beginning of what might otherwise seem a merely intellectual development."[2]

Lloyd has argued this thesis for some years, and has convinced many, and its application is seductive, at least at first reading, for the challenge to a concept as vague as that of "mentality" is always attractive, especially when it proposes to substitute practical, political influences for "airy-fairy" ideas of general mental orientation. But the Lloyd challenge will not quite stand, for a number of reasons. In the first place, in looking at science in the sixth century BCE, the proposal to substitute political democratic institutions for mentality to explain the shift to science stumbles on chronology. What Lloyd proposes might do for Athens in the fifth century, but will it do for Ionia in the sixth?[3] Lloyd sees that problem and tries to solve it. Connecting the development of science with the ideology of democracy, Lloyd tries to answer the chronological objection by citing Solon and Cleisthenes as creating democracy, "it was Cleisthenes who was responsible for establishing the full democracy at Athens, we should not forget that to some ancient writers it was Solon who initiated the democracy there."[4] That is true enough, but it does not face up to the fact that in these earlier stages of Aristotle's teleologically reconstructed history of democracy, there are no indications that the intense public debate, argumentation and polemic essential to Lloyd's argument had yet developed. How much public involvement was there in assemblies in mid-sixth century Athens – before or after the time of the tyrant Peisistratus? How political were the Athenians when they were first given their new institutions at the beginning of the century – if in fact it was done that early? Can we assume much public debate or sophisticated political argumentation before the growth of the empire and the concomitant wealth of Athens in the fifty years after the Persian Wars? So the political context might not explain the shift to science among the sixth century Greeks. Could it be that our explanation cannot be any better than the vague "mentality?" It is interesting that even Lloyd, in his attack on the concept, seems to need something like it, for time and again, in laying out the intensity of argumentation in the democratic institutions we know for Athens, he keeps referring to the agonistic characteristic of Greeks, "the competitiveness characteristic of so much of Greek intellectual life and culture."[5] But what is this if not mentality without the name?

Finally, in drawing his argument to its conclusion, Lloyd challenges "how a mentality, once acquired, can ever be modified. If the notion of a mentality is to have any force, it must correspond to certain recurrent and pervasive patterns of ideas, beliefs or behavior. But the more recurrent and stable these are thought to be, the more difficult it becomes to see how shifts and mentalities can occur, whether in individuals' mentalities in the short term, or in those of groups or whole societies in the long."[6] But this is exactly the point: the allegation of mentality – if I were to use the term – of the West is the notion that the attitudes and assumptions of Hellenism (or later) once they get into the system of thought, remain there; often they create contradiction, because new aspects of mentality do not eject the old in the way that conscious ideas can be abandoned.

I have examined this matter to such an extent because my own treatment of the Hellenic impact on my "mentality" accepts the existence of attitudes and assumptions that continued from ancient times into modern. I am the heir not only to the physical texts but to the accumulation of interpretations of which I am aware. Whether I use the word mentality or not, I assume the existence of such mental constructs, and further insist that they may not even be explicit to the Greeks or to us: they frame the way in which people see the world. While I agree with Lloyd that the assertion of such mental constructs is not really explanatory – it would be necessary to show how they came about for them to be truly explanatory – I argue that their existence is as much a fact of history as the political and agonistic behavior Lloyd selects as explanation.

---

[1] Lloyd (1990) p. 36.
[2] Lloyd (1990) p. 96.
[3] This point in particular is a difficulty for the long-standing Lloyd thesis, as is conceded by one of its supporters, Rihll (1999) p. 9.
[4] Lloyd (1990) p. 61.
[5] Lloyd (1990) p. 97.8
[6] Lloyd (1990) p. 136.

Bibliography

Authors and Works Cited

Acts of the Apostles.
Aeschylus, *Oresteia, Persians, Prometheus Bound.*
Alcaeus.
Amos.
Andocides, *On his Return.*
Antiphon, *On the Choreutes, On the Murder of Herodes, Prosecution for Poisoning.*
Aristophanes, *Clouds.*
Aristotle, *Constitution of Athens, de Anima, Metaphysics, Nicomachean Ethics, Organon, Politics, Posterior Analytics, Sophistical Refutations.*
Arrian, *Anabasis of Alexander.*
Colossians.
Confucius, *Analects, Doctrine of the Mean, Great Learning.*
Deuteronomy.
Dialogue with his Soul of the Man Tired of Life.

Diogenes Laertius.
Ecclesiastes.
Ecclesiasticus.
Ephesians.
Euripides, *Heracles, Hippolytus, Iphigeneia in Tauris, Medea, Orestes, Suppliant Women*
Exodus.
Ezra.
Galatians.
Genesis.
Herodotus, *Histories.*
Hesiod, *Eoiae, Theogony, Works and Days.*
Hippolytus, *Refutatio.*
Homer, *Iliad, Odyssey.*
I Ching
Isaiah.
James, Letter of.
Jeremiah.
Job.
John.

John, First Letter.
Jonah.
Josephus, *Jewish Antiquities, The Life.*
Leviticus.
Luke.
Maccabees 1.
Maccabees 2.
Marcus Aurelius, *Meditations.*
Matthew.
Mencius.
Numbers.
Peri Basileias.
Peter 1.
Peter 2.
Pindar, *Nemean Odes, Pythian Odes.*
Plato, *Apology of Socrates, Crito, Laws, Phaedo, Protagoras, Republic, Theatetus.*
Plutarch, *Life of Solon.*
Proverbs.
Psalms.
Samuel 1.
Sirach.
Shang Chu.
Shepherd of Hermas.
Shijing.
Shu Ching
Solon, Fragments, *Song to the Muses.*
Sophocles, *Antigone, Oedipus Tyrannus, Philoctetes.*
Spring and Autumn Annals.
Tacitus, *Annals.*
Theognis.
Thessalonians 1.
Theocritus, *Idyll* 17.
Thomas, *Gospel of.*
Thucydides.
Wisdom.
Xenophon, *Cyropaedia, Memorabilia of Socrates.*

Secondary Sources

Albertz, R. (1994) *A History of Israelite Religion in the Old Testament Period* Vol. II, *From the Exile to the Maccabees*, Louisville, Westminster John Knox Press.

Almeida, J. A. (2003) *Justice as an Aspect of the Polis Idea in Solon's Political Poems: A Reading of the Fragments in Light of New Classical Archaeology*, Leiden, Brill.

Ames, R. T., (2002) "Thinking Through Comparisons: Analytical and Narrative Methods for Cultural Understanding," in Shankman, S. and Durrant, S. W., eds. (2002) *Early China / Ancient Greece: Thinking Through Comparisons*, Albany, State University of New York Press.

BIBLIOGRAPHY

Arendt, H. (1971) *The Life of the Mind*, New York, Harcourt, Inc.
Armstrong, K. (2007) *The Bible: A Biography*, New York, Atlantic Monthly Press.
Arrian, *Anabasis of Alexander.*
Asselin, M. (1997) "The Lu-School of Reading of 'guanju' as Preserved in an Eastern Han fu," *Journal of the American Oriental Society*, 117, p. 435, n. 52.

Barnes, J. (1982) *The Presocratic Philosophers*, London, Routledge & Kegan Paul.
Bodde, D. (1991) *Chinese Thought, Society, and Science: The Intellectual and Social Background of Science and Technology in Pre-modern China*, Honolulu, University of Hawaii Press.
Brenner, A. and Fontaine, C. (1997) *A Feminist Companion to Reading the Bible: Approaches, Methods and Strategies*, Sheffield, Sheffield Academic Press.
Brickhouse, T. C. and Smith, N. D. (2000) *The Philosophy of Socrates*, Boulder, Westview Press.
Brooks, E. B. and A. T., "The Nature and Historical Context of the Mencius," in Chan, A. K. L. (2002).
Brown, T.S., in *Encyclopaedia Britannica*, III, 1974, s.v. Herodotus.
Burckhardt, J. (1998) *The Greeks and Greek Civilization*, transl. Stern, S, London, HarperCollins.
Burke, E. (1774) *Address to the Electors of Bristol*, November 3, 1774.

Carne-Ross, D. S. (1965) *Pindar*, New Haven, Yale University Press.
Chan, A. K. L., ed. (2002) *Mencius, Contexts and Interpretations*, Honolulu, University of Hawaii Press.
Chan, W-T. (1963) *A Source Book in Chinese Philosophy*, Princeton, Princeton University Press.
Chau, L. and Nyers, R.H. (1998) *The First Chinese Democracy: Political Life in the Republic of China on Taiwan*, Baltimore, Johns Hopkins University Press.
Chen, Li Fu (1986) *The Confucian Way: a New and Systematic Study of "The Four Books,"* [transl. of *Ssu Shu*] London. KPI Limited.
Chen, Li Fu. (1976) *Why Confucius Has Been Reverenced as the Model Teacher of All Ages*, New York, St. John's University Press, Asian Philosophical Studies No. 7.

BIBLIOGRAPHY

Cheng, C-Y., (1972) "Chinese philosophy: a characterization," in Naess, A., and Hannay, A., eds. (1972) *Invitation to Chinese Philosophy*, Oslo, Universitetsforlaget.

Ching, J. (1993) *Chinese Religions*, London, Macmillan.

Christ, C. P. (2003) *She Who Changes: Re-imagining the Divine in the World*, New York, Palgrave Macmillan.

Chroust, A-H. (1957) *Socrates, Man and Myth, The Two Socratic Apologies of Xenophon*, London, Routledge and Kegan Paul.

Conacher, D. J. (1980) *Aeschylus' Prometheus Bound: A Literary Commentary*, Toronto, University of Toronto Press.

Confucius, *Analects*, in Legge, J. (1960) *The Chinese Classics I*, Hong Kong, Hong Kong University Press.

Connor, W. R. (1971) *The New Politicians of Fifth-Century Athens*, Princeton, Princeton University Press.

Crombie, I. M. (1964) *Plato, The Midwife's Apprentice*, London, Routledge & Kegan Paul.

Davis, R. C. (1993) *The Paternal Romance: Reading God-the-Father in Early Western Culture*, Urbana, University of Illinois Press.

Del Veccio, A., introduction to Newton, I., (1962) *The Mathematical Principles of Natural Philosophy*, New York, Philosophical Library.

Dodds, E. R. (1951) *The Greeks and the Irrational*, Berkeley, University of California Press.

Doyle, R. J. (1984) *ATE: Its Use and Meaning: A Study in the Greek Poetic Tradition from Homer to Euripides*, New York, Fordham, University Press.

Dudek, L. (1994) *The Birth of Reason*, Montreal, DC Books, p. 65.

Eisler, R. (1987) *The Chalice and the Blade: Our History, Our Future*, New York, Harper and Row.

Euben, J. P. (1986) *Greek Tragedy and Political Theory*, Berkeley, University of California Press.

Euben, J. P. (1990) *The Tragedy of Political Theory: The Road Not Taken*, Princeton, Princeton University Press.

Farrar, C. (1988) *The Origins of Democratic Thinking: The Invention of Politics in Classical Athens*, Cambridge, Cambridge University Press.

Finley, M. (1991) *The Ancient Greeks: An Introduction to Their Life and Thought*, first publ. 1963, Harmondsworth, Penguin

Finnegan, R. (1977) *Oral Poetry, Its Nature, Significance and Social Context*, Cambridge, Cambridge University Press.

Fiorenza, E. S. (2001) *Wisdom Ways: Introducing Feminist Biblical Interpretation*, Maryknoll, NY, Orbis Books.

Fiorenza, E. S. (1983) *In Memory of Her: A Feminist Theological Reconstruction of Christian Origins*, New York, Crossroad.

Fiorenza, E. S. (1984) *Bread Not Stone*.

Fiorenza, E. S. (1992) *But She Said: Feminist Practices of Biblical Interpretation*, Boston, Beacon Press.

Fiorenza, E. S. (1993) *Discipleship of Equals: A Critical Feminist Ekklesialogy of Liberation*, New York, Crossroad.

Fiorenza, E. S. (1996) *The Power of Naming*, London, SCM Press.

Fiorenza, E. S. (1998) *Sharing Her Word*, Boston, Beacon Press.

Fiorenza, E. S. "You Are Not to be Called Father: Early Christian History in a Feminist Perspective," in (1993) *Discipleship of Equals*.

Fontaine, C. R. "The Abusive Bible: On the Use of Feminist Method in Pastoral Contexts," in Brenner, A. and Fontaine, C. (1997).

Fornara, C. (1971) *Herodotus, an Interpretative Essay*, Oxford, Clarendon Press.

Friedman, Thomas L. (2006) *The World is Flat: A Brief History of the Twenty-First Century*, New York, Farrar, Straus and Giroux.

Gadamer, H-G. (1998) *The Beginning of Philosophy*, New York, Continuum.

Graham, A. C. (1989) *Disputers of the Tao: Philosophical Argument in Ancient China*, La Salle, Open Court.

Graham, A. C. (1992) *Unreason Within Reason: Essays on the Outskirts of Rationality*, LaSalle, Open Court.

Graziosi, B., and Haubold, J. (2005) *Homer: The Resonance of Epic*, London, Duckworth.

Grene, D., and Lattimore, R. (eds.) (1959) *The Complete Greek Tragedies*, Chicago, University of Chicago Press.

Griffin, J. (1980) *Homer on Life and Death*, Oxford, Clarendon Press.

Griffith, M. (1977) *The Authenticity of Prometheus Bound*, Cambridge, Cambridge University Press.

Gunn, D. M., "Reflections on David," in Brenner, A. and Fontaine, C. (1997).

Guthrie, W. K. C. (1962-81) *A History of Greek Philosophy*, III.

Hadas, M. (1951) *Aristeas to Philocrates (Letter of Aristeas)* New York, Harper and Brothers.

BIBLIOGRAPHY

Hammer, D. (2002) *The Iliad as Politics: The Performance of Political Thought*, Norman, University of Oklahoma Press.

Hansen, M. H. (1987) *The Athenian Assembly in the Age of* Demosthenes: *Structure, Principles and Ideology*, Oxford, Basil Blackwell.

Hansen, M. H. (1996) "Liberty: Athenian vs. Modern Views," in Ober, J. and Hedrick, C., eds. (1996).

Harpur, T. (2004) *The Pagan Christ: Recovering the Lost Light*, Toronto, Thomas Allen.

Havelock, E. A. (1957) *The Liberal Temper in Greek Politics*, New Haven, Yale University Press.

Havelock, E. A. (1963) *Preface to Plato*, Oxford, Basil Blackwell.

Hillman, J. (2004) *A Terrible Love of War*, New York, Penguin Press.

Hobbes, T. (1651) *Leviathan*.

Hulse, J. W. (1995) *The Reputations of Socrates: The Afterlife of a Gadfly*, New York, Peter Lang.

Hunter, V. (1982) *Past and Process in Herodotus and Thucydides*, Princeton, Princeton University Press.

Jacoby, F. (1913) "Herodotus," *RE* Supplement II, col. 482.

Jaeger, W. (1943) *Paideia: The Ideals of Greek Culture*, transl. Highet, G., New York, Oxford University Press.

Jaspers, K. (1962) *The Great Philosophers: The Foundations* (transl. of *Die grossen Philosophen* (1957) ed. Arendt, H.) New York, Harcourt Brace & World.

Jaynes, J. (1976, 1990) *The Origins of Consciousness in the Breakdown of the Bicameral Mind*, Boston, Houghton Mifflin Company.

Jobling, D., "Methods of Modern Literary Criticism," in Perdue, L. G., ed. (2001) *The Blackwell Companion to the Hebrew Bible*, London, Blackwell Publishers.

Jobling, J. (2002) *Feminist Biblical Interpretation in Theological Context: Restless Readings*, Burlington, VT.

Jullien, F. (2000) *Detour and Access: Strategies of Meaning in China and Greece*, New York, Zone Books.

Kahn, C. (1996) *Plato and the Socratic Dialogue: The Philosophical Use of a Literary Form*, Cambridge, Cambridge University Press

Kallet L. (2001) *Money and the Corrosion of Power in Thucydides*, Berkeley, University of California Press.

Karlgren, B. (1950) *The Book of Documents*, Repr. Bulletin 82 from the Museum of Far Eastern Antiquities, Stockholm.

Karlgren, B. (1950) *The Book of Odes, Chinese Text, Transcription and Translation*, Museum of Far Eastern Antiquities, Stockholm.

Kerferd, G. B. (1981) *The Sophistic Movement*, Cambridge, Cambridge University Press.

Kim, J (2000) *The Pity of Achilles: Oral style and the Unity of the Iliad*, Lanham, Rowland and Littlefield.

King, K. C. (1987) *Achilles: Paradigms of the War Hero from Homer to the Middle Ages*, Berkeley, University of California Press.

King, T. (2003) *The Truth About Stories: A Native Narrative*, Toronto, Anansi.

Kirk, G. S. (1985) *The Iliad: A Commentary, vol. 1: books 1-4*, Cambridge, Cambridge University Press.

Kirk, G. S. and Raven, J. E. (1957) *The Presocratic Philosophers*, Cambridge, Cambridge University Press.

Knox, B. M. W. (1964) *The Heroic Temper: Studies in Sophoclean Tragedy*, Berkeley, University of California Press.

Kullmann, W. (1984) "Oral poetry theory and neoanalysis in Homeric research," *Greek, Roman and Byzantine Studies*, 25, pp. 307-23.

Lacey, A. E., "Our Knowledge of Socrates," in Vlastos, G. (ed.) (1971) pp. 22-49.

Lachenaud, G. (1978) *Mythologies, religion, et philosophie de l'histoire dans Herodote*, Thesis, Lille, 1976.

Lane, M. (2001) *Plato's Progeny: How Plato and Socrates Still Captivate the Modern Mind*, London, Duckworth.

Lateiner, D. (1995) *Sardonic Smile: Nonverbal Behavior in Homeric Epic*, Ann Arbor, University of Michigan Press.

Lattimore, R. (1960) *Greek Lyrics* (translated), 2nd edn., Chicago, University of Chicago Press.

Lee Teng-hui (1999) Quoted from "Confucian Democracy: Modernization, Culture, and the State in East Asia," *Harvard International Review* 1999, p. 18, in Ogden, S. (2002) *Inklings of Democracy in China*, Cambridge, MA, Harvard, p. 58.

Legge, J. (1960, repr. of 1935) *The Chinese Classics I*, Hong Kong, Hong Kong University Press.

Liddell, H. G., Scott, R., and Jones, H. S. (1940) *A Greek English Lexicon*, Oxford, Oxford University Press.

BIBLIOGRAPHY

Lloyd, G.E.R. (1990) *Demystifying Mentalities*, Cambridge, Cambridge University Press.

Lloyd-Jones, H. (1971, 1983) *The Justice of Zeus*, Berkeley, University of California Press.

Lord, A. B. (1960) *The Singer of Tales*, Cambridge, Mass., Harvard University Press.

Louden, B. (2006) *The Iliad: Structure, Myth and Meaning* Baltimore, Johns Hopkins University Press.

Luce, J. V. (1975) *Homer and the Heroic Age*, London, Thames and Hudson.

Macaulay, T. B. (1860) "On the Athenian Orators," in *Critical, Historical and Miscellaneous Essays*, Vol. I, New York, Sheldon and Company.

MacCary, W. T. (1985) *Achilles: Ontogeny amd Phylogeny in the Iliad*, New York, Columbia University Press.

MacDonald, D. R. (2000) *The Homeric Epics and the Gospel of Mark*, New Haven, Yale University Press.

Madison J. "To Thomas Jefferson, October 24, 1787," in Madison, J. (1999) *Writings*, New York, Library of America.

Martin, K. (1962) *French Liberal Thought in the Eighteenth Century*, London, Phoenix House.

Martin, R. P., (1989) *The Language of Heroes: Speech and Performance in the Iliad*, Ithaca, Cornell University Press.

McKay, H. A., "On the Future of Feminist Biblical Criticism," in Brenner, A. and Fontaine, C. (1997).

Meier, C. (1993) *The Political Art of Greek Tragedy*, Cambridge, Polity Press.

Mill, J. S. (1859) *On Liberty*, in Alexander, E., ed. (1999), *On Liberty*, Peterborough, Ont., Broadview Press.

Milne, P. J. "No Promised Land: Rejecting the Authority of the Bible," in (1995) *Feminist Approaches to the Bible*, Washington, D.C., Biblical Archaeology Society.

Morris, I. (1987) *Burial and Ancient Society: The Rise of the Greek City-State*, Cambridge, Cambridge University Press.

Mueller, L. (1996) *The Anger of Achillles: Mênis in Greek Epic*, Ithaca, Cornell University Press.

Mueller, M. (1984) *The Iliad*, London, George Allen & Unwin.

Munn, M. (2000) *The School of History: Athens in the Age of Socrates*, Berkeley, University of California Press.

Murray, O. (1993) *Early Greece*, Cambridge, Mass, Harvard University Press.

BIBLIOGRAPHY

Nagy, G. (1979, 2nd ed. 1999) *The Best of the Achaeans: Concepts of the Hero in Archaic Greek Poetry*, Baltimore, Johns Hopkins University Press.

Nagy, G. (1990) *Greek Mythology and Poetics*, Ithaca, Cornell University Press.

Nehamas, A. (1999) *Virtues of Authenticity: Essays on Plato and Socrates*, Princeton, Princeton University Press.

Neugebauer, O. (1962) *The Exact Sciences in Antiquity*, New York, Harper & Brothers.

Newton, I., (1962) *The Mathematical Principles of Natural Philosophy*, New York, Philosophical Library.

Nylan, M.. (2001) *The Five "Confucian" Classics*, New Haven, Yale University Press.

Ober, J. (1989) *Mass and Elite in Democratic Athens*, Princeton, Princeton University Press.

Ober, J. (1996) *The Athenian Revolution: Essays on Ancient Greek Democracy and Political Theory*, Princeton, Princeton University Press.

Ober, J. And Hedrick, C., eds. (1996) *Demokratia: A Conversation on Democracies, Ancient and Modern*, Princeton, Princeton University Press.

Ogden, S. et. al. (1992) *China's Search for Democracy: The Student and Mass Movement of 1989*, Armonk, N.Y.

Osborne, R. (1996) *Greece in the Making, 1200 – 479 BC*, London, Routledge.

Paine, T. (1792) *Rights of Man*, Part II, in Paine, T. (1942) *Basic Writings of Thomas Paine*, New York, Willey Book Company.

Parker, H. T. (1937) *The Cult of Antiquity and the French Revolutionaries*, repr. 1962, New York, Octagon Books.

Parry, M., ed. (1971) *The Making of Homeric Verse: The Collected Papers of Milman Parry*, Oxford, Clarendon Press.

Perdue, L. G., ed. (2001) *The Blackwell Companion to the Hebrew Bible*, London, Blackwell Publishers.

Podlecki, A.J. (1966) *The Political Background of Aeschylean Tragedy*, Ann Arbor, University of Michigan Press.

Poo, M-c. (1998) *In Search of Personal Welfare : A View of Ancient Chinese Religion*, Albany, State University of New York Press.

Popper, K. R. (1956) "The History of Our Time: An Optimist's View," Sixth Eleanor Rathbone Memorial Lecture, in Popper, K. (1963) *Conjectures and Refutation: The Growth of Scientific Knowledge*, London, Routledge.

Popper, K. R. (1962) *The Open Society and Its Enemies*, London, Routledge & Kegan Paul.

Popper, K. R. (1963) *Conjectures and Refutations: The Growth of Scientific Knowledge*, London, Routledge.

Popper, K. R. (1998) *The World of Parmenides: Essays on the Presocratic Enlightenment*, London, Routledge [first published 1977].

Powell, B. B. (2004) *Homer*, Malden, MA, Blackwell Publishing.

Rabel, R. J. (1997) *Plot and Point of View in the Iliad*, Ann Arbor, University of Michigan Press.

Rawls, J. (1971) *A Theory of Justice*, Cambridge, Mass., Harvard University Press.

Reinhartz, A., "Feminist Criticism and Biblical Studies on the Verge of the Twenty-first Century," in Brenner, A. and Fontaine, C. (1997) *A Feminist Companion to Reading the Bible: Approaches, Methods and Strategies*, Sheffield, Sheffield Academic Press.

Reinhold, M. (1984) *Classica Americana: The Greek and Roman Heritage in the United States*, Detroit, Wayne State University Press.

Rihll, T. E. (1999) *Greek Science*, Oxford, Oxford University Press.

Rist, J. M. (1989) *The Mind of Aristotle: A Study in Philosophical Growth*, Toronto, University of Toronto Press.

Roberts, J. T. (1994) *Athens on Trial: The Antidemocratic Tradition in Western Thought*, Princeton, Princeton University Press.

Rosemont, Jr., H. (1991) *A Chinese Mirror: Moral Reflections on Political Economy and Society*, La Salle, Open Court.

Rousseau, J-J. (1755) *Discourse on Political Economy*, in (1988) *Rousseau's Political Writings*, transl. Bondanella, J. C., New York, W. W. Norton and Company.

Rousseau, J-J. (1762) *On Social Contract*, in (1988) *Rousseau's Political Writings*, New York, W. W. Norton and Company.

Rousseau, J-J. (1964) *The First and Second Discourses*, transl. Masters, R. D. and Masters, J. R., New York, St. Martin's Press.

Rousseau, J-J. (1988) *Rousseau's Political Writings*, New York, W. W. Norton and Company.

Rutledge, D. (1996) *Reading Marginally: Feminism, Deconstruction and the Bible*, Leiden, E. J. Brill.

Sagan, E. (1991) *The Honey and the Hemlock: Democracy and Paranoia in Ancient Athens and Modern America*, New York, Basic Books.

Samuel, A.E. (1963) "Plutarch's Account of Solon's Reforms," *Greek, Roman and Byzantine Studies* 4, pp. 231–36.

Samuel, A. E. (1972) *Greek and Roman Chronology: Calendars and Years in Classical Antiquity*, Munich, Beck'sche Verlag, Handbuch der Altertumswissenschaft.

Samuel, A. E. (1984) "Between Marathon and Salamis: Aristotle's Views," *"MNHMH" Georges A. Petropoulos*, Vol. 2, pp. 287-309.

Samuel, A. E. (1988) *The Promise of the West: The Greek World, Rome and Judaism*, London, Routledge.

Samuel, A. E. (1992) "Text and Ideology in Hellenism," *Scripta Mediterranea: Writing and the Growth of Culture in the Mediterranean, Bulletin of the Society for Mediterranean Studies*, 12-13, 1991-1992, pp. 6–11.

Samuel, A. E. (1992) *The Greeks in History*, Toronto, Edgar Kent.

Santas, G. X. (1979) *Socrates: Philosophy in Plato's Early Dialogues*, London, Routledge & Kegan Paul.

Saul, J. R. (2001) *On Equilibrium*, Toronto, Penguin.

Schein, S. (1984) *The Mortal Hero: An Introduction to Homer's Iliad*, Berkeley, University of California Press.

Schmidt, W. H. (1984) *Old Testament Introduction*, New York, Crossroad (trans; of *Einführung in das Alte Testament*, 1979).

Shankman, S. (1994), *In Search of the Classic: Reconsidering the Greco-Roman Tradition, Homer to Valery and Beyond*, University of Pennsylvania Press, University Park.

Shaughnessy, E. L. (1997) *Before Confucius: Studies in the Creation of the Chinese Classics*, Albany, State University of New York Press.

Sima Qian (2002) *The Grand Scribes' Records, Vol. I, The Basic Annals of Han China by Ssu-ma Ch'ien*, ed. Nienhauser, W. H. Jr., Bloomington, Indiana University Press.

Sinclair, R. K. (1988) *Democracy and Participation in Athens*, Cambridge, Cambridge University Press.

Smart, J. (1985) *The Triumph of the West*, London, British Broadcasting Corporation.

Snodgrass, A. (1987) *An Archaeology of Greece: The State and Future Scope of a Discipline*, Berkeley, University of California Press.

Sommer, D. (1995) *Chinese Religion: An Anthology of Sources*, New York, Oxford University Press.

BIBLIOGRAPHY

Starr, C. J. (1990) *The Birth of Athenian Democracy: The Assembly in the Fifth Century B.C.*, Oxford, Oxford University Press.

Starr, C. J. (1987) *Past and Present in Ancient History* Publications of the Association of Ancient Historians 1, Lanham.

Stockton, D. (1990) *The Classical Athenian Democracy*, Oxford, Oxford University Press.

Stone, I. F., (1988) *The Trial of Socrates*, Boston, Little, Brown and Company.

Tanakh, A New Translation of The Holy Scriptures According to the Traditional Hebrew Text, 1985, Philadelphia, The Jewish Publication Society.

The Jerusalem Bible (1966) Garden City, NY, Doubleday.

Thornton, A. (1984) *Homer's Iliad: Its Composition and the Motif of Supplication*, Göttingen, Vandenhoeck & Ruprecht.

Toffler, A. (1965) *Future Shock*.

Trimble, P., "Eve and Miriam," in (1995) *Feminist Approaches to the Bible*.

Turner, F. M. (1981) *The Greek Heritage in Victorian Britain*, New Haven, Yale University Press.

Vellacot, P. (1984) *The Logic of Tragedy: Morals and Integrity in Aeschylus' Oresteia*, Durham, N. C., Duke University Press.

Vernant, J-P. and Vidal-Naquet, P. (1988) *Myth and Tragedy in Ancient Greece*, New York, Zone Books.

Veyne, P. (1988) *Did the Greeks Believe in Their Myths: An Essay on the Constitutive Imagination*, Chicago, University of Chicago Press.

Vlastos, G., ed. (1971) *The Philosophy of Socrates: A Collection of Critical Essays*, New York, Anchor Books.

Vlastos, G. (1991) *Socrates, Ironist and Moral Philosopher*, Ithaca, Cornell Univesity Press.

Von Glahn, R. (2004) *The Sinister Way: The Divine and the Demonic in Chinese Religious Culture*, Berkeley, University of California Press.

Wakeman, F. (1989) *He Shang* (River Elegy), Berkeley, University of California. reprinted in Ogden, S. et al. (1992).

Walcot, P. (1966) *Hesiod and the Near East*, Cardiff, University of Wales Press.

Wallach, J. R. (2001) *The Platonic political art: A Study of Critical Reason and Democracy*, University Park, University of Pennsylvania Press.

BIBLIOGRAPHY

Waltham, C. (1971) *Shu Ching, Book of History: A modernized edition of the translations of James Legge*, Chicago, Henry Regnery.

Wardy, R. (2000) *Aristotle in China: Language, Categories and Translation*, Cambridge, Cambridge University Press.

Weber, M. (1904-5) *Die protestantische Ethik und der Geist des Kapitalismus*, transl. (1930) *The Protestant Ethic and the Spirit of Capitalism*.

West, M. L. (1971) *Early Greek Philosophy and the Orient*, Oxford, Oxford University Press.

Whorf, B (1956) *Language, Thought and Reality*, Cambridge, MA, MIT Press.

Wilson, J. (2000) *Sense and Nonsense in Homer: A Consideration of the Inconsistencies and Incoherencies in the Texts of the Iliad and the Odyssey*, Oxford, BAR International Series 839.

Winnington-Ingram, R. P. (1983) *Studies in Aeschylus*, Cambridge, Cambridge Univesity Press.

Wofford, S. L. (1992) *The Choice of Achilles: The Ideology of Figure in the Epic*, Stanford, Stanford University Press.

Wood, E. M. (1996) "Demos vs. 'We the People,'" in Ober, J. and Hedrick, C., eds. (1996).

Woozley, A.J. (1971) "Socrates on Disobeying the Law," in Vlastos, G., ed. (1971) pp. 299-318.

Wu, J. S., (1972) "Western Philosophy and the Search for Chinese Wisdom," in Naess, A. and Hannay, A., eds, (1972) *Invitation to Chinese Philosophy*, Oslo, Universitetsforlaget.

Xu, Ben (1999) *Disenchanted Democracy: Chinese Cultural Criticism after 1989*, Ann Arbor, University of Michigan Press.

Zak, W. F. (1995) *The Polis and the Divine Order: The Oresteia, Sophocles and the Defence of Democracy*, Lewisburg, Bucknell University Press.

Zanker, G. (1994) *The Heart of Achilles: Characterization and Personal Ethic in the Iliad*, Ann Arbor, University of Michigan Press.

Zeitlin, F. I. (1996) *Playing the Other: Gender and Society in Classical Greek Literature*, Chicago, University of Chicago Press

Index

A

absolutes, 5, 52, 57, 65, 194
absolutism, 131, 132, 133, 134, 142
Academy, 62
Achilles, 127, 226, 289, 313
    and assertion of will, 301, 302, 303, 304, 305, 308, 317
    as hero, 301
    character development, 291, 295, 296, 299, 301
    choosing long life, 294
    grief, 296
    helping comades, 295
    mercy, 298
    nobility, 302
    revenge, 296
    wrath, 291, 293, 295, 297
Acts of the Apostles, 238, 250
Adam, 81
Aeschylus, 6, 21, 82, 88, 89, 90, 92, 215
Agamemnon, 93
agon, 291
Ahab, 207
Ajax, 293
Alcaeus, 112, 114, 123
Alcibiades, 169
Alexander the Great, 28, 62, 106, 138, 140, 214
Alexandria, 236
Ames, R., 75
Amos, 229
Anabasis of Alexander, 122
Analects, 131, 142, 144, 279
Anaxagoras, 44
Anaxarchus, 106
Anaximander, 263
Anaximenes, 262

Andocides, 195
Annals, 235, 241
Antigone, 83, 134, 190, 191, 192
Antiochus IV, 222
Antiphon of Rhamnous, 195, 196
apocalyptic vision, 243, 244, 246
Apollo, 100, 104
Apology, 29, 30, 33, 35, 36, 38, 42, 43, 44, 46, 47, 323
Archilochus, 114
Arendt, H., 26
Areopagus, 83, 93, 94, 103
arete, 35, 43, 54, 285
Aristeas, 140
aristocracy, 107, 109, 110, 112, 114, 128, 175, 291
aristocratic ideal, 52
Aristophanes, 28, 32, 96, 153
Aristotle, 31, 32, 33, 35, 37, 43, 45, 50, 62, 63, 64, 65, 67, 68, 69, 70, 71, 74, 110, 126, 149, 153, 159, 171, 177, 256
Armstrong, K., 12
art of accommodation, 75, 258
Assembly, 151
ate, 91, 94
Athena, 21, 83, 94
Athens, 14, 29, 114, 126
    constitution, 149, 150, 152, 165
    drama, 87
    fifth century, 90, 98, 111, 172
    fifth-century texts, 13
authoritarianism, 129, 133, 134, 135, 180
authority, 129, 130, 142, 181, 246, 256, 268
autocracy, 122, 127, 128, 134, 135, 136, 137, 138, 139, 141
autonomy, 84

B

Bar Kochba, 237
Barnes, J., 266
Baruch 2, 244
being and essence, 32, 259, 261, 266, 267
Bel and the Dragon, 229
benevolence, 132
Bible, 6, 206, 242
   and feminism, 217
body, 43, 58, 59
Book of Documents, 278. See *Shang Chu*
Book of History. See *Shu Ching*
Book of Songs, 143, 278. See *Shijung*
Boulé, 151, 152
Bronze Age civilization, 275
Buddha, 45
Buddhism, 221
Burckhardt, J., 176

C

catharsis, 196
Chen Li-fu, 19, 120, 280
Chiang Kai-shek, 120
Chinese civilization, 16, 109
Chinese language, 17, 23
Chinese philosophy, 75, 78, 108, 109, 118, 120, 129, 130, 142, 256, 258, 259, 261
   humanism, 119
   political, 129, 133, 143
Chinese religion, 219, 220, 221
Choephoroe, 92
Christian philosophy, 253
Christology, 246, 252
citizenship, 111, 116, 118, 148, 150
Cleisthenes, 150, 165
Cleon, 169
Clouds, 32, 96
Club of Rome, 314
colonizing movement, 110
Colossians, 257
community, 75, 78, 92, 110
Confucian philosophy, 21, 59, 67, 78, 84, 87, 121, 130, 133, 141, 162, 164, 180, 181, 221, 264, 313

Confucius, 45, 108, 119, 120, 129, 131, 133, 135, 142, 279
Constantine, 128
Constitution of Athens, 115, 117, 123, 149, 166, 171
Copernicus, 63
Corinth, 110
cosmic order, China, 199
cosmogony, 262
cosmos, 50, 59, 70, 71, 79, 91, 92, 94, 113, 187, 191, 192, 194, 199, 211, 216, 218, 219, 227, 230, 252, 259, 262, 263, 265, 267, 271, 282, 285, 300, 303, 304, 305, 307, 309, 313
court speeches, 195
courts, 115
Covenant with Abraham, 234
creation stories, 203
creative, 287
Creon, 134
Critique of Pure Reason, 43
Crito, 33, 38, 40, 41, 46, 47
Croesus, 100, 101
Cyropaedia, 145
Cyrus, 100, 101, 137, 138, 208

D

Daniel, 223, 229
Dao, 143
Daoism, 221
Darius, 101
Darkness at Noon, 121
David, 206
debate, 321
deference, 142
definition, 37, 41, 42, 64, 69, 107
   by universals, 32, 34
Delphic Oracle, 36
democracy, 14, 19, 44, 98, 107, 109, 115, 117, 128, 136, 137, 138, 146, 147, 148, 149, 150, 152, 153, 154, 155, 156, 157, 158, 159, 160, 161, 162, 164, 165, 166, 168, 170, 171, 172, 173, 174, 175, 183
   hostility to, 153
Democritus, 263
Demosthenes, 138
denigration of the body, 257
Descartes, R., 26

INDEX

Deuteronomy, 208, 210, 228, 229, 234
Dialogue with his Soul of the Man Tired of Life, 225
dikaiosune, 107
diobelia, 171, 172
Diogenes, 262
Diogenes Laertius, 241
Dionysius II, 62
discipleship of equals, 255
discipline, 129
Discourse on the Sciences and Arts, 183
distribution of wealth, 172
    Athens, 171, 172, 173
divination, 219
divine antagonism, 92
divine justice, 195
divine law, 42, 93, 94, 96, 190, 192, 197
divine order, 90, 94, 100, 187, 188, 189, 213
divine providence, 100
Doctrine of the Mean, 201, 279
Donation of Constantine, 128
dualism, 187
duality, 26, 43, 46, 59, 60
Dudek, L., 260

E

Ecclesia, 151
Ecclesiastes, 214, 225, 226, 229, 323
Ecclesiasticus, 229
eighteenth century, 43
elenchos, 36, 37
Empedocles, 263
Emperor, 233
energeia, 67
Eoiae, 113
Ephesians, 258
epic, 53, 107, 127, 143, 273, 285
Epicureanism, 225
Epicurus, 228, 230, 256
Epimetheus, 80
equality, 113, 130, 159, 161, 168, 169, 171, 173, 175, 176, 177, 179, 182, 254
equality of discipleship, 246
Essenes, 233

ethics, 34, 39, 41, 43, 65, 67, 84, 133, 142, 187, 190, 204, 209, 211, 212
Euben, J.P., 13
Eucharist, 252
Eumenides, 92, 94
Euripides, 84, 88, 89, 189, 191, 193, 195
Eve, 81, 86
exile, 207, 208, 214
Exodus, 207
Ezra 4, 244

F

feminist criticism, 21
feminist theologians, 242, 254
Finley, M., 51
Fiorenza, E.S., 240, 254
First Letter of John, 253
First Letter of Peter, 243
Forms, 49, 54, 57, 61, 63, 64, 65
formulaic diction, 272, 273
Fourth Philosophy, 233, 234, 237
franchise, 174
freedom of speech, 44, 53
Friedman, T., 315, 316
funeral oration, 137, 169, 171, 176
Furies, 83, 93, 94
Future Shock, 319

G

Gadamer, H-G., 262
Galatians, 257, 323
Galilee, 234, 236
Galileo, 63, 178
Genesis, 203, 207, 243, 267
gnosticism, 254
Golden Rule, 103, 189
Good, 68
Gospel of Thomas, 239
Gospels, 189, 235, 236, 238, 240, 241, 243
    composition, 239
    language, 247, 249
    synoptic, 238, 248
government, 119, 120, 131, 132, 133, 143, 153, 157, 158, 160, 182, 204
Graham, A.C., 18, 75
Graziozi, B., 283

INDEX

Great Learning, 279
Grote, G., 174
Guanzi, 141
guidance and constraint, 18, 22
Gunn, D., 205

H

Haemon, 192
Han Dynasty, 135
Hanson, M., 176
harmony, 76, 77, 78, 120, 130, 182
Hasmoneans, 224
Haubold, J., 283
He Shang, 162
heart-mind, 25
Hector, 296, 297
Hellenism, 15, 20, 21, 44, 71, 84, 95, 122, 135, 163, 177, 199, 214, 222, 253, 260, 268, 273, 291
   political theory, 135, 139, 141
Heracles, 189, 193
Herod Antipas, 235
Herod the Great, 232, 235
Herodotus, 98, 99, 100, 101, 102, 112, 125, 126, 136
Hesiod, 79, 84, 94, 109, 112, 113, 114, 117, 119
hierarchy, 78, 79, 119, 121, 129, 133, 181, 203, 205, 217, 218, 254, 261
Hillman, J., 9
Hippias, 91
Hippolytus, 193
historians, 34
historical causation, 98
Histories, 145
History, 5, 8, 10, 11
   Jewish view, 209, 210
Holy Spirit, 246
Homer, 52, 278, 281, 287
Hsün-Tzu, 108
hubris, 191, 192
human prosperity, 100
humanism, 119
Hyperbolus, 169

I

I Ching, 278

Iliad, 6, 79, 107, 127, 226, 271, 272, 273, 281, 286, 295, 310
   book ix, 310
   date, 274, 275, 276, 277, 287, 310
   glorification of war, 305, 306, 307
   influence, 283, 285, 286, 290, 309
   literary quality, 277, 280, 281, 283, 300
   patrarchy, 308
inalienable rights, 44
individual as sacrosanct, 121
individual autonomy, 121
inductive reasoning, 34
Iphigeneia in Tauris, 193
Isaiah, 207, 208, 211, 228, 229
Israel, 206

J

Jaeger, W., 260
Jason, 223
Jaspers, K., 45, 260
Jeremiah, 207, 208, 213, 228, 229
Jerusalem, 232
Jesus, 45, 231, 233, 234, 235, 236, 244, 245, 255
Jewish Antiquities, 223
Job, 178, 214, 215, 216, 229, 267
John, 238, 251, 258
John the Baptist, 235, 252
Josephus, 223, 233, 234, 235, 241
Judaea, 232
Judah, 206, 207
Judah Maccabaeus, 223
Judea, 233
justice, 30, 34, 37, 38, 40, 42, 52, 53, 60, 76, 82, 86, 92, 93, 95, 96, 97, 99, 100, 101, 102, 103, 104, 106, 107, 108, 112, 113, 114, 116, 117, 118, 120, 121, 122, 130, 133, 140, 187, 188, 189, 190, 191, 192, 194, 196, 197, 198, 200, 210, 211, 212, 215, 216, 262, 263
   as balance, 121
   civic, 93
   cosmic, 194

K

Kant, I, 43

INDEX

King, K., 306
King, T., 202
Kingdom of God, 236, 243, 245
knowledge, 35, 36, 37, 56, 188, 197
Knox, B., 304
Koestler, A., 121

L

Lao-tze, 279
Law, Jewish, 211, 212, 214, 216, 220, 223, 226, 233, 249
    Christian debate, 240
Laws, 55
Legalists, 135
Letter of James, 254
Leucippus, 263
Leviathan, 167
Leviticus, 189, 207, 210, 228, 229, 234
Libation Bearers. See *Choephoroe*
liberalism, 14, 19
liberty, 155, 157, 158, 159, 173, 174, 175, 224
Life (Josephus), 241
Life of Solon, 115, 117
limit, 101
Limit to Growth, 314
Lloyd, G., 15, 320
logic, 66, 69
Logos, 228, 252, 253
Luke, 238, 249, 250
Lyceum, 63
Lysias, 195

M

Maccabaean revolt, 222
Maccabees 1, 223, 224
Maccabees 2, 223
Macchiavelli, 139
Madison, J, 158
male supremacy, 205, 217, 218
male-female conflict, 82, 83
mandate of heaven, 120, 133, 138, 211
Marcus Aurelius, 141
Mark, 238, 241, 249, 311
matriarchy, 85
Mattathias, 223
matter, 26
Matthew, 238, 249, 258

Medea, 84, 193
Meditations of Marcus Aurelius, 141
Meier, C., 13
Melian dialogue, 95, 96
Memorabilia of Socrates, 38, 47
Mencius, 108, 119, 120, 131, 132, 135, 144, 145, 221, 279
Meno, 56, 57
mentality, 15, 21, 34, 52, 92, 95, 178, 274, 283, 307, 320, 321, 322, 323
    Calvinist, 190
Metaphysics, 32, 64, 72, 269
    1078 B 17-32, 32
Milton, J., 86, 178
mind, 25, 26, 40, 46, 54, 58, 59, 66, 71
    and body, 26
misogyny, 20, 80, 81, 84
moderation, 129
monarchy, 106, 107, 110, 128, 136, 137, 138, 139
    attributes, 140, 141
monotheism, 218, 219
Montaigne, M., 43
moral order, 92
morality, 34
Moses, 86
Mo-Tzu, 108, 221
Munn, M, 173
myth, 203
Mytilenean debate, 95

N

Nagy, G., 277
Nemean Odes, 201
New Testament, 314
Newton, I., 178
Nicias, 169
Nicomachean Ethics, 65, 66, 68, 72
Nietzsche, F., 43, 52
nomoi, 38
nomos, 39, 47, 96, 97, 102, 103, 170, 180, 188, 194
Numbers, 207
nurture, 130
Nylan, M., 61, 76, 180, 330

O

obedience, 129, 130, 133

341

INDEX

Obers, J., 14
objectification, 16, 264, 267
obligation, 129
observation, 69
Odysseus, 293
Odyssey, 107, 273
Oedipus, 134, 191
Oedipus Tyrannus, 191
Old Testament, 20, 82, 204, 205, 210, 217, 218, 261, 314. See Septuagint
oligarchy, 110, 112
oligarchy of 411, 196
On his Return, 197
On the Choreutes, 196
On the Murder of Herodes, 196
open society, 137
oracles, 100, 102, 220, 221, 230
oral poetry, 272, 276, 287, 310
Oresteia, 6, 20, 82, 83, 84, 92, 186, 198
Orestes, 189
Organon, 69
ostracism, 150

P

Paine, T., 118, 154, 158, 159, 166, 331
Palestine, 232, 236, 238
Pandora, 80
parent of the people, 132, 138
Parmenides, 263
Parry, M., 272
participation, 111, 148, 156, 160
patriarchy, 80, 83, 84, 203, 205, 217, 240, 268
Patroclus, 294
Peisistratus, 125, 126
Peloponnesian War, 29
Pentateuch, 227
Peri Basileias, 139
Pericles, 44, 97, 137, 153
Perses, 114
Persian Wars, 98
Persians, 90
persuasion, 122
Phaedo, 57, 61
Pharisees, 233, 236, 237
Philip II, 138
Philo of Alexandria, 10, 227
Philoctetes, 191, 200

philosophy, 33, 34, 35, 43, 49, 113, 157, 194
Phoenix, 293
physical reality, 69, 70, 71
physical world, 262, 263, 264, 266, 267
physis, 39, 40, 96, 97, 170, 179, 188, 194
physis-nomos antinomy, 39
Pindar, 101, 198
Plato, 6, 27, 28, 31, 32, 33, 34, 35, 44, 46, 49, 51, 52, 53, 54, 55, 56, 58, 60, 61, 62, 68, 76, 153, 177, 180, 188, 195, 253, 256, 274, 28
Platonism, 50, 51, 54
Plutarch, 117, 175
pneuma, 33, 247, 251
polis, 109, 110, 111, 117, 118, 122, 127, 148
Politics, 65, 143
pollution, 196
Polybius, 154
Pontius Pilate, 233
pope, 128
Popper, K., 15, 51, 60, 260, 261, 262, 269, 313, 314, 316, 319
Posterior Analytics, 72
power, 126, 127, 128
  abuse, 127
Presocratics, 260, 266
prohibition of debt slavery, 115
Prometheus, 80, 91
Prometheus Bound, 91, 187, 215
prophets, 207
Protagoras, 35, 61, 177, 187, 188, 200
Proverbs, 214
Psalms, 214, 229
psyche, 40, 48, 51
  immortality, 49
Ptolemy Philadelphus, 139, 140
public goods, 30
Pythagoras, 263
Pythian Odes, 198, 201, 323

Q

Qin dynasty, 108, 135

R

rationalism, 98

reciprocation, 131
Refutatio (Hippolytus), 269
relativism, 19, 98, 101, 142, 170, 186, 188, 189
religion, 204, 220, 222, 237, 259
religious matters as defence, 196, 197
ren, 132
representative government, 155, 158, 159
Republic, 53, 55, 56, 60, 65, 76, 287.
Revelation of John, 243, 244
rhapsodes, 276
righteousness (*yi*), 119
rights, 111, 113, 118, 130, 162, 179
Rights of Man, 166
River Elegy. See *He Shang*
Roberts, J., 154, 159
Roosevelt, F.D., 118
Rosemont, H., 21
Rousseau, J-J., 118, 157, 160, 175
Rutledge, D., 268

S

Sabbath, 223
Sadducees, 233, 236, 237
Sagan, E., 147
salvation, 254, 255
Samuel 1, 228
Sappho, 114
Saul, 206
science, 32, 69, 70, 260, 264, 265, 266
scientific method, 70, 71
seamless web, 19
Second Letter to Peter, 245
sense perception, 26, 32, 54, 63, 66, 67, 69, 187
Septuagint, 141
Sermon on the Mount, 244, 245, 249
shaking off of debts, 115
shamans, 219, 221
shame culture, 292
Shang Shu, 134
Shepherd of Hermas, 239
Shijing, 133
Shu Ching, 119
Shun, 119
Sima Qian, 133, 134, 145
sincerity, 19
Sirach, 229

Social Contract, 167, 175
Socrates, 27, 28, 29, 30, 31, 32, 33, 34, 35, 36, 37, 38, 39, 40, 41, 42, 43, 44, 46, 47, 48, 49, 52, 53, 54, 55, 56, 57, 58, 60, 61, 63, 65, 69, 151, 179, 180, 314, 319
  historical, 28, 39, 195
  ignorance, 33, 35, 37
  trial, 45
Socratic Problem, 31, 32, 49
Solomon, 206
Solon, 94, 99, 111, 112, 114, 115, 116, 117, 119, 123
Song to the Muses, 117
sophistes, 33
Sophistical Refutations, 72
Sophists, 34, 35, 39, 40, 170, 171, 177, 187, 188, 189, 197
Sophoclean hero, 192
Sophocles, 88, 89, 189, 191, 195
sophoi, 33
soter, 247
soul, 29, 30, 39, 40, 42, 43, 46, 48, 52, 53, 54, 55, 56, 57, 59, 61, 66, 67, 68, 71, 76, 140, 179, 222, 254, 257, 264
  immortality, 54, 57, 58
  primacy, 41
Sparta, 111
spirit, 40. see *pneuma*
Spring and Autumn Annals, 278
Spring and Autumn period, China, 108, 219
St. Augustine, 45
St. Paul, 237, 238, 240, 243, 246, 247, 248, 251
Starr, C., 11
Stoicism, 230, 256
Stoics, 227
Sun Yat-sen, 120
Suppliant Women, 92
synagogues, 230, 234, 236

T

Tacitus, 235, 241
teaching, 35
Temple, 223, 224, 232, 237
Ten Commandments, 103, 208, 209

texts, 12, 13, 20, 21, 22, 142, 217, 222, 231, 239, 243, 253, 256, 274, 280
  authority, 248
Thales, 262
Theatetus, 188
Theocritus, 139
Theocritus, *Idyll* 17, 139
Theognis, 112, 123
Theogony, 79, 80, 85, 113, 203, 262
theoi, 218
Theophrastus, 139
theoretike, 68
Theramenes, 169
Thessalonians 1, 257
Thucydides, 34, 95, 96, 97, 101, 102, 112, 123, 195, 284
Tiberius, 233
Titans, 91
tradition, 15, 20
tragedians, 34, 40, 42
tragedy, 52, 53, 87, 88, 89, 90, 99, 101, 196, 215
translation, 17
Trinity, 246
truth, 222
Turner, F., 176
tyranny, 91, 112, 125, 126, 128
  cause, 112

V

victory odes, 198
virtue, 54
Vlastos, G., 31
Voltaire, 118

W

Wardy, R., 17
Warring States period, China, 108
Way of Heaven, 143
Weber, M., 190
Wen, 133, 135
western civilization, 8, 9, 15
Whorf, B., 17
Wisdom, 214
Wofford, S., 307
Works and Days, 80, 81, 85, 113, 114, 122
writing, Chinese, 278, 280
  Greek, 278
Wu, 119
wu wei, 290

X

Xenophanes, 227
Xenophon, 28, 32, 38, 137, 195
xin, 25
Xu, Ben, 163

Y

Yahweh, 206, 207, 208, 214, 215, 216, 228
yi, 119
Yu, 119

Z

Zeus, 80, 91, 94, 117, 120, 189
Zhou, 108, 129, 133